Space, Drama, and Empire

Campos Ibéricos:
Bucknell Studies in Iberian Literatures and Cultures

Series editors:
Isabel Cuñado, Bucknell University
Jason McCloskey, Bucknell University

Campos Ibéricos is a series of monographs and edited volumes that focuses on the literary and cultural traditions of Spain in all of its rich historical, social, and linguistic diversity. The series provides a space for interdisciplinary and theoretical scholarship exploring the intersections of literature, culture, the arts, and media from medieval to contemporary Iberia. Studies on all authors, texts, and cultural phenomena are welcome and works on understudied writers and genres are specially sought.

Recent titles in the series:

Space, Drama, and Empire: Mapping the Past in Lope de Vega's Comedia
Javier Lorenzo

Dystopias of Infamy: Insult and Collective Identity in Early Modern Spain
Javier Irigoyen-García

Founders of the Future: The Science and Industry of Spanish Modernization
Óscar Iván Useche

Shipwreck in the Early Modern Hispanic World
Carrie L. Ruiz and Elena Rodríguez-Guridi, eds.

Calila: The Later Novels of Carmen Martín Gaite
Joan L. Brown

Indiscreet Fantasies: Iberian Queer Cinema
Andrés Lema-Hincapié and Conxita Domènech, eds.

Between Market and Myth: The Spanish Artist Novel in the Post-Transition, 1992–2014
Katie J. Vater

For more information about the series, please visit bucknelluniversitypress.org.

Space, Drama, and Empire

Mapping the Past in Lope de Vega's Comedia

Javier Lorenzo

BUCKNELL UNIVERSITY PRESS
LEWISBURG, PENNSYLVANIA

Library of Congress Cataloging-in-Publication Data
Names: Lorenzo, Javier, 1970– author.
Title: Space, drama, and empire : mapping the past in Lope de Vega's comedia / Javier Lorenzo.
Description: Lewisburg, Pennsylvania : Bucknell University Press, [2023] | Series: Campos ibéricos: Bucknell studies in Iberian literatures and cultures | Includes bibliographical references and index.
Identifiers: LCCN 2023004138 | ISBN 9781684484911 (paperback ; alk. paper) | ISBN 9781684484928 (hardcover ; alk. paper) | ISBN 9781684484935 (epub) | ISBN 9781684484942 (pdf)
Subjects: LCSH: Vega, Lope de, 1562–1635—Criticism and interpretation. | Politics in literature. | Imperialism in literature. | Space in literature. | Place (Philosophy) in literature. | LCGFT: Literary criticism.
Classification: LCC PQ6490.H5 L67 2023 | DDC 862/.3—dc23/eng/20230501
LC record available at https://lccn.loc.gov/2023004138

A British Cataloging-in-Publication record for this book is available from the British Library.

bucknelluniversitypress.org

Distributed worldwide by Rutgers University Press

For Jung-Ja, 빛

Contents

Illustrations

Note on Translations

Unless otherwise noted, all translations are mine. Translations quoted from sources include Miguel de Cervantes, *Don Quixote*, translated by Edith Grossman (New York: HarperCollins, 2003); and Gonzalo Fernández de Oviedo, *Fernández de Oviedo's Chronicle of America: A New History for a New World*, translated by Nina M. Scott, edited by Kathleen Myers (Austin: University of Texas Press, 2007).

Space, Drama, and Empire

Introduction

In a recent dissertation on the imperial literature of late nineteenth- and early twentieth-century Germany, Lisa Skwirblies argues for "a better understanding of the microphysics of colonial rule" that takes into account the "entangled histories" of theater and the colonial enterprise.[1]

Theater, Skwirblies contends, was a critical part of the "representational machinery" of German fin de siècle imperialism and played a central role in disseminating its "epistemologies, social practices, discourses, and ways of knowing."[2] This deep-seated interdependence between theater and empire comes as no surprise to critics of early modern drama, who in recent decades have explored the ways in which the *artes dramaticae* of the period interfaced with the imperial and expansionist policies of early modern European nations and their understanding and representation of non-Western cultures.[3] The Spanish *comedia* has not remained immune to these efforts, and this explains, at least in part, the current interest in transatlantic studies of the genre.[4] In many of these studies, as well as others concerned with the depiction of imperial expansion in dramatic form, the "script"—that is, the play's ability to plot or represent race, culture, and other significant markers of difference—usually takes precedence over the "scenario," understood here in its broad geographical and spatial sense as location or setting.

This type of omission comes at a high critical cost, for, as Edward Said has argued, it is impossible to conceive of Western colonialism or imperialism "without important philosophical and imaginative processes at work in the production as well as the acquisition, subordination, and settlement of space."[5] The significance of these processes for the study of the Spanish *comedia* becomes apparent, as I will argue in this book, in a handful of plays written by Lope de Vega in which the landscapes and historical scenarios of the past are used to foretell and legitimize the imperial present of Hapsburg Spain. Further, these plays underline expansion and the acquisition of territory as central features of the state designed by the Catholic monarchs and enlarged by their descendants. By pointing out the political significance of space in these plays, this book calls into question the idea of the comedia as a nonpartisan genre, free from the stain of ideology and aimed primarily at echoing the values and tastes of its paying audience. This apolitical position continues to be promoted in scholarly assessments of the genre, for example, in the following passage:[6]

> In assessing the possible linkage between the Hapsburgs' imperialist and domestic policies and the theater as a commercial enterprise or industry, it is thus crucial to bear in mind that the commercial theaters succeeded mainly because they met the needs of the new urban populations, and that consequently most of the ideas and sentiments expressed in these plays were meant to find a ready echo in the minds and hearts of those spectators. The dramatist's main aim was to appeal to the paying public, not to a noble patron, the Crown or the Church, all of whom were, however, accorded the customary and obligatory show of respect and allegiance in the text of many plays. Eventually realizing the growing economic and social importance of the theaters, Crown and Church sought to control them, especially on moral grounds; but . . . there is no compelling evidence to conclude that commercial plays were ever considered suitable vehicles for official imperialist or counter-reformist propaganda.[7]

There is no doubt that the enormous success of the Lopian comedia as an artistic and social phenomenon was due in large part to its ability to cater to the tastes of the masses who filled the *corrales de comedias* (public playhouses) in the major urban centers of early modern Spain. Nevertheless, the constant effort to recast the past in imperial terms through the use of space that we see in some of Lope's historical comedias reveals a deep complicity between the new dramatic genre established by *El Fénix* de España and the new imperial history developed in Spain under the Hapsburgs. The primary aim of this history was, as Fernando Wulff has argued, the production of "nuevas imágenes del pasado que explicaran y ensalzaran la posición alcanzada en el presente"[8] (new images of the past that could explain and celebrate the status acquired in the present). Similar to the new imperial history chronicled by Florián de Ocampo and the Jesuit Juan de Mariana, Lope, as Allan Paterson has suggested, looked into the past "for prefigurations of the order that would eventually emerge as the modern state, as if the nature of that state were continually being exposed and pre-enacted at critical junctures in its past."[9]

Lope's refashioning of those critical moments of Spain's past as imperial or proto-imperial episodes, I will argue, relied heavily on the use of space as a tool to legitimize expansion and territorial control. By focusing on this particular aspect of Lopian drama, my study fills a significant gap in comedia studies, where, as Javier Rubiera Fernández has contended, "normalmente se ha dejado de lado la cuestión del espacio"[10] (the question of space has been regularly marginalized) by subsuming it into the study of scenography or by simply ignoring it. The reasons for this neglect vary (the traditional subordination of space to time in the Western philosophical tradition, the prominence given to plot—and consequently to time—in Aristotelian and post-Aristotelian dramatic theory, the impact of semiotics in drama studies). However, they all underline the fact that space, as Ricardo Padrón has aptly noted in a study on the relationship between texts and maps in the early modern Hispanic world, "continues to look positively—even positivistically—innocent" to those engaged in the study of literature.[11] Surpassing this critical "age of innocence" requires looking at space not simply as the setting for action or as the handmaid of plot, but rather, as I try to do in this book, as a primary vehicle for the dramatic production and dissemination of ideology.

This connection between space and ideology has been largely neglected in the major studies on the relation between stage, text, and space in early modern Spanish drama that have been published in recent decades—those by Regueiro, Rubiera Fernández, and Sáez Raposo.[12] The semiotic *esprit de système* that animates these studies looks at drama as an enclosed system whose spatial rules and forms must be catalogued and explained and treats individual comedias or groups of comedias as syntagmatic manifestations of those rules and forms.[13] Their main goal is to examine the impact of space on "el funcionamiento del signo en la poética teatral" (the functioning of the sign in the poetics of drama) (Regueiro, *Espacios dramáticos*, 6) and to elucidate "qué recursos debieron emplearse a la hora de recrear en escena los espacios de la ficción dramática" (what resources were used to recreate onstage the spaces of dramatic fiction) (Sáez Raposo, *Monstruos de apariencias llenos*, 8). Going beyond this basic descriptive level of analysis to provide social and ideological reflections is seen as a desirable goal by these critics, but one that scholars should not prioritize over the meticulous examination and classification of the codes that regulate the use and functioning of space in the comedia:

> Es deseable tratar de ir más allá de un nivel descriptivo del texto, intentando proporcionar conclusiones de valor social o ideológico que permitan afirmar la significación del teatro dentro de la estructura cultural. Sin embargo . . . esta obligación de trascendencia hace que con frecuencia se precipiten las conclusiones, forzando los textos para que digan lo que se necesita que digan. Es preciso ante todo un análisis minucioso que tenga en cuenta todas las informaciones espaciales pertinentes. (Rubiera Fernández, *La construcción del espacio*, 96–97)
>
> (It is desirable to go beyond a descriptive level of the text to provide social and ideological conclusions that underscore the significance of theater within the

> cultural structure. However . . . this desire for transcendence often leads to premature conclusions and forces the texts to say what we need them to say. What is necessary, above all, is a meticulous analysis of the text that takes into account all the relevant spatial information.)

The type of inquiry these studies distrust and want to subordinate to the rigorous and seemingly infallible methods of *la semiótica teatral* takes center stage (pun intended) in this book. My aim is not to provide a meticulous account of the various codes and conventions Lope relied on to flesh out the different spaces represented or alluded to in his historical dramas, but rather to show how those spaces paint a picture of the past that reinforced the image of Spain as an imperial nation embraced by its monarchs. Lope's endorsement of this image reflects, I will argue, the impact on his comedias of the discourses of contemporary politics, cosmography, and historiography and underlines the cartographic role of his theater as a device that allowed audiences to gain their historical bearings as imperial subjects—namely, as subjects to a monarchy that claimed, as historian Anthony Pagden has put it, "supreme military and legislative power over widespread and diverse territories."[14]

The space I will discuss here primarily refers to the fictional setting where Lope situates the action of his plays—what drama critics call "imagined space" or "diegetic space," as opposed to "stage space" or "mimetic space"—that is, the enclosed physical area (usually coterminous with the stage) where the actors make themselves visible to the audience and play their roles.[15] Although the latter—through the use of costumes, music, and other effects—very often shaped and gave critical support to the former, it is crucial to keep in mind, as Ignacio Arellano has stated, that it was primarily through "los valores visuales de la palabra" (the visual effects of language) that dramatic space was constructed in the Lopian comedia. This type of theater aimed not to reproduce mimetically the places and venues chosen by the dramatist to situate the action of the play but rather to evoke such locales by stimulating the audience's imagination. This process was facilitated through description and other discursive devices that were typically blended into the speech of the characters or, less frequently, inserted into the playwright's stage directions. It happened even in those instances in which props, paintings, objects, and other types of *realia* were incorporated into the performance, for, as Rubiera Fernández has argued, "junto a esta posibilidad de que se concretizara y se visualizara sobre la escena un espacio construido con estos variados recursos no verbales, se encuentra la posibilidad, cumplida en todas las *comedias*, de que el espacio se cree mediante la palabra" (in addition to having space materialize and become visible onstage by using these manifold nonverbal resources, it was always possible—as it happened in every *comedia*—to use language to create space) (*La construcción del espacio*, 91). It was indeed this perceived capacity of language to figure forth and render visible places, landscapes, and settings that informed what this critic calls "la poética del espacio en la comedia barroca" (the poetics of space in Baroque drama) (55).

The way this poetics interfaced with other onstage components of the performance—music, costume, scenography—to flesh out the fictive space imagined by *el poeta* (the playwright) has been the object of much attention in a handful of critical studies published recently that posit a one-to-one, iconic relation between the verbal and nonverbal components of drama as the key to understanding the production and signifying power of space in the comedia.[16] Missing from these studies, however, is a similar commitment to examining the indexical and extramural dimension of this poetics, that is, the way it pointed to and interacted with social, political, religious, and cosmographical ideas of space that were produced outside the corrales and infiltrated the dramatic texts. These views preceded and informed, in many cases, the writing and staging of the comedias and gained wider circulation and social acceptance precisely through their adaptation to theatrical productions.

Foremost among the views I will discuss throughout this study were those that celebrated the power of the nation to acquire, control, and expand its territory, namely, its imperial vocation. The presence of these specific views of space in plays that explore select episodes of Spain's past underscores, in the words of Barbara Fuchs, "the continuities and interdependence [that existed] between the formation of early modern nations and their imperial aspirations."[17] The use of the adjective "imperial" in this context may seem misleading and imprecise. Lope and his contemporaries did not use the term *empire* to refer to the extended dominions of the Spanish crown. The terms they most frequently employed were *Monarquía*, *Monarquía Española*, or *Monarquía Católica*. Empire, in a strict sense, alluded to a political reality that was only in existence during the reign of Charles V (1519–1556), who in 1519 succeeded his grandfather, Maximilian I, as Holy Roman Emperor. Charles abdicated in 1556 in favor of his brother, Ferdinand, who then assumed control of all the Austrian lands belonging to the Hapsburgs. Charles's decision prevented his Spanish heirs from officially donning the mantle of emperors, but the diverse and global polity they governed, with its enormous military and financial resources, "was to remain, even after the abdication of Charles V in 1556 and the separation of the *Imperium* from the *Monarchia*, the only viable candidate for a true universal empire" (Pagden, *Lords of All the World*, 43).[18] This meant that Spain, as a nation, "came into being," as historian and cultural critic Joan Ramón Resina has argued, "as an empire,"[19] a fact that has often been ignored in studies on the relation between Lope's comedias and the formation of a national consciousness in early modern Spain.[20] The emergence and expansion of that consciousness were inextricably linked in Lopian drama to the celebration and legitimation of the unprecedented power acquired by the Hapsburgs as both national and "universal" monarchs—an operation that required an imperial reading and transformation of history in which space played, I will argue, a critical role.

My exploration of that role in this book covers the three main periods in which Lope, according to Antonio Carreño, consciously divided Spanish history in his drama: an initial period concerned with the foundation of the nation that dramatizes the struggle for supremacy between the Christian kingdoms of northern Iberia and the Muslim caliphate in the south; a middle period that explores the tensions between monarchy and aristocracy, which resulted from the increasing centralization of authority in the crown; and, finally, a period of peace and stability characterized by "la presencia de una monarquía (la de los Reyes Católicos) que instaura la idiosincrasia de los viejos valores (de los visigodos al Cid), y otorga sentido a la ya constituida nación como imperio"[21] (the presence of a monarchy—that of the Catholics Kings—that promotes the idiosyncrasy of the old values [from the Visigoths to El Cid] and gives meaning to the nation-empire that has already been formed). Lope's dramatic rendition of these three periods in his national history theater includes a series of spatial motifs that inscribe empire into the past and connect history to a present that sees itself mirrored, prefigured, and legitimized in the legends and memorable deeds performed by the kings and heroes of medieval Iberia.

My analysis of these motifs in the chapters that follow focuses on four comedias Lope wrote at the height of his career as a playwright: *El mejor alcalde, el rey* [The Best Justice, the King] (ca. 1620–1623), *Las famosas asturianas* [The Famous Women from Asturias] (ca. 1610–1612), *Las paces de los reyes y judía de Toledo* [The Monarchs' Reconciliation and the Jewess of Toledo] (ca. 1610–1612), and *Los guanches de Tenerife y conquista de Canaria* [The Guanches from Tenerife and the Conquest of the Canary Islands] (ca. 1604–1606).[22] All these works exemplify his commitment to dramatizing Spain's "grandezas de sus glorias / en elegantes historias"[23] (great glories / in elegant stories), as the gardener Fabio (Lope's fictional alter ego) declares in *El premio de la hermosura* [The Prize of Beauty] (ca. 1609–1620), and his reliance on space as a vehicle to imperialize the past.

My decision to focus specifically on these four comedias is based on the fact that they represent the two genres within Lope's historical theater that, according to renowned Lope scholar Joan Oleza, "están llamados a definir el drama del *Arte nuevo* de Lope en su madurez" (are destined to define the drama of Lope's *Arte nuevo* in its mature stage) ("Del primer Lope," xvi), dramas that adapt to the stage famous events that shaped the collective destiny of the nation (*dramas de hechos famosos públicos*) and dramas centered on the personal conflicts faced by individual historical actors (*dramas de hechos particulares*).[24] Lope composed dozens of comedias belonging to these two genres during his heyday as a playwright, outnumbering anything he wrote in other dramatic modalities in which he was also very prolific (urban, courtly, and hagiographical comedias, for instance).[25] The plays I analyze in this book represent only a small fraction of Lope's output as *dramaturgo de la historia*, a role in which he outperformed other dramatists of the period, but as a corpus they underscore the central part that space played in his "contribuciones [dramáticas] a la meditación contemporánea sobre la expansion imperial de España"[26] (dramatic contributions to the contemporary reflection on Spanish imperial expansion). Because the four "dramatic contributions" I examine here adapt to the stage events pertaining to the three major periods in which Lope divided Spanish history, they also provide a panoramic framework for understanding in overall terms his dramatic engagement with the past.[27]

These plays also highlight something that I hope will become evident in the pages that follow: Lope's concern with difference and with the relation between center and periphery, the local and the global, in his historical theater. The recurrent appearance of these two themes in his *comedias historiales* reveals his knowledge of the multiethnic reality of medieval Iberia and of the geopolitical factors—the growth of the monarchy, in particular—that shaped its history. It also reflects his awareness of the significance that these two issues continued to have for early modern Spaniards as their country struggled to maintain control over a vast polity made up of diverse and far-flung territories and with the uncomfortable legacy of its Semitic past. Lope's attention to these problems explains the constant overlap between past and present in his historical drama, an overlap that, as Anthony Cascardi has pointed out, creates the chronological illusion of "a future that is continuous with the past" (*Ideologies of History*, 4) in his theater and that relied on space to imperialize national history.

Such reliance, as I argue in chapter 1, reflects the peculiar status of the comedia as what Ricardo Padrón calls an "optical regime" (*The Spacious Word*, 97)—a system of representation in which distances shrink and subjects are allowed to move quickly, like a finger on a map, from one location to another. Lope took advantage of the comedia's adherence to this mode of representation to disseminate an image of medieval monarchy that resembled that of the imperial rulers of his day, who were often depicted in woodcuts, emblems, and other forms of propaganda as being able to materialize in every corner of their vast and scattered domains. This image, I will contend in more detail in chapter 2, colors the relationship between kingship and territory that Lope establishes in *El mejor alcalde, el rey*, a play in which the monarch, King Alfonso VII of León and Castile, is praised for his ability to impart justice in person in a remote corner of his realm, the wild and far-off kingdom of Galicia.

The imperialized image of medieval monarchy that we see in plays like *El mejor alcalde, el rey* finds a parallel, as I further maintain in chapter 1, in the expanding picture of the territory Lope includes in some of his national history dramas. The Christian kingdoms of medieval Iberia often appear in these plays as *figurae* or early incarnations of the expansive and sprawling empire ruled by the Hapsburgs. The link between this empire and its distant medieval predecessors was often formulated in spatial terms by early modern Spanish historians, whose writings emphasized the desire of northern Christian monarchies to enlarge their territory at the expense of the Muslim polities located to the south. As I will discuss in chapter 3, Lope clearly embraced this expansionist view of Spain's past in *Las famosas asturianas*, a play that recounts how the behavior of a group of women in the small and beleaguered kingdom of Asturias and León inspired their king, Alfonso II, "El Casto" (The Chaste), to take up arms against his Muslim overlord, the caliph of Córdoba, and trade confinement for expansion. The proto-imperial image of Asturias and León that Lope fashions in this play is underscored in a number of scenes that center on overcoming enclosure as a key political and geographical motif and highlight the ability of gender and onomastics to embody the drive for expansion that identifies this northern Iberian kingdom.

The final aspect of the relation between space, history, and empire I will examine in this book is the imperialized image of otherness Lope presents in plays that dramatize encounters and relationships with members of non-Christian communities. In these plays, Lope adapts new experiences related to difference collected in the present to the depiction of past events, reversing the strategy he adopts in his *dramas históricos de tema contemporáneo* (dramas on contemporary historical events), where, as critics have observed, the tendency is to depict contemporary imperial conflicts—those taking place in the Netherlands and the Americas, for instance—in a manner that recalls the struggle between Christians and Moors during the Reconquest of Iberia.[28] Space plays a key role, as I will argue in chapters 4 and 5 when discussing *Las paces de los reyes y judía de Toledo* and *Los guanches de Tenerife y conquista de Canaria*, in the elaboration of this anachronistic, "modernized" view of otherness that Lope promotes in his national history theater. This becomes apparent in the image presented in *Las paces de los reyes* of twelfth-century Castile as a polity endangered internally by traitors and infiltrators. This image, which the play chiefly associates with Raquel, the Jewish mistress of the Castilian King Alfonso VIII, reproduces in a medieval context the spatial anxieties that early modern Spaniards felt in relation to the *Moriscos*, Muslims who had converted to Catholicism during and after the *Reconquista*, whom the Spanish authorities accused of collaborating with the Turks to bring about the downfall of Spain as a Christian nation.

Similarly, the image of the Canary Islands as an ingestible and penetrable territory, both sexually and geographically, that Lope paints in *Los guanches de Tenerife* projects notions of space onto this archipelago that postdate their conquest by the crown of Castile in the latter half of the fifteenth century. As I discuss in chapter 5, these notions occupy a prominent place in the imperial and highly sexualized discourse of early modern cosmography and in the chronicles that described the distant and unfamiliar territories conquered and settled in the New World by the Spanish. The way Lope mobilizes these notions in *Los guanches* to re-enact the Castilian conquest of Tenerife in the late 1400s illustrates the central role that space plays in the imperialized view of the past he promotes in his drama.

Those delving into the pages of this study will undoubtedly find it strange that a book that bears the word "mapping" in its title does not actually contain any maps. My use of this term reflects the textualized view of cartographic and spatial representation that has gained currency in what both theorists and literary critics have called "the spatial turn"—a growing body of scholarship in the humanities dedicated to examining the role of space in literature and other cultural manifestations.[29] According to this view, "literature functions as a form of mapping, offering its readers descriptions of places, situating them in a kind of imaginary space, and providing points of reference by which they can orient themselves and understand the world in which they live" (Tally, *Spatiality*, 3). The view of Lopian drama I present in this book underlines this map-like function of literature, for it emphasizes how this new type of theater or *comedia nueva*, as Lope called it, allowed audiences to make sense of the place they occupied in the imperial polity they inhabited by presenting them with a coherent and comprehensive picture of the past.

This picture relied heavily on the effective manipulation of spatial motifs to establish, as Veronika Ryjik has put it, "una continuidad histórica desde los orígenes de la comunidad hasta su actualidad" (a historical continuity from the origin of the community to the present) (*Lope de Vega en la invención*, 43), making constant use of the signifying power of space to imperialize history. Theater, under this paradigm, became an ideal vehicle for "mapping" the hallowed roots and global destiny of the nation, serving thus, as British cultural geographer Denis Cosgrove has argued in relation to Elizabethan playhouses, as a "conspectus" for its members, namely, as "a place, region, or text in which phenomena are unified for public understanding."[30]

The dramatic geography that made this understanding possible cannot be divorced from the places where it was performed: the bustling corrales de comedias that peppered the urban landscape of early modern Iberian and American cities from the late sixteenth century onward. These budding public theaters, typically located in a rectangular courtyard surrounded by three- or four-story houses in the middle of the city, featured a thrust stage with very few props, minimal sets, and scant scenery that contrasted with the technically sophisticated stages that were used to perform masques and *dramas de corte* (courtly dramas) in the palaces and estates of the powerful.[31] Plays performed in this simple urban environment were characterized, as José María Ruano de la Haza has noted, by "the relatively small number of characters, stage machines, special effects and 'discoveries' involved in their staging" and thus enabled a type of drama in which location was primarily created though the allusive language of the playwright.[32]

Plays like *El arenal de Sevilla* [The Arenal Neighborhood of Seville] (1603) and *Barlaán y Josafat* [Barlaam and Josaphat] (1611), in which Lope, as Ruano points out, uses the speech of the characters to conjure up "the sights, smells, people, shops, buildings and streets of a whole city in the mind of the spectators, who only see in front of them an empty stage platform with a plain curtain as a backdrop" ("Lope de Vega and the Theater," 43), underscore how the minimalism of the corrales fostered a dramatic geography that, although technically limited, engaged the imagination of the audience through the evocative power of language. Lope, as I hope to demonstrate in this book, took advantage of this poetic opportunity that the sparseness of the corrales provided to reconfigure Spain's past in the image of its present and to design an imperial cartography that maximized the ideological power of space in his historical theater.

CHAPTER 1

Space and the Imperial Appropriation of the Past in the Lopian Comedia

Although not particularly alert to its political import in the comedia, critics have long recognized the distinctive role of space in the new dramatic practice established by Lope de Vega. As Javier Rubiera Fernández has stated in a study devoted to the perception and manipulation of space in early modern Spanish drama, "efectivamente, uno de los elementos más característicos de la comedia nueva, cuando se la compara con otras formas teatrales, es la variación en el lugar de la acción dramática"[1] (indeed, one of the most characteristic features of the *comedia nueva*, when compared to other dramatic modalities, is the variation in the setting for the dramatic action) (*La construcción del espacio*, 26). This fondness for shifting and diverse locations in the plays written by Lope and his followers has been linked to the priority given by these playwrights to fast, action-packed plots that, according to Rubiera, "es la clave de una comedia dirigida a un público impaciente y ávido de sucesos variados" (is the key to a drama that was addressed to an impatient audience hungry for diverse events) (26). More recently, however, Margaret Greer has attempted to link the spatial diversity characteristic of the Lopian comedia to the imperial context in which this new type of drama developed. Taking her cue from studies on the representation of urban landscape in Elizabethan drama, Greer suggests that the variety of spaces evoked and staged in the comedia made it possible for its audience to gain awareness of their belonging to an imperial polity, the reality and sheer magnitude of which would remain otherwise very difficult to grasp:

> Sin embargo, quisiera considerar con Uds. una relación que observo entre la densidad y extensión del mapa de los corrales y los textos dramáticos producidos para representarlos en ellos. Howard, al hablar del teatro urbano inglés, ha especulado que en una época en la que la gente común londinense no

> se movía mucho más allá de los límites de su barrio inmediato, parte de la función del teatro era familiarizarles con otras partes de la ciudad. La diversidad de espacios dramatizados en el drama del Siglo de Oro . . . ¿no podría haber ejercido una función parecida en la monarquía española? . . . Un buen número de comedias apoyan este autoconocimiento imperial. *El burlador de Sevilla* (o *Tan largo me lo fiais*) por ejemplo, nos lleva del palacio del rey de Nápoles, a un pueblo de pescadores en la costa cerca de Tarragona, al villorrio andaluz de Dos Hermanas, y a Sevilla.[2]
>
> (I would like, however, to ponder with you a correlation I have observed between the number and density of playhouse locations on the map and the dramatic texts that were produced to be represented in them. Howard, referring to Elizabethan urban theater, has posited the idea that, at a time when regular Londoners did not venture much farther than the boundaries of their neighborhood, the role of the theater was partly to make them familiar with other parts of the city. Could the diverse places dramatized in Golden Age comedias have performed a similar role in relation to the Spanish Monarchy? . . . A good number of plays support this idea. *El Burlador the Sevilla* (or *Tan largo me lo fiáis*) takes us, for instance, from the palace of the king of Naples to a fishing village on the coast of Tarragona and then to the Andalusian hamlet of Dos Hermanas and to Seville.)

Although unstated, Greer's view of the instrumental role of dramatic space in the formation of an imperial self-consciousness in early modern Spain owes much to Benedict Anderson's understanding of the impact of the printing press in the formation of the modern nation.[3] Just as the press made readers of a particular language aware of the scope and dimensions of the "national" territory they occupied, fostering a sense of connectedness, the spaces represented in the comedia, according to Greer, allowed theater audiences to know the vast political entity they inhabited and to bond as imperial subjects through the acquisition of that knowledge. Audience members who attended a performance of *El burlador de Sevilla* [The Trickster of Seville] had a chance, therefore, to get acquainted with "tanto el espacio percibido como el espacio concebido de la monarquía española del siglo XVII"[4] (both the perceived space and the conceived space of the Spanish monarchy in the seventeenth century) ("Espacios teatrales," X) and to feel part of that space as they saw don Juan and other characters move through it and sometimes meticulously describe it. The spatial limitations imposed by the architecture of the corrales may have also contributed significantly to this dual objective, for as Rubiera has noted:

> La posibilidad de mostrar en una misma pieza dramática acciones diversas en tiempos y lugares distintos es característica esencial, aunque no específica, de la comedia española del siglo de oro. La variedad de los lugares fingidos en

> los estrechos márgenes del espacio de la representación en el corral podía incluso obligar a la imaginación de los espectadores a volar en dos horas escasas por diversos países y regiones. (*La construcción del espacio*, 101)

> (The possibility of showing in the same play diverse actions taking place at different times and in different places is an essential feature—albeit not unique—of the Spanish Golden Age comedia. The variety of fictional places dramatized within the narrow margins of the stage in the corrales could even force the imagination of the audience to fly through different countries and regions in the space of barely two hours.)

Many of the spaces comedia audiences were able to "see" or hear about in the two or three hours they spent in the corrales were not, however, coeval, for playwrights often resorted to stories from the past to find in them material fit for their plays. This approach was especially true in the case of Lope de Vega. Out of the 314 plays that have been legitimately attributed to him, 84 (one-fourth of his theatrical production, approximately) belonged to what Menéndez Pelayo called more than a century ago "Crónicas y leyendas dramáticas de España"[5] (chronicles and dramatized legends of Spain)—a sizeable dramatic corpus inspired in the ballads, chronicles, and legends of medieval Iberia. As Alan Paterson has written, these plays were set in "a time and an environment which his audience could recognize as belonging to a period of the past through certain coordinates established by characters and events" ("Stages of History," 151).[6] How were these settings or "environments" of the past incorporated into the imperial consciousness of early modern Spain? How did Lope use them to instill a sense of collective imperial identity despite the chronological distance that separated his audience from such events? These are questions that critics of Lope's drama, concerned as they have been with explaining the way *El Fénix* articulates the relation between past and present in his national history theater, have thus far neglected.

Some critics have argued that in Lope's *comedias historiales*, we witness a clear and sustained effort to make the past embody the moral and political values of sixteenth- and seventeenth-century Spain—"en ellas se encontraba esencializada," David Roas has argued, "la idiosincrasia de los españoles del presente"[7] (in them one could find distilled the idiosyncrasy of present-day Spaniards). However, not enough attention has been devoted to analyzing the role of space in that effort or to understanding how the comedia's handling of spatiality fostered the attachment to a global polity rooted in and often identified with legends and specific episodes of the national past. To explain how space contributed to the imperialization of this historical and legendary material, I will focus in this chapter on three aspects of the Lopian comedia that underscore its commitment to the same principles of globalism and homogeneity that informed the imperial project of Hapsburg Spain: its shrinking of distances to emphasize global reach and omnipresence as key signifiers of power, its figural reading of history to inscribe expansion into the national past, and its depiction of old forms of difference in contemporary terms. My intention is not to prove that Lope's comedia became nothing more than a neat propaganda instrument at the service of the Hapsburg imperial agenda, but rather to show that the spatial principles that structured and were enacted through this genre converged with those embraced and publicized by the Spanish monarchy and its supporters through various media.

Abolishing Distance: The Comedia as Optical Regime

"Early modern culture," as Ricardo Padrón has written in a groundbreaking study on the emergence of cartographic literature in sixteenth-century Europe, "is not one for whom 'space' is something to be appreciated synchronically" (*The Spacious Word*, 97). In this culture, Padrón adds, space "is understood not as a surface but as a distance" (97), that is, as a stretch of territory to be covered and traversed. The practical implications of this understanding for early modern Europeans were perhaps most acutely felt in the arenas of politics, diplomacy, and the military. As historian Geoffrey Parker has stated: "Indeed, the delays and disruptions posed by distance complicated the actions of all early modern governments, from the transmission of orders and items of news to the dispatch of bullion and the continual movement of troops—and the greater the distance, the greater the disruption, and the longer the delay."[8]

For a country like Spain, engaged throughout the early modern period in territorial expansion and consolidation processes at home and outside its borders, the challenge and critical significance of distance as a constitutive element of space became more apparent than in any other European nation.[9] It is no surprise then, as Parker has underlined, that distance was considered "public enemy number one" (*The Army of Flanders*, 42) by the Spanish monarchy and that its defeat was constantly imagined and represented by those who wished to celebrate royal power and the possibility of its deployment on a global scale.

This attitude is perhaps best illustrated in those images of the crown that, taking as their focus the idea of omnipresence, praised the unique status of Spanish kings as *monarcae universales*, worldwide rulers. An early example of this is the woodcut that appears on the title page of Giuliano Dati's *Lettera dell'isole che ha trovato nuovamente il re di Spagna* [Letter on the Islands Newly Found by the King of Spain] (1493), a rendition in verse of Columbus's second letter, which shows King Ferdinand, "The Catholic," watching in real time the Spanish arrival in the Americas while sitting comfortably on his throne at court (figure 1.1). "The king's transoceanic gaze," Padrón has written concerning this image, "reduces the vast ocean sea to the status—in the language of a later age—of nothing but 'the pond' that separates Europe from America" (*The Spacious Word*, 123). The same could be said, I would argue, about the pointing gesture

Figure 1.1. Title page, Giuliano Dati, *Lettera dell'isole che ha trovato nuovamente il re di Spagna* (1493). Tracy W. McGregor Library of American History, Small Special Collections Library, University of Virginia.

Ferdinand makes with his left arm, which, half-stretched across the Atlantic, shrinks the distance between the American and European shores and brings the king's transatlantic possessions almost within his grasp.

The implicit statement about the breadth and depth of the monarch's authority contained in the woodcut is, needless to say, one neither cartographers nor colonial administrators would have been able to support, but its message regarding distance is one we repeatedly encounter in other images of kingly power produced for the Spanish monarchy during the early modern period. Thus, more than one hundred years after the publication of Dati's letter, in 1599, members of the Jesuit order

Figure 1.2. Emblem (bottom left), "Labore et constantia," from Domenico Fontana, "Mausolei Typus Neapoli in Funere Philippi II." In *Descriptio honorum qui Neapoli habiti sunt in funere Philippi II. Catholici Regis*. Bibliothèque Nationale de France, Ms. Latin 6175.

in Naples issued an emblem to commemorate the death of Philip II that reemphasized the king's ability to reach across vast distances and make himself present in all his territories while remaining fastened to his *Escorial* throne (figure 1.2). The emblem in question, attached to one of the four façades that supported the elaborate mausoleum that the architect Domenico Fontana had designed to summarize the meaning of Philip's reign, shows a drawing compass with one of its feet pinned down on a grassy floor while the other traces a circle around it.[10] Above and surrounding the compass, the Latin inscription *labore et constantia* (through labor and perseverance) let visitors to the mausoleum know, as John Marino has remarked, that "even if in life Philip stayed in Spain, his high and generous thought circumscribed the world and his undefeatable power circled the earth."[11] The power to overcome distance that Ferdinand exhibits in the Dati woodcut thus came to full realization in the person of his grandson, who, transformed into a measuring instrument, was able to prevail mentally over distance he could not cover corporeally as the ruler of an empire in which the sun never set.

We can identify the types of images produced by Dati and the Neapolitan Jesuits, however illusory and blatantly propagandistic they may be, with the emergence of what Ricardo Padrón has called "optical regimes," that is, systems of representation in which spatial and chronological distances are abolished and in which objects and places are presented synchronously. For Padrón, behind these optical regimes lie notions of spatiality that were not yet fully operational in early modern Europe, where space, following medieval models, was still "inseparable from the action of moving through it" and was conceived therefore as "something to be taken in diachronically" (*The Spacious Word*, 97).

Chronicles documenting the exploration and colonization of the Americas and epic poems recounting the deeds of famous conquistadors in the newly found territories across the Atlantic provide, according to Padrón, ample proof. In these documents, space is imagined in a linear, not a planar sense, and is thus represented "from the perspective of the earthbound traveler, moving from one location to another along a linear route" (94). Padrón has demonstrated the pervasiveness of this linear form of spatiality, inherited from the portolan charts and pilgrim guides of the Middle Ages, in the iconographic and textual depictions of space that were produced in the early modern Hispanic world. Consequently, he has argued for a less planar or map-oriented approach to the study of spatial representation in the literature of the period: "The hegemony of the gridded map is something from which we are only beginning to liberate ourselves, as we gradually shed our old definitions of maps and mapping and look for more inclusive language with which to think about territorial representation" (91).

Padrón's argument makes perfect sense in the types of texts he analyzes: prose and verse narratives in which the sequential structure of the plot restores and enhances the older sense of space as distance by forcing the reader to move from place to place along a protracted discursive and geographic itinerary. The same, however, does not hold for texts in which the focus is less on telling and more on showing, particularly those written for theatrical performance. In these texts, the emphasis is on witnessing, not on following, events, and the viewer can simply appear alongside the characters in those places where the action occurs without having to travel along the route that connects them. Dramatic texts, especially those affiliated with the new conventions of the Lopian comedia, frequently flaunt this nonlinear and instantaneous form of spatiality that Padrón refers to as an "optical regime" and resort, unsurprisingly, to the map as an apt metaphor for its conceptualization. Consider, for instance, the dialogue between *Curiosidad* and *Comedia* that opens act 2 of Cervantes's *El Rufán dichoso* [The Fortunate Ruffian], where the latter's ability to collapse distances is identified as the most distinctive and innovative feature of the new dramatic genre she represents:

CURIOSIDAD. Comedia.
COMEDIA. Curiosidad,
 ¿qué me quieres?
....
CURIOSIDAD. Véote, y no te conozco;
 Dame de ti nuevas tales
 Que te vuelva a conocer,
 Pues que soy tu amigo grande.
COMEDIA. Los tiempos mudan las cosas
 Y perficionan las artes,
 Y añadir a lo inventado

No es dificultad notable.
Buena fui pasados tiempos,
Y en éstos, si los mirares,
No soy mala, aunque desdigo
De aquellos preceptos graves
Que me dieron y dejaron
En sus obras admirables
Séneca, Terencio y Plauto,
Y otros, griegos, que tú sabes.
....
Ya represento mil cosas,
No en relación, como de antes,
Sino en hecho; y así, es fuerza
Que haya de mudar lugares,
Que, como acontecen ellas
En muy diferentes partes,
Voime allí donde acontecen,
Disculpa del disparate.
Ya la comedia es un mapa
Donde no un dedo distante
Verás a Londres y a Roma,
A Valladolid y a Gante.
Muy poco importa al oyente
Que yo en un punto me pase
Desde Alemania a Guinea
Sin del teatro mudarme;
El pensamiento es ligero:
Bien pueden acompañarme
Con él doquiera que fuere,
Sin perderme ni cansarse.[12]

(CURIOSITY. Comedia.
COMEDIA. Curiosity, what do you want from me? . . .
CURIOSITY. I see you and I barely know you. Tell me what's happened to you so I may recognize you again; for I am your good friend.
COMEDIA. Time changes things and perfects the arts, so adding to what has been invented is not so difficult. I did well in the past; and now, if you well consider me, I am not doing so badly, even though I do not abide anymore by those authoritative precepts that Seneca, Terence, Plautus, and others you know—Greeks—gave me and used in their revered works. . . . I represent now a thousand things, not in words, like before, but in deeds; and

> since they occur in very different places, I must change locations and go where they happen. So please excuse this nonsense. Theater has now become a map, where you can see London and Rome, Valladolid and Gante, less than a finger away from each other. Audiences care little if I move in one instant from Germany to Guinea without leaving the stage. Thought is light. They can come with me wherever thought goes without fear of getting tired, or of me getting lost.)

Critics who have commented on this dialogue have often noted how out of sync *Comedia*'s views are with the opinions on contemporary drama Cervantes expressed in other passages of his oeuvre.[13] The author of *Don Quixote*, so critical in some of his writings of the new style of theater introduced by Lope de Vega, has wholeheartedly embraced here its capacity to "mudar lugares," or change places and to incorporate different locations into one single plot.[14] Cervantes has even resorted in this passage to the same argument Lope employed a few years earlier in his *Arte nuevo de hacer comedias* [New Art of Writing Plays in This Age] (1609)—"los tiempos mudan las cosas" (time changes things)—to justify the drastic change of setting he will later introduce in act 2 of *El rufián*, which transports the audience from the mean streets of Seville, where the criminal career of Cristóbal de Lugo, the play's main character, begins, to a peaceful Dominican monastery in Mexico City where Lugo will attain sainthood.[15] The move from Seville to Mexico is mediated in Cervantes's play by the speech given by *Comedia* at the start of act 2. However, her words are not primarily intended to fill with discourse the distance between the two locations or to provide a narrative itinerary that may mimic for the audience "the perspective of the earthbound traveler" (*The Spacious Word*, 94), as Padrón has argued concerning prose texts written in this period. *Comedia*'s discourse is aimed, instead, at highlighting precisely how inoperative linear or discursive spatiality has become in the genre that she embodies and at making readers aware of the changes that have made that situation possible. Those changes have to do, as *Comedia* states, with the fact that playwrights prefer now to let the action unfold directly onstage instead of telling the audience about it through the speech of the characters: "Ya represento mil cosas, / no en relación, como de antes, / sino en hecho" (I represent now a thousand things / not in words, like before, / but in deeds) (*El rufián dichoso*, act 2, lines 1245–1247). This shift in practice, which *Comedia* implicitly identifies with the new style of drama sponsored by Lope de Vega, rendered obsolete the type of theater made popular a generation earlier by playwrights like the Valencian Cristóbal de Virués. The plays of Virués frequently contain lengthy narrative segments like the one he inserted in act 1 of his *Elisa Dido* (ca. 1580), in which the slave Delbora begs the Syrian Ismeria to give her a word-for-word account of Queen Dido's life before arriving in exile in Carthage:

ISMERIA. Con regalos mayores te prometo,
Quisiera aligerar, dulce Delbora,
La prisión que padeces en Cartago.
DELBORA. No la llames prisión, Ismeria mía,
A la dichosa suerte que poseo,
Que es agraviarme a mí y menguar el gozo
Que de ser de la Reina esclava tengo,
De quien te ruego, si hay espacio ahora,
Me digas, como ya me has prometido,
La notable salida de su tierra
Y el proceso admirable de su vida.
ISMERIA. Haré lo que deseas. Está atenta,
Que te diré palabra por palabra
Y te referiré cosa por cosa
Cuantas de los sucesos de la Reina
Son dinas de saberse, como aquella
Que mejor que otro alguno y de más cerca
Los ha visto, por ser, como ya has visto,
Quien más a cerca está de su persona.
Escucha, pues.[16]

(ISMERIA. With better care, I promise you, would I like to relieve, sweet Delbora, the burden of your captivity in Carthage.

DELBORA. Do not call captivity, dear Ismeria, the good fortune I enjoy, for that would be an insult to me and would lessen the joy I feel at being the queen's slave. Please tell me now, if you have the time, about her remarkable exodus from her land and the amazing story of her life, for you promised me.

ISMERIA. I will do what you wish. Pay attention, and I will tell you word for word everything worth knowing about the queen. No one knows or has seen these things better than me, for I am, as you know, the one closest to the queen. Therefore, listen carefully.)

The long account Ismeria provides in the next three hundred lines to explain to Delbora why Queen Dido left her native Syria to found and settle a new city on the Lybian coast is, quite tellingly, absent in Gabriel Lasso de la Vega's *Tragedia de la honra de Dido restaurada* [Tragedy of Dido's Honor Restored] (1587), which, as Alfredo Hermenegildo has argued, "sigue los caminos de la presentación integral de la historia en escena, acercándose así de modo claro y eficaz al modelo de la 'comedia nueva' [de Lope]"[17] (opts for presenting all the story onstage, adopting thus, clearly and efficiently, the model of Lope's "comedia nueva"). The changes that Hermenegildo has identified in Lasso's play underscore the hypermimetic agenda that, under the influence of Lope, Spanish playwrights began to embrace in the late 1580s, an agenda that, though still relying heavily on language to sustain the plot, curtailed narration in order to represent things "no en relación . . . / sino en hecho" (not in words . . . / but in deeds) (act 2, lines 1245–1247), as *Comedia* puts it in *El rufián dichoso*.

This innovative and self-conscious privileging of mimesis over diegesis allowed Lope and other dramatists influenced by his *comedia nueva* to set their dramas in distant locations "sin necesidad de 'hacer camino'" (without making the journey there), as Aurelio González has argued ("Espacio y dramaturgia cervantina," 901), in relation to *El rufián dichoso*, and to use space in a synchronous or quasi-synchronous manner in their plays. This practice materializes, for instance, in Lope's *Los españoles en Flandes* [The Spanish in Flanders] (ca. 1597–1606), in which Alessandro Farnese, the new leader appointed by Philip II to put down the Protestant rebellion in the Netherlands, travels the distance between Italy and Flanders in the space of a few hundred verses and is able to appear in Naples, Milan, and Brussels in the same act.[18] Farnese's journeying, his earthbound movement "from one location to another along a linear route" (Padrón, *The Spacious Word*, 74) is, with the exception of a few isolated references to horses and travel clothes, virtually absent in Lope's play, which focuses on the loyalty, prowess, and exemplary conduct of the new royal appointee. That this should happen in a play that, to a significant extent, thematizes travel, the movement of troops, and the crown's efforts to maintain control over distant territories clearly indicates that the spatiality at work in the comedia radically differs from the linear and protracted treatment of space that is prevalent in other texts of the period. The remarkable shrinking of distances that takes place in *Los españoles en Flandes* must have made its audience feel that Naples and Brussels were indeed, as Cervantes's *Comedia* boasts in *El rufián dichoso*, less than a finger away from each other and that the many countries, regions, and provinces that spanned the breadth of the Spanish Empire could be reached "sin del teatro mudarse" (without leaving the theater) (*El rufián dichoso*, act 2, line 1260).

The way of perceiving, understanding, and representing space fostered by the Lopian comedia was thus, one must conclude, very close to the synchronicity that Padrón has identified with the optical regime of the map and to the geographical wishful thinking that informs the many depictions of Spanish kings as *monarcae universales* that we find in emblems, woodcuts, and other propagandistic images from this era. Like these images, the comedia effectively promoted a view of space that, by abolishing or significantly shrinking distance, conferred on audiences the power to reach and make themselves present in all the regions of the known world in only a few verses. Whether that fostered a better understanding of empire as a vast and heterogeneous polity is something that can only be conjectured. What is certain, however, is that the new spatial regime instituted by the Lopian comedia allowed theatergoers to occupy a position in the political and geographical imaginary of the period that was otherwise routinely reserved for the global monarch they served. This experience surely had an empowering effect on the public, but it also ensured ideological subjection. If the comedia allowed audiences to enjoy global reach and feel like universal rulers for the span of a few hours in the corrales, it also instilled in them a perception of space that converged with and ultimately reinforced the power of the monarchical and aristocratic elites who ruled the Spanish empire. That perception concerned not only the places and scenarios where contemporary events unfolded but also those of the past. This had a critical impact, as we shall see in chapter 2, on the image of Alfonso VII of Castile (1105–1157) as omnipresent ruler that Lope presents in *El mejor alcalde, el rey* [The Best Justice, the King], an image that redefined the identity of this twelfth-century monarch in contemporary terms and that imperialized the episode of Spanish history dramatized in this comedia.

Empire across Time: Space and the Figural Reading of History in the Comedia

The comedia's use of space to imperialize the past was as much the result of the new shifts in dramatic practice that Cervantes described in *El rufián dichoso* as it was the consequence of a close reading of history—national history, in particular—that paid special attention to the rhetorical and ideological strategies employed by historians to link the past to the present. These strategies materialized in discursive form the dual mission that Renaissance humanism assigned to history as an intellectual and, more importantly, a civic enterprise.[19] That mission entailed, on the one hand, providing early modern rulers with a practical frame of reference to govern their subjects in a virtuous manner and, on the other, fostering a strong sense of national identity by extracting from the past a common ancestry that individuals ruled by the same prince or inhabiting the same territory could claim as their own. The former required approaching the past from an ethical and pedagogical perspective in order to tease out models of civic conduct that could guide and authorize political action in the present.[20] The latter was often achieved by subjecting past events to the same exegetical techniques that interpreters of Scripture had used during Late Antiquity and the Middle Ages to make the Old and New Testaments cohere and plot a single, unbroken doctrinal line from Genesis to Revelation. Applying these techniques to the reading and writing of history allowed past acts and actors to retain historical specificity and appear simultaneously as *figurae*—prefigurations of personages and events to come that were both real and historical.[21] This figural interpretation of history allowed, for instance, the Jesuit historian and political theorist Juan de Mariana to claim in his *De rege et regis institutione* [On the King and the Royal Institution] (1598) that the decline of the medieval House of Trastámara was a sure sign of the impending collapse of the Hapsburg dynasty and to present Philip II's unwavering defense of Catholicism as prefigured by the campaigns launched by the Trastamaran king Henry III (1379–1406) to expand the Christian faith in medieval Iberia.[22] Lope was well aware of the figural techniques employed by Mariana and other contemporary historians to link the past to the present and did not hesitate, as Alan Paterson has argued, to incorporate them into his national history dramas:[23]

> Lope seems to have been guided by an underlying pattern in contemporary history writing, which did not divide the past into the now familiar periodicities but which rather looks into the past for prefigurations of the order that would eventually emerge as the modern state, as if the nature of that state were continually being exposed and pre-enacted at critical junctures in its past; it is on such a view of history, not dissimilar to the prefigurative readings that were made in Scriptural exegesis, that the exemplarity of the past is based. ("Stages of History," 154)

The "prefigurative readings" Patterson refers to in this passage are often lodged in Lope's drama in the prophetic speeches that characters close to the monarch give to highlight a specific historical event. The event in question is described in detail and treated as a specific historical occurrence, but it is also used to prognosticate the emergence of a political order that will come to fruition in the years or centuries to come. More often than not, that order is the universal monarchy devised and ruled by the Hapsburgs, thus making the event performed or described onstage the seed of an empire awaiting its historical fulfillment. This empire *in nuce*, the contours of which Lope is able to glimpse in the isolated episodes of national history he dramatizes, can be clearly discerned, for instance, in the prophecy that a Gypsy woman makes to Queen Sancha in act 3 of *El primer rey de Castilla* [The First King of Castile] (ca. 1598–1603) after her husband, count Ferdinand of Castile, defeats King Bermudo of León in the battle of Támara:

> GITANA. Por años cuarenta y siete
> Reinaréis príncipes santos,
> Y tú dos más que tu marido,
> Reina, vivirás dos años.
> De vosotros irá siempre
> Castilla el reino aumentando,
> Llamándose reyes de ella,
> Emperadores romanos.
> Será vuestra España toda,
> Discurriendo siglos largos,
> Nápoles, Milán, Sicilia,
> Y otros mil reinos cristianos,

La Oriental y Occidental
Del Indio.[24]

(Gypsy Woman. You will reign as holy princes for forty-seven years; and you, my queen, will outlive your husband by two years. With you two on the throne, Castile will always grow bigger, and their kings will call themselves Roman emperors. All Spain will be yours, and, after many centuries, so will be Naples, Milan, Sicily, and a thousand other Christian kingdoms, as well as the East and West Indies.)

There is no denying that the prophecy delivered here to Queen Sancha serves to intensify, as Veronika Ryjik has argued, the moment of geopolitical transition dramatized by Lope in this play: "A partir de este momento, el reino astur-leonés 'viene a ser / segundo reino,' mientras que la historia de España se convierte en la historia de Castilla" (From this moment on, the kingdom of Asturias and León will "become / a secondary kingdom," while the history of Spain will become the history of Castile) (*Lope de Vega en la invención*, 69). Such a reading, however, overlooks how the prophecy also underlines the figural approach to history that Lope often adopts in his national history drama, allowing him to connect struggles for internal sovereignty in the past to processes of external expansion in the present. These processes are overtly alluded to in the reference to the Indies, Naples, Milan, Sicily, "and a thousand other Christian kingdoms" the Gypsy woman makes in her speech. Her mention of all these territories does more than simply subsume the history of Spain within the history of Castile, as Ryjik has stated. It imperializes the past by planting in it the seed of a universal monarchy that will be incarnated centuries later by the Hapsburgs.

The careful enumeration of territories under Hapsburg control in the prophecy made by the Gypsy woman also serves to underscore the critical role that space plays in Lope's imperial transformation of national history through the use of *figurae*. This feature of his drama has escaped the attention of even those who, like Geraldine Coates, have recently highlighted the dramatist's fascination with the spatial dynamics that govern the chronicle accounts he employed to write his historical comedias.[25] The impact of such fascination goes beyond the value Lope placed on symbols like walls, battlements, and doors to communicate the desire to defend or gain entry to a territory and extends to the larger signifying power attached to space in contemporary chronicles that express Spain's imperial destiny as a nation. This tactic appears, for example, in the seemingly contradictory use of confined spaces that Lope frequently employs to represent conquest. These spaces are commonly alluded to in early modern chronicles—both in new works and in those that were republished—when describing the battles and military campaigns waged against Islam by the Christian kings of the Iberian Peninsula. Consider, for instance, how the royal chronicler Florián de Ocampo depicted the gathering in Toledo of the Christian troops that, under the leadership of King Alfonso VIII of Castile (1155–1214), would go on to defeat the Almohad forces of Caliph Al-Nasri at the famous battle of Las Navas in 1212. In his widely read *Crónica general de España*, a text Lope repeatedly consulted to write his comedias, Ocampo provided the following description:

> Y porque en las angosturas de la ciudad no fuesen ellos apremiados, el noble rey don Alfonso . . . dioles fuera de la ciudad en la ribera del rio Tajo huertas y huertos y otros vergeles de deleite en que tomasen solaces y sabores, que él hiciera criar para tomar la su real majestad sabores y solaces cuando él en esa çiudad fuese y quisiese salir a andar.[26]

> (And to avoid having the soldiers constrained within the narrowness of the city, the noble King Alfonso . . . placed them in orchards and pleasant gardens outside Toledo, on the banks of the Tagus, so they could rest and enjoy themselves in those places he had built to enjoy and relax himself when he visited the city and wanted to stretch his legs.)

The orchards and gardens outside of Toledo where Alfonso's troops are relocated and allowed to set up camp forecast the vast geographical expanse south of the Tagus that will be conquered and settled after the victory at Las Navas. Historically speaking, however, the occupation of this territory was preceded by a long period of confinement that kept the Christian kingdoms of medieval Iberia enclosed within the northern half of the peninsula, a period that the text of the *Crónica* alludes to by referring to the narrow spaces ("las angosturas") where Alfonso's troops had been quartered in Toledo.

Thus, the local landscape of the city and its surroundings unveils a spatial pattern that the attentive reader could link to another crucial episode in the long fight against Islam in medieval Iberia: Pelayo's victory against the invading army of the Umayyad Caliphate in the narrow valley of Covadonga in 722. Pelayo's ability to turn the tide of Spanish history by transforming the *angostura* or narrow space where his army had been cornered into a site that would mark the beginning of Christian Iberia's long march south to conquer the homeland was regularly celebrated by early modern Spanish historians, who wasted no opportunity to turn "la insigne Cueba donde se hizo fuerte el Rey D. Pelayo, y de donde comenzó sus Conquistas"[27] (the illustrious cave where King Pelayo made himself strong and from where he began his conquests), as the royal chronicler Ambrosio de Morales wrote in his *Corónica general de España* [General Chronicle of Spain] (1572), into a veritable symbol of Spain's prowess and expanding vocation. Lope, as I will argue in chapter 3, adhered to this familiar confinement/expansion pattern employed by contemporary historians to codify Spain's imperial destiny in *Las famosas asturianas* [The Famous Women from Asturias].

This play dramatizes the decision made by a group of ninth-century Asturian women to fight their Moorish overlords and thereby persuade their monarch to set their kingdom on a path to expansion.

Lope's incorporation of this spatial motif into the plot of *Las famosas asturianas* allowed him to present an isolated, legendary episode from the past as a prefiguration of a political order that, glimpsed first in the victory obtained by Pelayo in Covadonga, would culminate centuries later in the project of an all-Catholic, universal monarchy sponsored by the Hapsburgs. We could attribute the complex spatial and chronological overlap at work in a play like *Las famosas asturianas* to the fact that, as Herbert Lindenberger has posited, "historical plays are at least as much a comment on the playwright's times as on the periods about which they are ostensibly written."[28] However, that would only serve to subsume Lope's historical theater within a larger interpretative paradigm that blatantly ignores the dramatist's reliance on space and figural patterns of reading to exploit the full political meaning of history.[29] The critical role these two factors played in Lope's effort to imperialize the past in his national history theater becomes apparent, as I will argue in my discussion of *Las famosas asturianas*, in plays that dramatize episodes of beleaguerment and territorial contraction during the *Reconquista*. In these plays, Lope maximizes the signifying power attached to space in historiographical discourse to make the past and present cohere within a grand imperial narrative that highlights Spain's resolve to expand its borders at critical moments in history. The episodes chosen by Lope to familiarize his audience with this grand narrative appear linked in contemporary historiography to specific locales and spatial configurations. Lope was able to exploit the full political meaning of these settings by subjecting history to the type of figural reading that, according to Paterson, informs many of his *comedias historiales*.

Old Others in New Clothes: Space and the Representation of Difference in the Comedia

The vanishing of distances and the fulfillment of expansive prophecies that inscribe empire into the nation's past often materialize in Lope's historical dramas at the expense of those whom Spanish culture traditionally considered its others: Muslims (Moors) and Jews. These others are stripped of their land and incorporated into a national and proto-imperial polity that views its relationship to the territory as mediated by the moral and ideological imperatives of religion. This perspective is hardly surprising, for, as Anthony Pagden has noted, Spanish views on expansion "had since the eleventh century been inextricably bound in with the language and cultural traditions—as well as the mythology—of the *Reconquista*" (*Lords of All the World*, 92). These traditions invariably promoted the annexation and settlement of territory as a means to expand the Christian faith and to assert the authority of the Catholic Church. The Lopian comedia's adherence to these ideals of the *Reconquista* explains why, according to Walter Cohen, its depiction of conquest and conflict in contemporary settings is, more often than not, modeled on patterns inherited from the Middle Ages: "The late sixteenth-century Golden Age national history play, regardless of its temporal and geographical setting, tends to emphasize the struggle between Catholic Spain and its infidel, external foes. When the dramatized events postdate the Reconquest, the structure of the Christian/Mooor struggle is simply shipped abroad, for instance to the New World in *Arauco domado* or to Flanders in *El asalto de Mastrique*."[30]

However, along with this tendency to transfer long-standing notions of otherness to new settings, there is a parallel effort in Lope's theater to adapt new experiences related to differences to the events and historical scenarios of the past. This is an aspect of Lopian drama that has not received much attention from critics, who, in general, have been content with repeating that "los procesos de alterización, típicos de cualquier empresa imperial, se adaptan en España al esquema antitético familiar moros-cristianos" (othering processes, typical of every imperial enterprise, are adapted in Spain to the familiar, antithetical model of Moors vs. Christians) (Ryjik, *Lope de Vega en la invención*, 175).[31] Such adaptation, however, as I will argue in chapters 4 and 5 while discussing *Las paces de los reyes y judía de Toledo* [The Monarchs' Reconciliation and the Jewess of Toledo] and *Los guanches de Tenerife y conquista de Canaria* [The Guanches from Tenerife and the Conquest of the Canary Islands], is concurrent in Lope's comedia with an effort to depict old encounters with the other in a manner that reflects and absorbs newer experiences collected in the present. The echo of these experiences in Lope's historical drama reinforces his desire to imperialize the past and his reliance on space to fulfill that goal.

One way Lope mobilizes space in his theatrical works to project contemporary views of otherness onto the past is by promoting the theme of infiltration. The ability of certain non-Christian characters to insinuate themselves into the circles of power of Christian society and threaten them from within reflects a contemporary problem the Spanish monarchy had to confront repeatedly throughout the early modern period, and features in some of his national history plays. The first visible manifestation of this problem was in 1558, when Spanish religious authorities discovered the existence of Protestant cells in Seville and Valladolid led by two prominent humanists, Dr. Constantino Ponce de la Fuente, who had been Charles V's confessor, and Dr. Agustín Cazalla, a former court preacher. The cells, remnants of earlier communities of mystics or *alumbrados* that had blossomed in Spain under the influence of Erasmus, had virtually no impact on the religious and political life of the country. However, their discovery had a significant psychological impact on both the authorities and the general population.[32] Their appearance in two of the largest urban centers in Castile called into question, as historian J. H. Elliott has argued, the ability of the Spanish authorities to keep the country insulated from its external enemies: "Was even Castile, the most Catholic land in Christendom, to be tainted by the Lutheran heresy? In the feverish climate of the 1550s the discovery of Protestants in the heart of Spain seemed very alarming, threatening as it did new dangers at a time when the Church and the Inquisition thought themselves to have successfully barred the gates against the advance of heretical doctrines."[33]

The problem these Protestant cells unveiled was magnified a decade later when the Morisco population living in the old Moorish kingdom of Granada revolted due to the oppressive laws that were passed banning the use of Arabic and prohibiting Moorish dress and customs. Although the revolt was primarily a local affair driven by the many grievances caused by the enforcement of the new laws, rumors that the Turks had thrown their support behind the rebel leaders made the Spanish authorities think of this episode as part of a more considerable effort to undermine the political and religious integrity of the country from inside its borders.[34] This perception, unjustified in light of what we now know about Turkish plans to become involved in Spain's internal affairs, had nevertheless a critical impact on the collective psyche of the Hapsburg elites. As Antonio Feros has noted, it conjured up the image of a triumphant Islam planting the crescent once again on Spanish soil: "The authorities believed that the Moriscos were doing more than merely fighting to maintain their identity within the Hispanic community: they were really conspiring against the King of Spain, through real or imagined alliances with North African princes or the Grand Turk—not only in pursuit of Granada's independence but above all to restore Islamic rule in the Peninsula."[35]

Later events, like the decree signed in 1609 by Philip III expelling *all* Moriscos from Spain and the plans drawn up by his successor, Philip IV, to banish Portuguese New Christians from all the realms of the Hispanic monarchy, further demonstrated that Spain could not consider itself safe. This understanding created deep anxiety about the truth and validity of the inside/outside dichotomy set in place by the Spanish monarchy to assert its role as defender of the Catholic faith and upset the spatial certainties that Spaniards identified with that role. Exacerbated by the fear of Semitic intrusion that permeated Spanish society from the late Middle Ages and throughout the early modern period, it colored the view of the past that Lope presented in many of his national history plays and the relation between space and otherness that he established. Like their early modern counterparts, the monarchs of medieval Castile seem unable in these plays to safeguard the territory they rule effectively and protect it from infiltration. This inability, as I will argue in chapter 4 in relation to *Las paces de los reyes y judía de Toledo* [The Reconciliation of the Monarchs and the Jewess from Toledo], shows Lope's clear awareness of the possibilities that space offered as a vehicle for exporting contemporary perceptions of otherness to the past and for imperializing the history of medieval Iberia.

That awareness also surfaces in the use Lope makes of spatial images and motifs related to penetration and ingestion to dramatize conquest in premodern colonial environments. Those images and motifs, borrowed from contemporary sources depicting the peoples, foodstuffs, and landscapes of the Americas, allowed Lope to present the invasion and colonization of those environments in terms that had gained broad currency in the spatial imagination of his culture and therefore to imperialize the past, once again, in his national history theater. The use of this strategy is evident, as I will discuss in chapter 5, in the unmistakable link Lope establishes in *Los guanches de Tenerife* between the conquest of the island kingdom of Tenerife—annexed to the crown of Castile in 1496—and the discovery and settlement of the New World. The connection between these two distant imperial scenarios is now taken for granted by historians, who see in the Spanish annexation of the Canaries a testing ground for "the forging of new methods which would come into their own in the conquest of the New World" (Elliott, *Imperial Spain, 1469–1716*, 58).[36] That connection, however, was far from obvious to Lope's audience. The conquest and settlement of the "Fortunate Islands" were, as Eyda Meridiz has argued, long-forgotten events for Lope's contemporaries until the Dominican Alonso de Espinosa published *Del Origen y Milagros de la Santa Imagen de Nuestra Señora de la Candelaria* [On the Origin and Miracles Performed by the Holy Image of Our Lady of La Candelaria] in 1594:

> The friar's main purpose was to record an account of the origin of the Virgin of Candelaria and of the miracles ascribed to her in Tenerife. . . . In the third book he narrated the history of the conquest and colonization of Tenerife at the behest of Ferdinand and Isabella and under the military direction of Alonso de Lugo. . . . Espinosa's work, despite his religious subject, was one of the first to re-articulate the history of the Canary Islands, which had been widely mistold or simply ignored due to the discovery and colonization of the New World.[37]

Like Espinosa, Lope was able in *Los guanches de Tenerife* to bring to the attention of his contemporaries an important episode of Spain's past that had all but disappeared from the pages of history.[38] However, as opposed to the friar, whose primary concern was to provide his readers with a well-researched historical account of the cult of the Virgin of La Candelaria, Lope decided to concentrate in his play on the desire for possession of the territory that drove the invading Spaniards. This change in focus allowed him to incorporate into *Los guanches* images of the territory as penetrable and edible that were common in the gendered discourses of early modern cosmography and historiography. The presence of this perspective in the play proves that, along with a tendency to medievalize difference in his drama, Lope also tried to imperialize the past by portraying historical encounters with the other according to the representational codes of contemporary imperial culture. This latter trend, which relied heavily on a skillful manipulation of space to overcome chronological barriers, was also in part responsible, as I will argue in chapter 2, for the Americanized picture of medieval Galicia that Lope paints in one of his best-known comedias, *El mejor alcalde, el rey*.

CHAPTER 2

"Que los reyes nunca están lejos"

EMPIRE AND METATHEATRICALITY IN *EL MEJOR ALCALDE, EL REY*

"¿Con qué pagaría un rey un hechizo," wondered the playwright and royal chronicler Juan de Zabaleta in his *Errores celebrados* [Revered Mistakes] (1653), "con el cual . . . se pudiera hacer a un mismo tiempo presente en todos sus estados donde, causando alegría, se granjeara amor y respeto?"[1] (How much would a king pay for a spell that would allow him . . . to make himself present simultaneously in all his territories, where, making his subjects happy, he could obtain from them love and respect?). Written over a century and a half after the woodcut on the title page of Giuliano Dati's verse rendition of Columbus's second letter to King Ferdinand of Aragón (figure 1.1), Zabaleta's question bears witness to the enduring concern with distance in the literature of early modern Spain. That concern, present always in the minds of those engaged in the contemplation and representation of power, is also vividly reflected, I will argue in this chapter, in Lope de Vega's *El mejor alcalde, el rey* [The Best Justice, the King] (ca. 1620–1623), a play long considered one of the dramatist's masterpieces.[2] The central conflict driving the plot of *El mejor alcalde*—the kidnapping and rape of a peasant woman (Elvira) in twelfth-century Galicia by a depraved nobleman (Don Tello de Neira) and her betrothed's search for justice at the court of King Alfonso VII of León and Castile—has led scholars to classify this play as a "peasant honor drama" or *comedia del honor villano*. Further, many have identified in it the same critique of seigneurial abuse and idealization of peasant values that we see depicted in *Fuenteovejuna* (ca. 1611–1618) and *Peribáñez y el comendador de Ocaña* [Peribáñez and the Commander of Ocaña] (ca. 1605–1612), two plays with which *El mejor alcalde* is said to form a trilogy.[3] However, as Donald Larson has argued, *El mejor alcalde* differs substantially from *Fuenteovejuna*, *Peribáñez*, and other peasant honor plays due to the role that Lope assigns to the figure of the monarch, whose centrality is clearly advertised, as this critic has observed, in the title of the play:[4]

> Nevertheless, there is a significant difference that distinguishes *El mejor alcalde, el rey* from the other two plays. In *Fuenteovejuna* and *Peribáñez* the peasant heroes react to the heinous actions of the villainous nobleman by taking matters into their own hands and killing him. These two works, then, are honor plays, plays in which the dramatic interest centers on the vengeance undertaken by the male protagonist, or protagonists, in order to recover honor that was diminished or destroyed because of the predatory behavior of another male. In *El mejor alcalde*, however, there is no vengeance as such, although there is a bloody punishment, and the focus of the play is quite different from that of a typical honor play. As the title itself of the work indicates, that focus is on the celebration of monarchy.[5]

The kind of monarch Lope celebrates in *El mejor alcalde* is one who, like the yearning despot described by Zabaleta, is willing to go to significant lengths to assert his authority in all the territories he rules, including traveling in person to the distant *campos de Galicia* (Galician fields), where the ill-fated Elvira is being held by her rapist. This type of king embodies onstage an idea of the relationship between monarchy and territory that, although unfeasible in the expansive and highly bureaucratized state governed by the Hapsburgs, was nonetheless constantly invoked, as I discussed in chapter 1, in contemporary depictions of Spanish kings as *monarcae universales* that periodically appeared in emblems, woodcuts, and other propagandistic representations of the period. The purpose of these images was to disseminate and provide visual support for what historian J. H. Elliott has called the "central fiction of the Spanish Monarchy" in the early modern period[6]—the idea that the king could make himself present in all the territories of his vast and scattered empire and rule, as jurist Juan de Solórzano y Pereira wrote in his *Política indiana* [On the Government of the Indies] (1648), "como si fuera Rey solamente de cada uno de ellos"[7] (as if he were king only of each one of his kingdoms). Lope de Vega's *El mejor alcalde* clearly subscribes to this fiction and projects it onto the past by rescuing from the historiographical record an anecdote about a twelfth-century monarch who traveled to the far end of his realm to act as *alcalde* (high justice) in a rape case involving a lecherous and refractory aristocrat.

The imperialized image of the past that Lope is able to construct by bringing to the stage this minor episode of medieval history is greatly enhanced, I will first contend in this chapter, by his decision to reproduce in a medieval context the same image of peripheral lands that he employed two decades earlier in *Arauco domado* [Arauco Tamed] and *El nuevo mundo descubierto por Cristóbal Colón* [The New World Discovered by Cristopher Columbus]—two plays written between 1598 and 1603—to justify Spain's conquests in the New World. This image, popularized in early modern European book culture through the writings of Herodotus, Euripides, Ovid, and Seneca, depicts marginal or "exorbitant" territories as places naturally inhabited by violent and depraved peoples and therefore in need of corrective action from a civilized center.[8] Lope adopted this classically inspired view of borders and marginal regions in *El mejor alcalde* to characterize the actions and behavior of Don Tello and to legitimize the intervention of King Alfonso in far-off Galicia. In so doing, he brought the small segment of Spanish history he dramatized in his comedia into alignment with the present and with the spatial codes he employed a few years earlier to justify *monarchia universalis* in his so-called "American plays."

This effort to recast the past in contemporary, imperial terms is further reinforced, I will argue, by the way Lope reinterprets the designation given to King Alfonso VII of León and Castile in the historiographical tradition he drew upon for the composition of his play. In this tradition, Alfonso is referred to as *Emperador de las Españas* (emperor of Spain) on account of his annexation of La Rioja and other territories belonging to the Crown of Aragón in 1134. However, in *El mejor alcalde*, the king's appellation refers to a much broader plan of territorial expansion that links the monarch's journey to Galicia to punish Don Tello to his unspoken desire to conquer Seville and Granada in the Moorish south. This wider geographical scenario in which Lope reframes Alfonso's designation as emperor allows him to portray the king as a worthy predecessor of the *monarcae universales* of early modern Spain.

Travel and the ability to quickly cover the distance between León and Galicia also play an integral part in Lope's refashioning of Alfonso's image in the likeness of the universal monarchs of his day. This aspect of the monarch's image, which Lope extends to Sancho, Elvira's betrothed, to tighten the alliance between king and vassal in the play, does not merely serve, however, as a device to foster social cohesion and monarchical sentiment in *El mejor alcalde*. Because audiences in the corrales could also "travel" swiftly from one geographical location to another during the performance of a play, the king and Sancho's journeys to and from Galicia also serve to highlight the status of Lopian theater as an "optical regime"—a system of representation in which audiences were able to experience space in a synchronous or quasi-synchronous manner, regardless of distance.[9] Travel thus performs, I will finally argue, both a political and a metatheatrical role in *El mejor alcalde, el rey*.

Empire and Exorbitance: Taming the Exotic in Medieval Galicia

As with most any history play by Lope, careful consideration of his engagement with the primary source is essential. The comedia's closing verses, uttered by Sancho, draw explicit attention to the chronicle that inspired Lope to write his play:[10]

Sancho. Y aquí acaba la comedia
Del mejor alcalde, historia
Que afirma por verdadera
La corónica de España:
La cuarta parte la cuenta.[11]

(Sancho. Here ends the comedia of the best justice; a true story, according to the *Chronicle of Spain*, which tells it in its fourth volume.)

The passage alluded to here—from book IV of Florián de Ocampo's 1541 *Crónica de España* (fol. 375r)—relates how, during the early years of his reign, King Alfonso VII of León and Castile was petitioned to intervene in a legal dispute by a Galician peasant who had his lands unlawfully seized by a local lord or *infanzón* named don Fernando (Don Tello in Lope's comedia). The king first wrote a letter to the *infanzón* asking him to restore the lands he had usurped, but, when told by the peasant his injunction had been ignored, King Alfonso decided to pay a visit to Don Fernando in Galicia and serve justice in situ. The king thus traveled incognito all the way from his court in Toledo to the northwestern edge of his realm and, after consulting with the local judge or *merino*, ordered Don Fernando hanged from the doorway of his residence. This event, the chronicle tells us, is how Alfonso acquired his reputation as "príncipe muy justiciero" (a very just king) (*Crónica de España*, fol. 375v) among his subjects and brought peace and justice to the territory of Galicia.

Lope closely follows the text of Ocampo's *Crónica* in his comedia but inserts several significant changes in the plot. The most important of these, as Donald Larson has noted, is the incorporation of a female character, Elvira, into the story, thereby switching the focus of the altercation between the dispossessed peasant and his lord:

> In his reworking of the incident from Ocampo, Lope has taken care to supply his male characters—Alfonso himself, Sancho, the peasant, and Don Tello, the nobleman—with a specificity of identity that is largely missing in the source work. He has, furthermore, placed them in surroundings that not only serve to ground the action of the play, but that, with their obvious mythic overtones, also function to enhance its thematic concerns. Finally, he has added another major character, Elvira, the betrothed of Sancho, and she is, in some sense, the crux of the plot, for in Lope's retelling of the story, what Don Tello steals from Sancho is not his lands, but Elvira, his intended wife. ("Rape, Redress, and Reintegration," 127)

The insertion of Elvira into the plot and the ensuing shift from a drama focused on land ownership to one concerned with *honra* or honor has been related by scholars to the remarkable emotional efficacy Lope assigns to this theme in the reflections he wrote on his dramatic practice in *El arte nuevo de hacer comedias en este tiempo* [New Art of Writing Plays in This Age] (1609), where he states that "los casos de la honra son mejores, / porque mueven con fuerza a toda gente"[12] (honor stories are best because they move all people). This critical opinion is warranted, but it should not overshadow the fact that, as Alan Paterson has argued, "distance and the tension between remote Galicia and León form a significant and emphatic geopolitical motif throughout the play" ("Stages of History," 151). This much-neglected aspect of the comedia is key to understanding the imperialized image of medieval Iberia that Lope presents in *El mejor alcalde*. This depiction echoes his dramatization of the imperial present in his American comedias and reflects his familiarity with the moralized conception of borders and marginal territories that permeated the discourse of classical history, geography, and literature.

As a promiscuous and rebellious strongman living on the edge of his king's dominions, Don Tello embodies the association between peripherality and moral transgression that is frequently evoked in classical culture whenever the topic of geographical remoteness is raised. For the poets, historians, and geographers of the ancient world, as John Gillies has written, there was a natural link "between monstrosity, margins, and sexual promiscuity" (*Shakespeare and the Geography of Difference*, 13) that made characters living in or coming from terminal or borderland territories morally suspect. Based on this link, Gillies has asserted, the ancient other or "barbarian"—the quintessential dweller of the border—was often constructed "in terms of an idiom that recapitulates geographic 'exorbitance' as moral transgressiveness" (18) and was made to exemplify the point that "to *be* [italics in original] at the edge is to be abominable":[13]

> Such places [margins] were not merely "uninhabited" but "uninhabitable" (in the active sense of Horace's *terras domibus negatas*); their very nature seeming to conspire with the "infamous promiscuity" of the abortive races (monstrous, savage and barbarous) which possessed them. Hence, in the words of Seneca the Elder, "all that is primitive and incomplete in nature has retreated to this far refuge"; simply to *be* [italics in original] at the edge is to be abominable: "if this were not an evil thing, it would not lie at the end of the earth." (13)

Gillies analyzes the traces of this ancient view in Shakespearean tragedy, where what he calls "exotics"—characters who live in or come from territories at the edge of what Europeans considered the civilized world—are habitually depicted as posing a moral, sexual, or political threat to the communities that host them due to their innate transgressiveness.[14] This transgressiveness, a natural consequence of the remote geographical location where these exotics hail from, is also clearly on display in Don Tello's behavior: his kidnapping and eventual rape of Elvira highlight the blatant disregard for morality and authority the nobleman exhibits throughout the play. The connection between these offenses and Don Tello's provenance is made plain at various points in *El mejor alcalde*. For instance, we see this connection in the description of Don Tello that Sancho provides in act 2 when he first visits Alfonso's court in León to request help from the monarch. Sancho's portrayal of the wayward nobleman underlines the link between Don Tello's *exorbitant* location—marking him as a "soberbio infanzón" (an arrogant nobleman) who lives far away from the king—and his immoral behavior in a manner that echoes the relation between marginality and transgressiveness established by classical culture:

> SANCHO. Es tan famoso,
> Que desde aquella ribera
> Hasta la romana torre
> De Hércules es respetado;
> Si está con un hombre airado,
> Sólo el cielo le socorre.
> Él pone y él quita leyes:
> Que éstas son las condiciones
> De soberbios infanzones
> Que están lejos de los reyes. (act 2, lines 1432–1440)

> (SANCHO. So great is his reputation that from this riverbank to the Roman Tower of Hercules everyone respects him. Heaven help the man who crosses him. He makes and unmakes the laws, for this is the way arrogant noblemen who live far away from the king behave.)

Similar to what we read in the classical authorities and Shakespearean drama, Don Tello's lawlessness and lack of morality are closely related here to his marginal location—his living, in Sancho's words, "far away from the king." The correlation between exorbitance and trangressiveness he embodies would have reminded Lope's audience, perhaps, of another figure popular in early modern Spanish drama—the "wild man," a character living at the edge of civilization whose geographical marginality reflected, according to Harrison Meadows, the inability of early modern Spanish society "to disavow the existence of perpetual threats lurking at the margins of the social order."[15]

Don Tello's Galician identity heightens the dangers associated with these marginal spaces that he and his classical and contemporary counterparts inhabit. During much of the early modern period, as historian Camilo Fernández Cortizo has noted, Galicia was a patchwork of peripheral "cotos y jurisdicciones de señores particulares"[16] (domains and fiefdoms belonging to individual nobles) and loosely governed by an isolated *Audiencia* or high court. This authority was created to address "los desórdenes imperantes"[17] (the prevailing disorders) that had marked that territory since the second half of the fifteenth century. Although the Crown had been able to exert greater control over this remote and unruly land since the 1580s as a result of Philip II's annexation of Portugal and his campaign against piracy and Protestantism in the Atlantic, for the most part, the provinces and fiefdoms belonging to the medieval Kingdom of Galicia would continue to occupy, as María del Carmen Saavedra Vázquez has argued, "una posición excéntrica"[18] (a peripheral position) within the administrative and geopolitical structure of Hapsburg Spain.[19] This description illustrates the fact that, even within Iberia, "controlar el espacio de los límites del imperio" (controlling the space on the borders of the empire) was "una tarea lenta y titubeante"[20] (a slow and uncertain task) for the Spanish monarchy.

Given this context of Galicia's exorbitance and disorderliness, it is not surprising, as Sofía Eiroa has observed, that the literature of Golden Age Spain should contain so many "ideas preconcebidas sobre la calidad moral de los Gallegos"[21] (preconceived ideas about the moral fiber of Galicians). Indeed, it clarifies the standard representation of this northwestern region as "el fin del mundo" (the end of the world), a borderland territory separating the known from the unknown and apt, therefore, to spawn the same wild and abnormal creatures one could find in the strange and liquid world that it bordered. One of the authors who more actively contributed to the dissemination of this latter image of Galicia was, according to Miguel Ángel Teijeiro Fuentes, Lope de Vega.[22] The list of examples from his comedias that this critic has provided to support this view omits, surprisingly, *El mejor alcalde*, perhaps because, unlike the other plays Teijeiro Fuentes has examined, it does not incorporate the leitmotif phrase "fin de la tierra" (end of the world) as a geographical descriptor.[23] This absence notwithstanding, Lope's drama makes a deliberate attempt to link Don Tello's way or conduct—his "condición," as Sancho puts it—to the terminal land he rules. In act 1, for instance, Elvira's father, Nuño, describes Don Tello as "poderoso en Galicia / y *reinos más extraños*" (italics added) (powerful in Galicia and in *stranger kingdoms*) (act 1, lines 194–195). The implication of exorbitance present in these words becomes more apparent in the indirect reference to the nobleman as a "fierce giant" that Sancho makes in act 2 when he recalls his whittling of a tall tree in the woods surrounding his village after hearing about Elvira's kidnapping.[24] Sancho's words link monstrosity, margins, and sexual promiscuity in a manner that brings to mind Gillies's identification of the classical view of boundaries or *fines mundi*:

> SANCHO. Llevaba yo, ¡cuán lejos de valiente!,
> Con rota vaina una mohosa espada;
> Llegué al árbol más alto y a reveses
> Y tajos igualé sus blandas mieses.
> No porque el árbol me robase a Elvira,
> Mas porque fue tan alto y arrogante,

> Que a los demás como a pequeños mira:
> Tal es la fuerza de un feroz gigante. (act 2, lines 1059–1066)

(SANCHO. I was carrying—what a poor display of courage—a broken sheath and a rusty sword. I approached the tallest tree and leveled it by slashing its soft branches. Not because the tree had taken Elvira from me, but because it is so tall and arrogant that it looks down on the other trees. Such is the power of a fierce giant.)

Sancho's characterization of Don Tello in this passage as a "fierce giant" and Nuño's description of the nobleman's domain as a faraway borderland extending over Galicia and "stranger kingdoms" are absent in the text of the 1541 *Crónica de España* that Lope used as the inspiration for his comedia. In Ocampo's history, Don Tello (Don Fernando) is simply referred to as "el infanzón" and the territory he rules as "aquel lugar do era el infanzón" (that place where the nobleman lived) (fol. 375r).

Lope's departure from his source here is, I suggest, a clear indicator of his play's indebtedness to ancient perceptions of marginality and the moral views those perceptions support. To this classical baggage, Lope adds allusions to contemporary views of Galicia as a peripheral and unruly territory. Anticipating the play's culmination, Sancho's whittling of the "tall and arrogant" tree on the outskirts of his village—a manifest allegorization of Don Tello—is also a sign of the fate that awaits the Galician nobleman in *El mejor alcalde*. His death in the last act is unmistakably foreshadowed by the image of the tree yielding to the slashes of Sancho's sword. The latter, moreover, can also be interpreted as an allegory of the bond between monarchy and peasantry that Lope will enshrine, in characteristic fashion, at the end of the comedia. The whittled tree, in parallel, signifies the geographical path King Alfonso will "clear" to reach and punish Don Tello in far-off Galicia.

It is worth noting that Lope's appeal to geographical notions rooted in classical sources to flesh out the conflict between center and periphery in *El mejor alcalde* is made in relation to a distant episode from the medieval past. Lope's interest in medieval Spanish history is typically marked, as Joan Oleza has acknowledged, by a conscious effort to break cultural ties with classical antiquity: "El papel asignado por el Renacimiento a la Antigüedad grecolatina se traslada ahora al pasado nacional, buscando en él su mitología propia" (The role assigned by the Renaissance to Greco-Roman antiquity is transferred now to the national past, and in it Lope searches for a national mythology) ("Del primer Lope," xxxi). Most of the comedias the dramatist set in medieval Iberia show, therefore, little or no trace of the impact of classical spatiality. That trace is much more pronounced in plays that dramatize events closer in time to Lope and his audience, like his so-called "American" comedias. In those plays, it is common to find echoes of what Gillies has called the "mythic" or "poetic geography" of the ancients, including the belief that the natural tendency toward depravity and disorder of peripheral territories justifies their oversight and control by a civilized imperial center.[25] This is an idea that we find plainly uttered, for instance, in *Arauco domado*, a play in which Lope eulogizes Don García Hurtado de Mendoza, conqueror of Chile, and legitimizes Spain's military intervention in the "Antarctic Pole"—the southernmost territory in the Hapsburg domain—through the character of Rebolledo, an ensign in don García's army:[26]

REBOLLEDO. No viene así don García
Ni plata intenta buscar,
Que viene a pacificar
Su bárbara rebeldía,
Pues es verdad que estos no son
De los indios desarmados
Que hallaba en selvas y prados
Como corderos Colón,
Sino los hombres más fieros,
Más valientes, más estraños
Que vio este polo en mil años. (act 1, lines 944–954)[27]

(REBOLLEDO. Don García has not come here with that purpose in mind; neither has he come searching for silver. He has come to put down their barbaric rebellion, for these are not the unarmed Indians Columbus found in meadows and rainforests, meek as lambs. These are the fiercest, bravest, and strangest men this corner of the world has seen in a thousand years.)

Like Alfonso's intervention in Galicia, Don García's presence in Chile is motivated by the transgressive behavior of a distant population presented as exotic and markedly different. Their defiance of the established order and rules of conduct—their barbaric rebellion—is directly linked to their "polar" or exorbitant location. Lope's use in *Arauco* of expressions like "bárbaro polo" (barbaric Pole) in act 3, line 1627 and "bárbaros suelos" (barbaric land) in act 3, line 2071 describe the territory to be conquered by Don García, in both geographical and moral terms, and invites consideration of the ideological connections between this play and *El mejor alcalde*.

These connections between geographical remoteness and political or moral errancy extend to the depiction of the Spanish arrival in the Americas in *El nuevo mundo descubierto por Cristóbal Colón*, a play composed in the same period of Lope's career as *Arauco domado*. In *El nuevo mundo*, the Columbian landing on the pristine and remote beaches of Guanhaní—"adonde nunca nadie ha llegado"[28] (where no one has ever set foot)—is preceded by an offense that implies a similar causal relation between exorbitance and moral transgression underpinning the behavior of Don Tello in *El mejor alcalde*. Dulcanquellín, the local ruler, has kidnapped a married woman, Tacuana, and forced her to become his wife, violating her will and that of her husband, the Haitian *cacique* or chieftain Tapirazú. Dulcanquellín's transgression against the social, moral, and religious codes of both his society and Lope's is not a colorful note the dramatist adds to his portrayal of the "natives." As Veronika Ryjik has noted, the chieftain's offense was committed right before the arrival of Columbus and his men at Guanahaní, thereby rendering his transgression an event that both triggers and legitimizes the arrival of the Europeans on American soil:

> Antes de la llegada de los españoles, los vemos festejar el desposorio de Dulcanquellín con la bella haitiana Tacuana. Como nos enteramos casi inmediatamente, el cacique ha raptado a Tacuana a su legítimo esposo y ha decidido celebrar la boda sin el consentimiento de la dama, quien, consecuentemente, lo denuncia como "tirano." . . . Ese en este estado de desorden social y emocional en que se encuentra la comunidad indígena en el momento de la llegada de las naves de Colón. (*Lope de Vega en la invención de España*, 192)
>
> (Before the arrival of the Spanish, we see them celebrate the nuptials of Dulcanquellín with the beautiful Haitian woman Tacuana. Almost right away, we find out that Dulcanquellín has taken Tacuana from her legitimate husband and has decided to celebrate the wedding without her consent. She, accordingly, accuses him of being a "tyrant." . . . This is the state of social and emotional upheaval the indigenous community is in when Columbus's ships arrive.)

As Ryjik observes, Lope presents a line of reasoning in which marginality and transgressiveness call for a corrective intervention from the center, much as in *El mejor alcalde*.[29] Lope's adherence to this logic to dramatize both Spain's arrival in the New World and a distant episode of rape and aristocratic rebellion in twelfth-century Galicia reveals that the depiction of the national past in his theater was influenced by the same classically inspired, moralized view of space that informed his portrayal of overseas expansionism in the early modern era. Awareness of how this conception of space impacted his national history drama as a whole underlines his familiarity with the cultural and intellectual legacy of the ancients. More importantly, it signifies his willingness to use that familiarity to legitimize and project back into the past an idea of kingship and of the relationship between monarchy and territory that echoed contemporary views of the king as a *monarca universal*—a ruler empowered and legitimized to intervene in every corner of his domain, no matter how distant he may be from the places where he is needed. This reframing of history according to the spatial codes of the present culminates in *El mejor alcalde* with Alfonso's decision to travel to far-off Galicia to punish the dissolute and rebellious Don Tello at the end of the play. The king's sojourn—overshadowed in Ocampo's chronicle by the journey the monarch takes through Galicia to pacify the land after Don Tello's trial and execution—occupies a central place in *El mejor alcalde*, where it plays a crucial role in Lope's refashioning of Alfonso as *Emperador de las Españas* in terms akin to those employed by the *monarcae universales* of his day. The king's trip also underscores, as I will argue in the last section of this chapter, the bond Lope's play seeks to establish between the monarch and his subjects—in particular Sancho, Elvira's betrothed—and the overall functioning of the Lopian comedia as an optical regime, a mode of representation in which distances shrink and space can be experienced synchronously by the audience.

The Making of a Universal Monarch: Alfonso's Journey to Galicia

Although Alfonso's decision to travel to Galicia occurs in the closing stages of *El mejor alcalde*, there is no denying that, thematically and ideologically, the monarch's trip is the most significant event in Lope's comedia after Elvira's abduction in act 1. The journey allows Alfonso to display his power as a universal monarch; turn the remote Galician village where his vassals live into a tangible, meaningful place within his realm; and acquire a concrete, physical presence before his subjects. Drawing on the framework provided by Ernst Kantorowicz in *The King's Two Bodies*, Alfonso's trip makes it possible for the monarch to transition from *body politic* (his symbolic and transcendental role as representative of the entire polity) to *body natural* (the reality of his physical presence as a human).[30]

The significance of the monarch's journey in Lope's comedia is underlined by the use of the play's title in the dialogue of act 3. The insertion of titles in Spanish dramatic texts of the early modern period was, as José Antonio Rodríguez Garrido has observed, a strategy often employed by playwrights to confer "un tono sentencioso"[31] (a solemn tone) on specific segments of their dramas. Lope's use of this tool to lend gravity to Alfonso's journey is embedded in the curt response Alfonso gives to Sancho when the latter tries to persuade him to stay in León and send in his stead a regular judge or *alcalde* to Galicia to prosecute Don Tello:

REY. Yo he de ir a Galicia,
Que me importa hacer justicia.
Y aquesto no se publique.
SANCHO. Señor, mirad que no os toca
Tanto mi bajeza honrar.
Enviad, que es justa ley,
Para que haga justicia,
Algún alcalde a Galicia.
REY. El mejor alcalde, el Rey. (act 3, lines 1727–1776)

(KING. I *will* go to Galicia, for it is my responsibility to impart justice; and let no one know about this.

SANCHO. Sire, my lowly state makes me undeserving of an honor like this. Send to Galicia a regular judge to impart justice, for that is what the law requires.

KING. The best judge, the king.)

Critics who have commented on this passage have focused on how Alfonso's adoption of the role of *alcalde* betrays, on the one hand, a longing for a more personalized form of rule among Lope's contemporaries and, on the other, a desire to reinforce the image of the monarch as a just prince that Ocampo presents in his *Crónica*. McKendrick and Varey have related Alfonso's role as high justice in Sancho's case to the yearning among seventeenth-century Spaniards for a more direct involvement of their monarchs in the business of government and the administration of justice.[32] In contrast, Paterson has described the king's intervention as an exemplary demonstration "of a feudal right of custom" that was "in resonance with the juridical-moral notions of Kingship in Lope's own time" ("Stages of History," 151). Yet from a political point of view, Alfonso's decision to travel north and administer justice in person in Galicia echoes the commonly held view among early modern Spanish political theorists that, quoting again Juan de Solórzano y Pereira's *Política indiana* (1648), "los Reinos se han de regir y gobernar como si el Rey que los tiene juntos, lo fuera solamente de cada uno de ellos" (kingdoms must be ruled and governed as if the king who holds them all together were king only of each one of them) (671). Such views, disseminated frequently through images like the one representing King Philip II in the shape of a compass in the Jesuit emblem discussed in chapter 1 (figure 1.2), are clearly evoked in the statement that closes the letter King Alfonso writes to Don Tello in act 2 to demand the immediate release of Elvira before his departure for Galicia:

> En recibiendo ésta, daréis a ese pobre labrador la mujer que le habéis quitado, sin réplica ninguna; y advertid que los buenos vasallos se conocen lejos de los reyes, y que los reyes nunca están lejos para castigar los malos—El REY. (122)[33]
>
> (Upon receiving this letter, you will return to this poor peasant the wife you took from him, no questions asked; and be warned that distance tests the mettle of good vassals, and that kings are never too far away to punish the bad ones.)

Like the universal monarchs imagined by Solórzano y Pereira and other theorists of Lope's day, the king is never far away from his subjects and can rule and punish them as if he resided where they live. This extraordinary ability to reach across space and overcome distance to be close to his vassals allows Alfonso to hold in check, as Sancho puts it in act 2, the conduct of "soberbios infanzones / que están lejos de los reyes" (arrogant noblemen / who live far away from the king) (act 2, lines 1439–1440). It also enables Lope to give the Castilian-Leonese king the characteristics of a universal monarch of his own time. This critical aspect of the play is reinforced by the way Lope recontextualizes the designation given to Alfonso as "Emperor of Spain" from its original significance in medieval Castile to one more attuned to early modernity.

Alfonso inherited his title of emperor from his grandfather, King Alfonso VI of León and Castile (1040–1109), and adopted it officially in a ceremony held at the León Cathedral on the feast of Pentecost (May 26) in 1135. The ceremony was meant to celebrate the king's newly attained status as a feudal lord over Aragón after occupying La Rioja and other territories belonging to Ramiro, "The Monk," who had occupied the Aragonese throne in 1134 after the death of his brother, Alfonso, "The Battler."[34] The new position of power in which the Castilian-Leonese monarch found himself after his victories over Ramiro of Aragón prompted him, as Ocampo wrote in his *Crónica*, to assume the title of emperor with the support of his prelates and noblemen:

> Así fue que este rey don Alfonso, que hasta aquí se llamaba rey de España, pues que hubo hecho con su hueste al reino de Aragón de esta guisa y ganó los lugares que contado habemos y tornó por fuerza al rey don Ramiro que reinaba entonces su vasallo . . . tornóse derechamente para León. . . . Y pues que vino con sus altos hombres y con sus prelados a departir y veían como era señor de estos tres reinos de Castilla y León y Aragón demandóles allí si tenían por bien de rey de España que le llamaban y de llamarle emperador de las Españas. Y los prelados y los ricos hombres y toda la corte, viendo como el rey movía buenas razones y derechas y que entendían bien todo el hecho de lo que decía, tuviéronlo por bien y dijeron que les placía lo que él hacía y dijéronle y aconsejáronle que se coronase y que allí adelante que se llamase emperador de las Españas. (fol. 372r)

> (And so it happened that this king Alfonso, heretofore called King of Spain, forced king Ramiro to become his vassal after subduing Aragon with his army and conquering the places we have mentioned . . . Then, king Alfonso returned straight to León. . . . And there, confirming with his prelates and noblemen his lordship over these three kingdoms of Castile, León, and Aragon, asked if they would agree to call him Emperor of Spain. Seeing that the king argued well his point and that they understood everything he said, the noblemen, the prelates, and the entire court agreed and said they were pleased by what he had done. They also advised him to get crowned as emperor and to call himself Emperor of Spain henceforth.)

In Lope's comedia, Alfonso's title as Emperor of Spain differs substantially in meaning from its use in Ocampo's chronicle, for it refers to the king's desire to extend his dominion beyond the borders of Christian Iberia. This desire can be historically related to the king's campaign to conquer Almería and other important strongholds in northern Andalusia in the 1140s, but there is no evidence, as scholars have noted, that Alfonso's expansion to the south was linked to his assumption of the imperial title in 1135.[35] His short-lived conquests in lands now belonging to the provinces of Córdoba, Jaén, and Almería were primarily the result, as Carlos Ayala Martínez has pointed out, of "the crusade idea that undergirded the legal construction of his reign."[36] We cannot therefore identify them with the type of wide-ranging hegemony we associate with the classical notion of empire.[37] That notion, however, is very present in *El mejor alcalde*, where the king's status as "emperador soberano" (sovereign emperor) is used to highlight his broad territorial ambitions. The impact of this notion in the play is evident in the way Sancho salutes the monarch when he visits his court for the second time in act 2 to inform him about Don Tello's refusal to release Elvira:

> SANCHO. Emperador soberano,
> Invicto rey de Castilla,
> Déjame besar el suelo
> De tus pies, que por almohada
> Han de tener Granada
> Presto, con favor del cielo,
> Y por alfombra a Sevilla,
> Sirviéndoles de colores
> Las naves y varias flores
> De su siempre hermosa orilla. (act 3, lines 1639–1648)

> (SANCHO. Sovereign emperor, undefeated king of Castile, let me kiss the sole of your feet, which, God willing, will soon use Granada for their pillow and tread on Seville as on a carpet dyed with the colors of the myriad flowers and ships that deck its ever-beautiful banks.)

Even though, as we have seen, Alfonso's title as *Emperador* was primarily used to designate his status as king of León and Castile and his suzerainty over parts of Aragón in Ocampo's chronicle, Lope uses it here to advertise the king's participation in a grand project of expansion that places the monarch in Seville, on the banks of the Guadalquivir. Sancho's tacit reference to the famous river clearly tinges Alfonso's project with classical and global overtones, for, as Paul Carranza has noted, rivers were often used "as symbols of imperial power and objects of military conquest" in both ancient and early modern literature.[38] In Spain this practice became enshrined in the description of Charles V as a new Julius Caesar crossing the Rhine that Garcilaso de la Vega, Lope's favorite poet, included in his Second Eclogue:

> Tomábale en su seno el caudaloso
> Y claro río, gozoso de tal gloria,

Trayendo a la memoria cuando vino
El vencedor latino al mismo paso.[39]

(The wide and famous river received him in its bosom, overjoyed with such honor, recalling the time when the famous Latin victor came to the same spot.)

Sancho's broadening of Alfonso's aspirations attests to Lope's effort to transform this monarch into a global ruler in *El mejor alcalde*, an effort that finds additional legitimation in the way his trip to Don Tello's estate is presented in the closing segment of the play. The king's journey to the northwestern edge of his realm is obviously designed to parallel the journey that he, according to Sancho, will be able to take one day as "sovereign emperor" to subject southern Iberia to his authority. The link the play establishes between these two momentous events is emphasized by the picture Sancho paints for the king of the flowery banks of the Guadalquivir in Seville. Sancho's charming tableau of the famous river's "ever-beautiful banks" echoes the one he employs in act 1 to describe the flower-covered Galician fields lapped by the Sil, where he and Elvira live:

SANCHO. Nobles campos de Galicia,
Que a sombras destas montañas,
Que el Sil entre verdes cañas
Llevar las faldas codicia,
Dais sustento a la milicia
De flores de mil colores;
Aves que cantáis amores,
Fieras que andáis sin gobierno,
¿habéis visto amor más tierno
En aves, fieras y flores? (act 1, lines 1–10)

(SANCHO. Noble Galician fields, which under the shade of these skirt-shaped mountains, coveted by the reedy Sil, nourish an army of colorful flowers; you birds, singing of love, and you beasts, living unrestrained, have you ever seen a tenderer love among your kind?)

The violent and erotic overtones of this description, underlined by the presence in it of words and expressions like "faldas" (skirts), "codicia" (coveting), and "sin gobierno" (unrestrained), foreshadow the brutal fate that will befall Elvira later on in the play.[40] More importantly, the connection between this picturesque riverside landscape and the one embedded in Sancho's depiction of the Guadalquivir reveals that Alfonso's trip to Galicia must be interpreted with an eye to the imperial march south that Sancho describes in his salutation to the king. What the Ocampo chronicle describes as a personalized attempt by the monarch to confront injustice and aristocratic disobedience in a remote corner of his kingdom is thus transformed in *El mejor alcalde* into a celebration of the overwhelming power and reach of the Spanish monarchy. This view impels Lope to endow a twelfth-century monarch with the same powers of omnipresence that Hapsburg propaganda attributed to the global rulers of sixteenth- and seventeenth-century Spain.

Alfonso's assumption of these powers redefines his identity as emperor according to the early modern conception of *monarchia universalis*. The resulting transformation culminates the imperialized image of the past that Lope elaborates on in the play by incorporating the same moralized view of space that he employed years earlier to celebrate Spain's conquests in the New World. Such a view, borrowed from the ancients, shapes the relation between center and periphery in *El mejor alcalde* by legitimizing the king's intervention in a faraway locale, where morality and his authority have been flouted. The instrument Lope uses to bring the center and periphery closer in his play—travel—also has a critical metatheatrical dimension, the significance of which has been overlooked by critics. As a device that obliterates the distance separating León from Galicia, travel emblematizes, as I will discuss next, the synchronic view of space that characterizes Lope's *comedia nueva* as a system of representation.

What Is in a Trip? *El mejor alcalde* as Optical Regime

As mentioned above, Alfonso's journey to Don Tello's estate occupies a much more prominent place in *El mejor alcalde* than in Ocampo's chronicle. This dimension results from the dramatist's decision to omit from his play the final section of Ocampo's account, which deals with Alfonso's stay in Galicia after Don Tello's execution. In this section of his chronicle, Ocampo relayed Alfonso's restless activity as a judge and the fear he was able to instill in his subjects following his punishment of the lusty and unruly aristocrat:

> Entonces el emperador anduvo descubierta y manifiestamente por Galicia toda, y apaciguó toda la tierra, y grande fue el espanto que todos los hombres de la tierra tuvieron por este hecho, que no fue ninguno osado en toda su tierra de hacer tuerto a otro. Y esta justicia y otras tales como estas hizo el emperador, por que era muy temido de todas las gentes, y vivía cada uno en lo suyo en paz. (fol. 376v)
>
> (Then, the emperor traveled openly and undisguised through all Galicia, pacified the land, and instilled so much fear in its inhabitants that no one dared do wrong to their neighbor. This act of justice and others like it made the emperor much feared by all his subjects and encouraged them to live peacefully, minding their own business.)

Lope's omission of this passage in *El mejor alcalde* makes the king a more appealing figure for his audience. Instead of a monarch who uses the law to rule by fear, we have, as McKendrick has noted, "a provider of national health and harmony" (*Playing the King*, 36) who uses his broad authority as Emperor of Spain to bring order and justice to a territory situated at the edge of his domains. The play's focus, therefore, is not so much on the depiction of Alfonso as a "just king," as Ocampo describes him in his chronicle, but on the monarch's ability to dispense justice despite the distance that separates him from his subjects.[41] This shift in focus explains why the trip Alfonso makes from his court to Galicia occupies only fifty-three verses in Lope's comedia. The short rest the monarch demands after he arrives at Don Tello's estate also contributes to shortening the length of his trip in the eyes of the audience:

REY. Bueno
    Está aquesto por agora.
    Caballeros, descansemos,
    Para que a la tarde vamos
    A visitar a Don Tello. (act 3, lines 2110–2114)

(KING. This is good enough for now. Gentlemen, let's rest so that we may visit Don Tello in the afternoon.)

Alfonso's statement gives the audience the impression that he has been riding for just a few hours to cover the distance from León to Galicia—an unrealistic notion, despite the relative proximity between these locales—and clearly drives home the point made earlier in his letter to Don Tello that "kings are never too far away to punish bad subjects."

Alfonso's words also serve to tighten the bond that Lope establishes throughout the play between the monarch and Elvira's betrothed, Sancho, whose staunch sense of honor, untainted (non-Semitic) ethnic background, and respect for social hierarchy make him the ideal representative of the type of *demos* Lope typically extolls in his national history theater. This bond is expressed in the final segment of *El mejor alcalde* through the parallel Lope establishes between Alfonso's trip to Galicia and the first trip Sancho takes from his remote village to León to inform the king about Elvira's kidnapping. Sancho's trip, like the monarch's, is extremely short. It is completed while Don Tello and his sister, Feliciana, speak briefly about the nobleman's chances to seduce Elvira by offering her land and expensive presents—a segment that occupies barely 70 verses (from lines 1245 to 1315) in the comedia's text.

The shortness of Sancho's trip also allows Lope to extend the bond between peasant and monarch to the play's audience. That audience, after decades of exposure to Lopian theater, would have been used to quickly transporting themselves "from London to Rome" and "from Valladolid to Gante," as Cervantes wrote in *El rufián dichoso.* As a result, they must have felt naturally inclined during the performance of *El mejor alcalde* to see their experience in the corrales mirrored in the brief journeys that both Alfonso and Sancho make between León and Galicia. This aspect of the play, unnoticed by critics, underlines the presence of a strong metatheatrical component that sheds light on the Lopian comedia's understanding of space and its functioning as an optical regime in which distances are drastically shortened.[42] This system, widely used in the maps and charts produced in the sixteenth and seventeenth centuries by the expert group of cosmographers that worked for the Spanish Crown to chart its empire, was largely ignored, Ricardo Padrón has argued, by the writers of the period. Their view of space adhered for the most part to that presented in the itineraries and portolan charts that sailors and travelers had employed since the Middle Ages. These charts and itineraries stressed the notions of distance and duration by depicting space "from the perspective of the earthbound traveler, moving from one location to another" (Padrón, *The Spacious Word*, 74). Such visualizations were therefore inimical to the development of a planar or map-like view of space that emphasized synchronicity and the possibility of swiftly moving between distant locations.

The discursive itineraries—mostly descriptions and short travel narratives—embedded in the epics and chronicles of sixteenth- and seventeenth-century Spain and Spanish America indeed prove, as Padrón has observed, that this medieval model of spatiality was alive and well in the written culture of the early modern Hispanic world. However, the abrupt change of settings and shrinking of distances that we witness in new genres like the Lopian comedia do not support the idea that this conception of space was all-pervasive in the literature of the period. Testimonies of artists like Cervantes, who witnessed with both wonder and envy the rise of Lopian drama, are, as I discussed in chapter 1, illuminating in this respect. The same is true of other late sixteenth-century playwrights who, writing a decade or so before Lope, provided *El Fénix* with valuable examples and ideas that would later be developed in his theater. Consider, for instance, what the poet, playwright, and historian Lupercio Leonardo de Argensola wrote in the opening address to the public in *La Alejandra* (ca. 1580), a traditional Senecan revenge play, in which Tragedy takes to the stage to boast about her ability to make the audience travel in a very short time from Zaragoza to "the great city of Memphis," in the middle of Egypt:[43]

TRAGEDIA. Imagináis quizás que estáis ahora
Contentos en la noble y fuerte España,
Y en la insigne ciudad de Zaragoza,
Ribera del antiguo padre Ibero,
....

Y estáis (¡O desdichados de vosotros!),
¿en dónde, si pensáis?, en medio Egipto,
Ribera del famoso y ancho Nilo,
En la grande ciudad llamada Menfis,
En donde reina y vive un rey tirano,
Cuyo fuerte palacio veis presente:
Aquí la casa real tiene su asiento,
Aquí se albergan hoy los infernales.
Mirad en poco tiempo cuántas tierras
Os hace atravesar esta tragedia;
Y sí, si en ella veis algunas cosas
Que os parezcan difíciles y graves,
Tenedlas, sin dudar, por verdaderas,
Que todo a la tragedia le es posible,
Pues que muda los hombres sin sentido
De unos reinos en otros, y los lleva.[44]

(TRAGEDY. You imagine, perhaps, that you are now at ease in strong and noble Spain, in the illustrious city of Saragossa, on the bank of old father Ebro . . . But you are, oh, poor you, what do you know, in the middle of Egypt, on the bank of the wide and famous Nile, in a great city called Memphis, ruled by a tyrant whose palace appears before your eyes. There the royal house has its seat, there the infernal creatures take up their residence. See how many countries this tragedy has made you cross in such short time. And if you discover in it things that are somber and hard to understand, consider them true. Everything is possible in tragedies, for they make men move from one kingdom to another without noticing and transport them.)

The type of spatiality Argensola associates here with the allegorical figure of Tragedy would become, one decade later, a staple feature of Lope's *comedia nueva*, in which the main appeal for theatergoers was, as Francisco Ruiz Ramón has argued concerning *Fuenteovejuna*, its capacity to take audiences "de la plaza del pueblo al salón del trono" (from the village square to the throne room) (*Celebración y catharsis*, 19) in the blink of an eye. This distinctive feature of Lopian drama is thematized in *El mejor alcalde* through the experiences of Sancho and King Alfonso. Their ability to quickly shuttle between León and a remote corner of Galicia epitomizes the distanceless and quasi-synchronous idea of space that Lopian drama embodied as an optical regime, an idea prefigured in the power Argensola's Tragedy assumes to transport audiences in a short time from one kingdom to another. Lope exploited this notion of space repeatedly in his national history comedias and established through them a relationship with the territory that contrasted sharply with the one represented in the chronicles and epic narratives of the period.

In Lope's plays, characters and audiences are not earthbound and forced to move slowly and linearly through the landscape. Instead, they are allowed to glide through the terrain and appear where they need to be in a very short amount of time. This experience, so characteristic, as Padrón has argued, of optical regimes like the map, is one that Lope took care to highlight in *El mejor alcalde* by playing down the impact of distance in Sancho and King Alfonso's journeys. The metatheatrical element present in their trips underscores the signifying power of space in Lope's historical drama, an aspect of his theater that comes through again, as I will discuss in the next chapter, in *Las famosas asturianas* [The Famous Women from Asturias], a play he wrote a decade or so before *El mejor alcalde*. In this earlier and much less known comedia, space is used to promote a figural understanding of history rooted in the beliefs and practices of contemporary historiography, which conceptualized empire as the result of a drive toward expansion that was present in Spanish history from its remote beginnings.

CHAPTER 3

Born to Expand

SPACE, *FIGURA*, AND EMPIRE IN *LAS FAMOSAS ASTURIANAS*

By advertising its own historiographical genesis through the mouth of Sancho at the end of act 3, *El mejor alcalde* underlines the central role that, as Joan Oleza has written, history and historiographical discourse played in the evolution of Lopian drama at the turn of the seventeenth century: "Es probable que el cambio más profundo experimentado en la trayectoria del Fénix a partir de 1599 sea el traslado mayoritario de su dramaturgia, con armas y bagajes, al campo de la historia" (The most substantial change Lope's career underwent from 1599 onward was probably the broad shift to history in his drama) ("Del primer Lope," xxvii). This shift to history as the preferred ground for the development of a distinct and innovative dramatic practice was naturally impacted by the apparent interest in all things Visigothic that early modern Spanish historiography developed to feed a long-standing narrative of national consolidation and territorial expansion that, following medieval models, sought to establish a Gothic origin for both monarchy and nation in Spain.[1] Works belonging to this historiographical corpus typically depict the global polity inherited and enlarged by the Hapsburgs as either a continuation or a revival of the Visigothic monarchy that ruled Spain before the Arabic invasion of 711 and that was later restored in the early medieval kingdom of Asturias and León after the famous victory over the Moors, won by the legendary chieftain Pelayo in Covadonga (ca. 720). This "neo-Gothic" view of Spain as a nation was so pervasive among early modern Spanish historians that, as Lucia Binotti has written, "one could say that it is the construction of the Gothic past that separates Renaissance Spanish historiography from its closer and more influential models, Florentine and Venetian humanistic historiography of the fifteen and sixteenth centuries."[2]

Along with this effort to uphold Visigothic Iberia as the cradle of Spain, early modern historians also highlighted the Roman ancestry of Spanish kings, who were frequently depicted as continuing the civilizing and conquering mission once assigned by God to the *Imperium romanum*.[3] Yet, even in the works of those more closely affiliated with this Romanizing trend, it is not uncommon to find explicit references to the Visigothic pedigree of early modern Spanish monarchs and the subjects they ruled.[4] Thus, Pedro Mexía, official chronicler for Holy Roman Emperor Charles V, wrote in his unfinished *Historia del Emperador Carlos V* [History of the Emperor Charles V] (1551) that Charles, like his grandparents, King Ferdinand of Aragón and Queen Isabella of Castile, descended from "la muy alta y muy poderosa y antiquísima sangre y casa de los invencibles reyes godos, que de Castilla se hizieron reyes y señores"[5] (the most noble, powerful, and ancient blood and lineage of the invincible Gothic kings, who became lords and monarchs of Castile). Similarly, Gonzalo Fernández de Oviedo proudly stated in his likewise unfinished *Historia General y Natural de las Indias* [General and Natural History of the Indies] (1557) that "Godos son y españoles los que estas nuestras Indias hallaron" (it was Goths and Spaniards who discovered these Indies), a fact that, in his view, clearly proved that "España mucho más deve gloriarse de sus godos y de sus propios naturales españoles, que no de los beneficios ni industria de la gente romana"[6] (Spain should take much more pride in its Goths and its native inhabitants than in all the benefits and expertise it obtained from the Romans). Statements like these, outlandish as they may seem, contributed to the consolidation of an ideology that was so widespread in early modern Spanish historiography that, as J. N. Hillgarth has written, "for many sixteenth- and seventeenth-century Spaniards the whole history of Visigothic Spain seemed contemporary history."[7]

The functioning of this ideology, which linked Visigothic Iberia to the imperial Spain of the Hapsburgs, was predicated on a figural understanding of history that interpreted past events as both incarnating their material and chronological individuality and foreshadowing episodes and experiences that would materialize centuries later. Historians, under this conception, looked back at the past in order to peer into the future, perusing the historical record to find in it the shape of things to come. Space played a critical role in this hermeneutic operation: the depiction of Spain as a nation destined to expand in dominion and power from its remote Visigothic beginnings required the ability to inscribe expansion into the small and fragile polities of yore. That ability was often displayed, as I discussed in chapter 1, in the depiction of caves, hideouts, and other places of confinement regularly featured in the work of early modern Spanish historians.

This approach can be seen at work, too, as I will argue in this chapter, in *Las famosas asturianas* [The Famous Women from Asturias] (ca. 1610–1612).[8] This play recounts how the Asturian-Leonese King Alfonso II, "The Chaste," (791–842), inspired by the behavior of a bellicose noblewoman named Doña Sancha, rebelled against the authority of the caliph of Córdoba by refusing to pay the yearly tribute of one hundred maidens demanded by his Moorish overlord for the survival of his kingdom.[9] This well-known episode of Spain's legendary past, dramatized elsewhere in *Las doncellas de Simancas*, a comedia of uncertain authorship that has sometimes been attributed to Lope, is presented in *Las famosas asturianas* as prefiguring the process of expansion that Spain would become immersed in at the outset of the early modern period.[10] Key to Lope's figural interpretation of history and his depiction of Asturias and León as an expanding, proto-imperial polity in *Las famosas asturianas* is his association of this beleaguered neo-Visigothic kingdom with the motif of triumph over confinement that early modern Spanish historians often employed in their works to represent Spain's imperial destiny. The political significance of this spatial motif in the play surfaces in Lope's depiction of Alfonso's arrival and crowning in León, the capital of his kingdom, as a new monarch. Subsequently, it is crucially reinforced by the critical contributions that onomastics and gender make to the representation of Asturias and León as a territory destined to expand beyond its borders.

From Confinement to Expansion: Alfonso in León

Lope's decision to imperialize the past in *Las famosas asturianas* by exploiting a spatial motif dear to contemporary historians should come as no surprise, given the inclusion of this play in part eighteen of his *Comedias*. In this part, as David Arbesú reminds us, "Lope publicó sus más famosos alegatos a favor de llevar la historia a las tablas"[11] (Lope penned his most famous pleas in favor of dramatizing history). These *alegatos* or short manifestos often revolve around the idea that national history plays provide continuity and disseminate on a larger scale the work of historians. Thus, in the preface to *La campana de Aragón* [The Bell of Aragon]—the comedia that immediately follows *Las famosas asturianas* in part eighteen—Lope writes the following:

> Nadie podrá negar que las famosas hazañas o sentencias, referidas al vivo con sus personas, no sean de grande efecto para renovar la fama desde los teatros a la memoria de las gentes donde los libros lo hacen con menor fuerza y más dificultad y espacio.[12]
>
> (Nobody can deny that famous exploits and words, when conveyed live onstage, can bring back fame to the memory of people better than books, which do this less forcefully, with greater difficulty, and by taking up more time.)

One of the things Lope was intent on transferring from history books to the stage in his national history dramas was the image of Visigothic Iberia as a polity that, shrinking in size after the Arab invasion of 711, had resurrected itself centuries later to expand and conquer the world under the Hapsburgs. This image was frequently evoked in contemporary historiographical accounts of the fall of the Visigothic kingdom and made readily available in passages like the following, in which the Jesuit Juan de Mariana (1536–1624), whose work Lope knew well, links the collapse of Visigothic rule in eighth-century Iberia to the subsequent formation of a worldwide empire under the Hapsburgs:[13]

> Cayó pues el reino y gente de los godos, no sin providencia y consejo del cielo, como a mí me parece, para que después de tal castigo de las cenizas y sepultura de aquella gente naciese y se levantase una nueva y santa España, de mayores fuerza y señorío que antes era; refugio en este tiempo, amparo y columna de la religión católica, que como compuesta de todas sus partes y como de sus miembros termina su muy ancho imperio, y le extiende, como hoy lo vemos, hasta los últimos fines de levante y poniente.[14]
>
> (The kingdom of the Visigoths then collapsed, but not, in my view, without the consent and foresight of Heaven, for, after this punishment, a new and holy Spain, stronger and more dominant, was born and rose out of the grave and ashes of that people, a country that in this age has provided protection and support to the Catholic religion and that, constituted by many parts and members, has formed a wide empire that extends, as we see it today, to the farthest corners of the east and the west.)

Mariana depicts the fall of the Visigoths as a providential event that would allow Spain to break out of the confines of its "sepultura" (grave) and stretch its borders "to the farthest corners of the east and the west" centuries later. This illustration reinforces the description of Spain's cradle, Pelayo's hideout in Covadonga, which we find in the work of fellow historian and royal chronicler Ambrosio de Morales, who in 1573 wrote a detailed account of his journey to the old kingdoms of León, Galicia, and Asturias at the behest of Philip II. Morales portrayed the "insigne Cueva" (illustrious cave) where Pelayo took refuge and defeated the Moors as a "harta estrechura" (very narrow) place, hemmed in by an equally narrow and foreboding landscape: "lo estrecho del valle y el torcer con vueltas, y el ser sus lados más peñas, que no montañas, hace una aspereza espantosa no dejar más de anchura de cuanto el río Diva lleva de corriente" (because the valley is narrow and with winding turns, and its slopes are covered with rocks, it looks terribly wild and it barely allows enough space for the river Diva to run through it) (*Crónica general*, 63). Out of the "estrechura" or narrow passage where he and his men were confined, Pelayo was able to carve out a new and expansive destiny for Spain whose contours can be glimpsed in the rushing waters of the Diva, which overflowed with blood the day Pelayo vanquished the Moors:

> Del pie de la peña hasta una vara, o poco más del llano, se descuelgan dos chorros derechos de agua con gran ruido, y de otro lado sale otro gran golpe de agua, que juntándose con los chorros en una balsa, sale de ella el pequeño río Diva, que entonces, como el arzobispo don Rodrigo encarece, creció y se hizo

> grande con la sangre de los moros, durándole muchos días el correr muy teñido con ella. (Morales, *Crónica general*, 63)

> (From the base of the rock [where Pelayo's cave stands], five feet or more down into the plain below, two straight jets of water plunge, making a great noise; from the other side of the rock, another big jet pours, joining the first one in a pool from which the tiny River Diva flows. Back then, as Archbishop Rodrigo admiringly states, the river swelled and made itself bigger with the blood of the Moors, which stained the water for many days.)

Accounts like this made legendary episodes like the one dramatized in *Las famosas asturianas* particularly attractive for those who, like Lope, were intent on disseminating and memorializing "los principios y medios por donde [España] se encaminó a la grandeza que hoy tiene" (the beginnings and middles by which [Spain] arrived at its present greatness), as Mariana wrote in his *Historia de España* (li).

The figural and spatial appeal of those beginnings was heightened by the growing sense of decline that had spread through Spanish society in the early 1600s, when Lope turned to history as a primary source of inspiration for his dramas. The early decades of the seventeenth century saw Hapsburg Spain retreating on many fronts and for the first time contemplating curtailing its imperial ambitions. This contemplation was the result of the new policy of nonaggression adopted by Philip III and his chief minister, the Duke of Lerma, who, faced with an insurmountable financial crisis, had signed a peace treaty with England in 1604 and a humiliating truce with the Dutch rebels in 1609.[15] The more restrained role this policy imposed on Spain as an imperial power sent the country into "an orgy of national introspection" (Elliott, *Imperial Spain, 1469–1716*, 300) and led many writers and intellectuals of the period, as Veronica Ryjik has argued, to propose a return to the values of the past as a means to reawaken Spain's imperial consciousness and legitimize its recent history:

> Enfrentados con el declive de un imperio que sólo hace medio siglo gozaba de una hegemonía incuestionable en el mapa europeo, los intelectuales de la época a menudo se refugian en la idealización del pasado glorioso . . . explican el desastre actual por la desviación de los valores propios de aquella edad heroica y propagan el retorno a estos valores como única solución. (*Lope de Vega en la invención*, 13)

> (Faced with the decline of an empire that only half a century before enjoyed uncontested hegemony in Europe, Spanish men of letters of the time took comfort in the idealization of the glorious past . . . they explain Spain's current collapse as caused by a deviation from the values that defined that heroic age and promoted the return to those values as the only solution.)

The impact that this return to the old values of Visigothic and Reconquest Iberia had on Spain's understanding and embracing of its imperial destiny is clearly emphasized in a number of scenes in *Las famosas asturianas* in which space occupies the center of dramatic attention. The critical importance of these scenes has been overlooked by scholars, whose interest in the play, on the whole, has been scarce and limited mostly to issues of race, gender, and national identity.[16] The stark set of contrasts (moral, religious, and linguistic) that Lope establishes between Christians and Moors and his flouting of gender conventions by making the leading female character, Doña Sancha, a "superior representative of masculine valor" (Burningham, "Beleaguered Hegemony," 135) explains why critics have been overwhelmingly drawn to these specific aspects of the comedia. However, I will argue that space also plays a key role in shaping the political message of *Las famosas asturianas*, which seeks to imperialize the past and figuratively connect it to the present by establishing expansion as an original, defining feature of the universal monarchy ruled by the Hapsburgs.

The pivotal contribution of space to this ideological operation can be first gleaned in the frantic scene of pursuit that opens the play, which features the newly crowned King Alfonso II of Asturias and León running through the streets of León to escape a murder attempt by the local nobility. Alfonso, who has just arrived in León to assume the responsibilities of government after a short exile in Navarre due to the usurpation of the throne by his uncle, the bastard Mauregato, takes refuge in a nearby monastery. Once there, he is forced into confinement by his pursuers, a situation akin to the one his kingdom will face a few scenes later when Audalla, a commander sent to León by the caliph of Córdoba, arrives in the city and surrounds it in order to force the king to pay the yearly tribute agreed upon by Mauregato: one hundred maidens to be paid by the Asturian and Leonese nobility.[17]

The proleptic value of this opening scene clearly underlines the running motif of the play: overcoming enclosure and rejecting spatial constrictions. This motif, clearly echoed in Mariana's account of Spain's passage from its grave to a wide empire after the fall of the Visigoths and in Morales's description of Pelayo's hideout in Covadonga, will acquire its full political import in act 3, when Doña Sancha persuades her fellow countrymen and her king to take up arms against the invading Moors. However, its significance can already be glimpsed at the outset of the comedia, as Alfonso is quickly released from the monastery where he is confined by the Asturian nobleman Don Nuño Osorio, who, with a small band of followers, sends the king's pursuers on the run and swears loyalty to the new monarch. Alfonso's liberation triggers the following enthusiastic speech from the Asturian leader:

Nuño. Fágavos Dios, rey sesudo,
Tan temido y acatado
Que tenga el vueso reinado

Al más envidioso mudo.

....

Veáis las vuesas banderas
Sobre las aguas del Tajo,
Aunque vos cueste trabajo
El conquerir sus fronteras,
Y si vos socede bien
Lleguen a Guadalquivir,
Y aun al mar oso decir,
Que puedan nadar también.
Crezca vuestra renta al año
Treinta mil maravedís . . . [18]

(NUÑO. May God make you, judicious king, so feared and obeyed that your reign mutes the most envious. . . . May you see your banners on the Tagus, though you suffer to conquer its banks; and, if you are successful, may your banners reach as far as the Guadalquivir, and even the ocean, so they may swim too. May your income grow by thirty thousand *maravedís* every year . . .)

This speech by Nuño is critical for recognizing the central role of space in the figural economy of *Las famosas asturianas* and the play's effort to bring the past into compliance with the imperial present of Hapsburg Spain. Nuño presents the newly arrived monarch with a grand new vision for the kingdom of Asturias and León, a vision that turns confinement into expansion and sets this small, beleaguered territory on an imperial course by making conquest its raison d'être. The expansive destiny Nuño lays out for Alfonso is highlighted, as it was in *El mejor alcalde*, by the reference he makes to the Tagus and the Guadalquivir, two major rivers that, following the classical tradition, operate as symbols of imperial power and military prowess.

Given Alfonso's shaky hold on power at this point, such a vision may seem hopelessly optimistic or unduly ambitious, but the audience quickly realizes its critical significance a few scenes later, when Alfonso enters the *Alcázar* (royal fortress) in León to take possession of the building as his official residence. The speech the king delivers at this momentous event clearly shows him embracing Nuño's vision and committing himself to it as he solemnly swears by the *casuella* or holy chasuble of Saint Ildephonsus—a relic transported to Asturias by the Visigoths of Toledo after the Arab conquest of their city—to expand the borders of his kingdom beyond the banks of the Tagus and to take his royal banner all the way to Africa:[19]

REY. Fago voto solene a las relicas
Y a la casuella santa de Ilefonso,

Con todas las demás, santas y ricas,
De procurar ponerle en riba el Tajo,
Porque espante los moros andaluces
Sin perdonar cansancio nin trabajo.
Este león salió de la montaña,
Maguer que non se crían en Asturias,
Y así sospira por salir de España.
En África los hay, allá sospecho
Que volverá, no digo que vencido,
Mas a triunfar con vitorioso pecho. (act 1, lines 663–674)

(KING. I solemnly swear by the relics and the holy chasuble of Saint Ildephonsus, and by all the other rich and holy relics, to plant my banner on the banks of the Tagus to frighten the Andalusian Moors, without regard for tiredness or effort. There are no lions in Asturias, but this one came out of the mountains and is yearning to leave Spain. Lions come from Africa. I suspect that is where this one wants to return, not in defeat, but rather to triumph with victorious spirit.)

It is worth noting that this plan of programmatic conquest is communicated to the Asturian and Leonese aristocracy (and, by extension, to the play's audience) before Audalla and his Moorish troops arrive in León to collect the payment of one hundred maidens owed to the caliph of Córdoba. The image of Asturias and León as a territory destined for expansion that Lope paints in *Las famosas asturianas* is therefore present in the play from its outset and is not the result of a natural response to foreign invasion or the spontaneous desire to safeguard the homeland, as some critics have argued. To view Nuño and King Alfonso "not as rapacious subjects who jealously covet someone else's object, but as protective mediators who must safeguard what is ignobly coveted by others" (Burningham, "Beleaguered Hegemony," 139) is to seriously misread Lope's play and distort its political message. Lope does not view expansion simply as a reactive phenomenon triggered by external aggression or the intolerable demands of an invading culture, but rather as an inherent feature of the newly formed neo-Visigothic kingdom of Asturias and León. This feature will shape the history of this territory in the comedia and allow Lope to present to his audience an early avatar or *figura* of early modern Spain.

Concerning this latter point, it is essential to realize that the expansive scenario Alfonso outlines in his speech at the *Alcázar* is not confined to the geographical borders of his kingdom or those of the nation as understood by the play's audience. The king, likened in his speech to the lion that flutters on his royal banner, "sospira por salir de España" (yearns to leave Spain) (line 671) and set foot in Africa "a triunfar con vitorioso pecho" (to triumph with victorious spirit) (line 674). Thus, Lope links a remote, legendary episode of Spain's early medieval past to the first phase of overseas expansion in the history of his country, a phase defined by the request made in 1504 by Queen Isabella of Castile to her heirs—Princess Juana and Philip of Hapsburg—in her testament: "que no çesen en la conquista de Africa e de pugnar por la fe contra los ynfieles" (do not quit conquering Africa and fighting for the Christian faith against the infidels) (quoted in de la Torre, 1974).[20]

The limited and short-lived influence Spain was able to exert in Oran, Algiers, and other spots along the North African coast during the early modern period reveals just how difficult it was for the Queen's Hapsburg successors to fulfill her wishes.[21] However, this did not deter Lope. By appropriating in *Las famosas asturianas* the triumph-over-confinement motif that historians like Mariana and Morales had used to imperialize post-Visigothic Iberia, he was able to figuratively connect Alfonso's plan for the enlargement of his kingdom to the efforts of the Hapsburg monarchs to expand into Africa and beyond. To reinforce this figural connection, Lope identifies Alfonso's expansive agenda, as I will discuss next, with the main female character of the play, Doña Sancha, a quarrelsome *asturiana* whose name, attitude, and relationship to the landscape embody the proto-imperial image of Asturias that Lope fashions in act 1 through the speeches of Nuño and King Alfonso.

Empire Incarnate: Doña Sancha and the Territory

The prominent role that expansion and the triumph-over-confinement motif have in *Las famosas asturianas* underscores the ideological ties that bind Lope's play to early modern Spanish historiography. If the former depicts a kingdom eager to break out of its borders and carry its banner proudly into Africa, the latter was primarily written, as Richard Kagan has argued in relation to Mariana, to provide "the unequivocal evidence needed to explain Spain's path to glory."[22] This path started in the narrow cave, where Pelayo and his men defeated the invading Arabs in Covadonga, and culminated in dominion on the global stage under the Hapsburgs. The critical contribution of space to the representation of that path in *Las famosas asturianas* is emphasized by the relations Lope establishes in the comedia between gender, landscape, and onomastics. Lope associates the Asturian-Leonese kingdom with the family name and personality of the manly and outdoorsy Doña Sancha, a young *asturiana* who refuses to be taken quietly to the caliph as payment for the freedom of her kingdom. Further, she rejects the narrow comforts of home for the wild and open spaces of the sierra, reinforcing the triumph-over-confinement motif that structures the plot of the play and contributing substantially to prefiguring Alfonso's beleaguered domain as the expansive state ruled centuries later by the Hapsburgs.

Critics who have discussed the character and behavior of Doña Sancha in Lope's play have traditionally portrayed her as an example of what Melveena

McKendrick has called *la mujer varonil*, a popular female type found in seventeenth-century Spanish comedias, in which women are sometimes given the ability to perform manly activities (warfare and hunting, for instance) or assume certain masculine traits (physical strength, courage). More specifically, within the taxonomy created by McKendrick to study the *mujer varonil*, Doña Sancha exemplifies what this critic calls *la mujer guerrera* or a warrior woman, an uncommon subtype that, in McKendrick's view, has little more than an ornamental role in the plays where it appears: "Compared with the Amazon and the woman leader, the ordinary *mujer guerrera* of the seventeenth-century Spanish stage is an insignificant creature, and her appearance is on the whole as unremarkable as that of the commonest form of the *mujer vestida de hombre*, the female page."[23]

Doña Sancha's incarnation of the "unremarkable" subtype identified by McKendrick can be seen, for instance, in act 1, where she is featured holding a spear and chastising a bear she has just killed, and again in act 2, where she is seen pursuing Moors through the mountains of Asturias despite her father's order to stay home.[24] However, there is more to this Asturian *guerrera* than the mere embodiment of a stage typology. Lope's audience is quickly made aware of this when, early in the play, Doña Sancha is compared to a lion by Don Laín de Lara, a refined gentleman from León who woos her and asks for her hand in marriage. Don Laín, having just been rejected by Doña Sancha and finding out that she is traveling incognito to León to witness Alfonso's coronation at the *Alcázar*, complains bitterly about his wretched state and points out how well Doña Sancha's destination reflects her cruel nature:

LAÍN. Non queda más helado y pavoroso,
Zambulléndose el sol, el pajarillo
Que de uno y otro pálido ramillo
Fabricaba su nido artificioso,
Que yo sin ti, dulce desdén hermoso,
Tanto, que de vivir me maravillo,
. . . .
¿Vaste a León? Bien faces, que ese nome
Conviene a tu crüel naturaleza. (act 1, lines 410–419)

(LAÍN. The little bird that tries to build its nest with pale branches is less cold and frightened when the sun goes down than I am without you, sweet and beautiful disdain. So much so that I wonder how I am still alive. . . . You are going to León? Wise decision, for that name suits your cruel nature.)

Don Laín's analogy establishes a deep and long-lasting connection in the play between Doña Sancha and the Asturian-Leonese kingdom, a territory with a name identified with the royal emblem of the lion. This connection echoes the one Lope established a few years earlier in another historical drama, *La varona castellana* [The Castilian Tomboy] (ca. 1597–1603), through the character of María Pérez. An indomitable and fierce maiden, María dressed as a page boy and assumed a male identity under the name *León*, joining the Leonese and Castilian forces fighting neighboring Aragón during the war waged for control of northeastern Castile in the twelfth century. Lope chose María's *nom de guerre* carefully in *La varona castellana*, for, as Luzmila Camacho Platero has explained, "the lion is . . . a symbol of the kingdom of León's coat of arms. María adopts the name of León and, by doing so, she becomes the personification of her kingdom."[25] This association between María and the territory she fights for becomes even more evident, as Camacho Platero has noted, after she captures a lion that has been let loose at the court of the young Castilian King Alfonso XI and takes prisoner the Aragonese king, Alfonso "El Batallador," at the battle of Los Altos de Barahona. Through this latter exploit, Camacho Platero adds, María reaches the zenith of her career as a *mujer guerrera* and manages to occupy the place reserved for the young Castilian monarch as a symbol of the kingdom:

> Lope, like many other playwrights from this period, needed to make the female warrior aware of her superiority, thus allowing her to distinguish herself from women and men, making possible her temporary transgression as a male, and letting her be the symbol of her kingdom. It is her superiority over men and women that allows her, and not the young King Alfonso, to embody the symbol of León: She is León. ("Political and Gender Transgressions," 6)

Like María, Doña Sancha is also León. Her role as living emblem of the Asturian-Leonese kingdom, first glimpsed in the remarks Don Laín makes about her "cruel nature" when she leaves for León to attend King Alfonso's coronation in the *Alcázar*, becomes increasingly apparent as Lope turns his attention to onomastics in *Las famosas asturianas*. This aspect of the play is foregrounded for the audience by Don García, Doña Sancha's father, who, approaching an advanced age and wanting to leave no loose ends before he dies, tells his daughter about his plans to marry her to Don Laín, a member of the distinguished Lara clan. Don García's discourse, built on paronomasia, reflects the "goût prononcé pour la sémantisation du nom propre"[26] (deep fondness for the lexicalization of proper names) that, as François Rigolot has argued, characterizes the literature of sixteenth- and seventeenth-century Europe and highlights the political significance that names and their rhetorical manipulation have in Lope's play, especially when references to geography or the territory are involved:

> DON GARCÍA. Fija, yo tengo ya bastantes años
> Para cuidar en la vecina muerte,
> Que, como con el tiempo el edificio
> Se va desmoronando y es indicio

De que amenaza ya total rüina,
Así en la edad la muerte se avecina.
Cuando de estas paredes, de humo llenas,
Se van cayendo a tierra las almenas,
Non me permitas, non, morir sin gusto,
. . . .

DOÑA SANCHA. Nunca he sido
Desobediente, ¡oh padre!, a tus quereres.
¿Qué estado al tu pracer donarme quieres?
DON GARCÍA. El de casada, fija de mios ojos,
Para que el abolengo de mi casa,
Ya que non se dilate por varones
Del apellido de León, leones,
Se destienda por fembra tan leona
Que más face honoranza que baldona.
Es Laín un fidalgo bien sesudo,
Home de pro para la paz y guerra,
Y que tiene solar en muesa tierra.
Los Laras son famosos caballeros,
Y este mancebo escurre de su alcurnia
Atán derechamente como debe. (act 2, lines 1001–1028)

(DON GARCÍA. Daughter, I am old enough to be concerned with approaching death, for as time dilapidates buildings and signals their total collapse, so age announces looming death. As the battlements fall from these walls, darkened with smoke, do not let me, I beg you, die without humoring me. . . .

DOÑA SANCHA. Father, I have always complied with your wishes. What status do you wish to bestow on me?

DON GARCÍA. The married status, my dearest daughter, so that I, not being able to perpetuate my lineage through lions, men bearing the León family name, may perpetuate it through you, brave lioness. Laín is a judicious nobleman, a worthy man in both war and peace, and his ancestral home is in this land. The Laras are distinguished noblemen, and this young man is truly a chip off the old block.)

Similar to what happens in *La varona castellana*, in which María, the main female character, is able to symbolize the polity she fights for due to the masculine name she adopts when she joins the army disguised as a page boy, Doña Sancha is made to embody the territory she hails from on account of her family name: León. The charge given to her by her father to extend the family lineage through her marriage to Don Laín must be interpreted, therefore, not only in biological but also in geopolitical terms. Seen from this perspective, the future *leones* that Don García imagines *destendiéndose* or disseminating from Doña Sancha's womb express more than the genealogical ambitions of an elderly paterfamilias. They also embody the inherently expansive nature of a kingdom that "yearns to leave Spain," as King Alfonso put it in his speech at the *Alcázar*, and express the final goal of extending its borders beyond the sea. Thus, implicit in Don García's wishes for a long and fruitful descent is a process of territorial expansion in which the local—the ancestral home or *casa solar*—and the global—Alfonso's expanding kingdom—cohere and join destinies like two sides of the same coin.

This expansion process is also inscribed in the relation Doña Sancha maintains with her surroundings throughout the play, a relation that explicitly privileges wild and open spaces over enclosed domestic settings. The geopolitical implications of this relation can be gleaned from the exchange Doña Sancha has with Don Laín de Lara right before she rejects him as a suitor and leaves for León to witness King Alfonso's coronation at the *Alcázar*. The setting of the dialogue, the mountains surrounding Doña Sancha's ancestral home in Asturias, inspires this Iberian lioness to make a passionate defense of her active lifestyle and to state emphatically her dislike for the comforts of home, which she finds oppressive and contrary to her nature:

LAÍN. El cultivado jardín
Conviene a la tierna dama,
Que non la nevada sierra;
Que, como al home la guerra
Acuciadora de fama,
Tal a la fembra la paz,
El estrado y la labor.
DOÑA SANCHA. Damas que cuidan de amor
Fallen sentadas solaz.
Yo, Laín, en este sino
Y en este planeta fui
Nacida al mundo, que a mí
Non me alegra el oro fino
En el dosel y el estrado,
Ni menos la mora alfombra,
Sinon la apacible sombra
Que facen olmos al prado.
Más precio esperar aquí
Que un jabalí fiero asome
Que oír blanduras de un home,
Puesto que fembra nací. (act 1, lines 293–313)

(LAÍN. The well-tended garden, and not the snowy sierra, becomes the tender lady, for just as war, bringer of fame, suits men, so does peace, cushioned seats, and needlework suit women.

DOÑA SANCHA. May ladies who care for love find pleasure sitting down. The sign and planet I was born under, Laín, makes me appreciate the peaceful shade that the elm trees make in the field more than fine gold, canopies, cushioned seats, and, most certainly, the Moorish carpet. I would rather wait here for a wild boar to appear than listen to the flattering words of a man, despite being a woman.)

Given the political and geographical associations attached to Doña Sancha's family name in Lope's comedia, her rejection of well-tended gardens, canopies, and cushioned seats reflects more than the standard departure from the spatial constraints of gender typically associated with the *mujer varonil* in early modern Spanish drama. The status Doña Sancha enjoys as a living emblem of the Asturian-Leonese territory makes it possible for Lope's audience to interpret the spatial references in her speech not only as a statement of gender defiance but also as a defense of the expansive impetus that defines the land she embodies and a rejection of the spatial and geographical restrictions imposed on it by political subjection. That refutation is underlined by the specific reference to the Moorish carpet Doña Sancha makes in her response to Don Laín, which clearly points beyond the narrow limits of the home and alludes to the political situation of the Asturian and Leonese kingdom, hemmed in by the forces commanded by Audalla and subject to the authority of the caliph of Córdoba. To the Moorish carpet that adorns the snug and restricted space of the home, Doña Sancha opposes "the peaceful shade that the elm trees make in the field," expressing a firm dislike for enclosed spaces that anticipates the political destiny of her kingdom.

That expansive future, perfectly outlined in the speech King Alfonso delivers at the *Alcázar*, is also hinted at in the contrast between the well-tended garden and the snowy sierra that Don Laín makes while pleading his case for marriage with Doña Sancha. Her dislike of the former and preference for the latter highlights her unwomanly behavior and the ideas of care, confinement, and control that, as Fernando Copello has argued, are commonly associated with gardening in early modern texts: "Le jardin est peut-etre à l'opposé du milieu naturel puisqu'il s'agit d'un milieu naturel modifié, arrangé, maquillé, perdant ainsi son essence meme, devenu quelque chose d'autre"[27] (the garden stands perhaps as the opposite of the natural environment because it is a type of environment that has been modified, organized, made up, and has lost therefore its very essence and become something else). Doña Sancha's rejection of the garden as a space where nature can be tamed and contained is clearly in tune with the running motif of Lope's play. Indeed, as landscape historian J. B. Jackson has argued, gardens are symbolically related in Western culture to the idea of an enclosure; their traditional meaning in modern Indo-European languages "seems to indicate less what our dictionaries define as 'a plot of land used for the cultivation of flowers, vegetables, and fruit' than it does an enclosure or container."[28] Sebastián de Covarrubias, the famous seventeenth-century Spanish lexicographer, echoed this traditional meaning at the end of the entry he wrote for the word *jardín* (garden) in his *Tesoro de la lengua castellana o española* (1611):

> Huerto de recreación de diversas flores y yerbas olorosas, con fuentes y cuadros repartidos con muchos lazos, y obra que llaman los latinos *topiaria*, de mesas de arrayán y de otras yerbas. Este nombre jardín es alemán, *latine dicitur viridiarium* ... El padre Guadix, si no me engaño, dice ser arábigo ... Otros van más a lo castellano, y dizen que jardín es quasi *guardín*.[29]
>
> (Orchard for recreation with diverse flowers and fragant herbs, with fountains and square flowerbeds arranged with many ropes, which the Romans called *topiaria*, with tables covered with myrtle and other herbs. This name, *jardín*, is German, and in Latin it was called *viridiarium* ... Father Guadix, if I am not mistaken, states that it comes from Arabic ... Others are more inclined to think its origin is Castilian, and they say that *jardín* is almost *guardín*.)

Given that Covarrubias considers the last meaning and etymology—*guardín* (from the verb *guardar*, to protect, to defend, to enclose)—closer or more familiar to speakers of Castilian, it is reasonable to think that Lope's audience was alert to the spatial implications of Doña Sancha's rejection of the well-tended garden and would have discerned the political meaning implicit in that rejection. That meaning could have been easily surmised by the audience after they listened to the Moorish commander Audalla speak to one of his aids at the end of act 1 about the increasing daring and adventurousness of the Asturian people. Coming right after Doña Sancha's rejection of the cozy life of confinement offered her by Don Laín de Lara, Audalla's words clarify that the Asturians' refusal to live within the borders imposed on them by their master, the caliph, is but an extension of the anti-confinement stance proudly adopted a few moments earlier by Don García's daughter when she chooses the snowy sierra over the well-tended garden:

> AUDALLA. Pues quédese la gente en este monte
> En tanto que [Alfonso] las parias nos concede,
> Que somos pocos para estar más cerca
> Y cada día crecen los cristianos
> En número, en valor y atrevimiento,
> Y bajan de esas sierras ciento a ciento. (act 1, lines 434–439)
>
> (AUDALLA. Let our people stay on this mountain while we negotiate the payment with [Alfonso], for we are too few to get any closer and the Christians grow day by day in number, courage, and daring, coming down from these sierras by the hundreds.)

These Asturians, who descend the sierras daily by the hundreds and overstep the boundaries set by the caliph, reaffirm and amplify the position adopted earlier by Doña Sancha toward Don Laín, a position that—although informed by the conventions associated with the dramatic type of the *mujer guerrera*—encapsulates the expanding ethos of the territory Doña Sancha embodies in *Las famosas asturianas*. Lope's decision to have the people of Asturias also embrace this ethos allows him to sustain and further develop the triumph-over-confinement motif that structures the plot of the comedia and that links the Asturian-Leonese kingdom and Hapsburg Spain. This connection, firmly established in the speeches given by Nuño and King Alfonso in act 1 and through the role Doña Sancha plays as a living emblem of her kingdom, is critically reasserted in act 3, as I will argue next, when both Nùño and the king, spurred by Doña Sancha, decide to confront the caliph's men and take a more aggressive stance against their Muslim overlord. Adopting this stance allows them, as Bruce Burningham has argued, to regain their "archetypal [masculine] role as defenders of the defenseless" ("Beleaguered Hegemony," 132) and enables Alfonso to start fulfilling the destiny of his kingdom as a proto-imperial polity bound for expansion.

Manly Kings, Expanding Kingdoms: Fighting Enclosure with *Brío*

Act 3 of *Las famosas asturianas* advances and connects several issues that regularly feature in Lope's national history dramas. These themes include the role of the monarch as both embodiment and guardian of the honor of the kingdom and "the growing realization," as McKendrick has argued in relation to peasant honor dramas, that kings "could not afford to disregard the power of the *demos*" (*Playing the King*, 169).[30] These two specific concerns are inscribed in the statement from Audalla quoted above, in which the Moorish commander complains about the growing number of Asturians who descend the sierras daily to settle beyond the boundaries established by his master. Audalla's words make it clear that King Alfonso has not been able to fulfill his obligations as the defender of the honor of his realm and that his actions trail behind those of his subjects, who understand better than him the expansive destiny of the territory they inhabit. Therefore, King Alfonso will have to play catch-up with his vassals in Lope's comedia and prove himself worthy of the *demos* and the territory he rules.

That opportunity will arise when Nuño, ordered by Alfonso to transport to Audalla's camp the hundred maidens he owes to the caliph, finds himself unable to carry out the king's command due to a "caso extraño," or bizarre event that puzzles both him and his men. In this scene, the women they are escorting, led by Doña Sancha, remove their clothes on their way to the Moorish camp only to cover themselves at the sight of Audalla and his troops. Asked by Nuño to explain this strange and disturbing behavior, Doña Sancha offers the Asturian leader the following explanation:

Doña Sancha. Atiende, Osorio cobarde,
Afrenta de homes, atiende
Porque entiendas la razón,
Si non entenderla quieres.
Las mujeres non tenemos
Vergüenza de las mujeres;
Quien camina entre vosotros
Muy bien desnudarse puede,
Porque sois como nosotras,
Cobardes, fracas y endebres
Fembras, mujeres y damas,

. . . .

Pero cuando vi los moros,
Que son homes, y homes fuertes,
Vestime, que non es bien
Que las mis carnes me viesen. (act 2, lines 2333–2350)

(Doña Sancha. Listen, cowardly Osorio, affront to men. Listen so you can understand the reason, if indeed you want to understand it. Women are not ashamed of other women's bodies. Whoever walks among you can do so naked, for you are like us: cowardly, frail, and vulnerable females, women, ladies. . . . But when I saw the Moors, who are men, truly strong men, I had to get dressed, for it is not appropriate for me to show them my body.)

What Doña Sancha and her fellow "females, women, and ladies" want, as critics have pointed out, is to elicit from Nuño and his men a more virile response in defense of their kingdom by "calling their archetypal manhood into question" (Burningham, "Beleaguered Hegemony," 135). That response will not be long in coming, for Nuño, spurred by Doña Sancha's rebuke of his conduct, quickly resolves to disobey the king's orders and, with the help of the women he is escorting, engage Audalla and his men in battle. His decision will allow him to instantly regain his manhood by defeating "el hombre más bravo / que de África vino a España" (the bravest man that came from Africa to Spain) (*El mejor alcalde*, act 1, lines 365–366) and, more importantly, persuade his monarch to adopt a more aggressive attitude toward the Muslim invaders. The effect of Nuño's decision on King Alfonso is revealed in the closing scene of *Las famosas asturianas*, in which Nuño asks the monarch to consider for a moment what he would have done if his manhood had also been placed in doubt by Doña Sancha:

Nuño. Socedió lo que ya sabes,
Así los cielos te fagan
El más dichoso, buen Rey,

En todas las tus andanzas,
Que juzgues lo que ficieras
Si en aquel prado te hallaras
Viéndote llamar mujer
. . . .
REY. Quedo, Osorio, todos somos
Homes—de Dios por la gracia—.
Non soy yo fembra, ¡ma Dios!,
Maguer que Casto me llaman,
Que el Casto fue por virtud,
Non porque el brío me falta,
Que una cosa es non querer
Y otra la fraqueza humana. (act 3, lines 2671–2692)

(NUÑO. What happened, you already know. May Heaven make you, good king, most fortunate in all your endeavors to consider what you would have done if you had found yourself in that field being called a woman.

KING. Easy, Osorio. We are all men here, by the grace of God. I am no woman, though they call me "The Chaste." That name refers to my virtue, not to a lack of vigor. For it is one thing to refrain, and quite another to be weak.)

There is no denying that Alfonso's masculinity, now under siege, serves as the driving factor behind his change of attitude at the end of the comedia. The king, asked by Nuño to step for a moment into his shoes and face the accusations leveled against him by Doña Sancha, is forced, like his subordinate, to reassert his manhood in front of his subjects by taking a more belligerent stance against his enemies. Doing so requires the monarch to highlight the positive moral connotations associated with his nickname, "El Casto," and to play down its connection to the sphere of women, a connection Covarrubias made explicit in the entry for *casto* (chaste) in his *Tesoro de la lengua castellana o española*: "Vale puro, continente, opuesto al deshonesto y dado al vicio de la lujuria. Las mujeres que guardan lealtad a sus maridos se llaman castas" (It means pure, continent—opposite to dishonest and given to the vice of lust. Women who are faithful to their husbands are called chaste) (Covarrubias Horozco, *Tesoro de la lengua*, 283).[31] In order to appear *casto*—that is, not driven by sexual appetite—and manly at the same time, Alfonso also portrays himself in front of Nuño as not lacking in *brío* (vigor), a quality Covarrubias associates with courage, loudness, and other common masculine traits in his *Tesoro*:

Esfuerzo, ánimo, valor, coraje, erguimiento y altiveza . . . Algunos quieren brío sea nombre francés, derivado de la palabra *bruit, sonitus, tumultus, tumultuatio*, porque el brioso con su altiveza va haciendo ruido y hablando alto. No tener brío, ser un hombre manso, tardo en su movimiento y acciones. (206)

(Effort, spirit, valor, courage, uprightness, and pride . . . Some have argued that *brío* is a French noun, derived from the word *bruit*, *sonitus*, *tumultus*, *tumultuatio*, because a person with *brío* makes noise and talks loud due to his pride. A man lacking *brío* is tame and slow in his movements and actions.)

By presenting himself as both *casto* and full of *brío* when facing Nuño and his vassals, the king appropriates for himself attributes that are masculine and feminine. Thus, his status at the end of the play mirrors that of Doña Sancha, both woman and warrior, throughout the comedia, a status she transfers to her fellow *asturianas* and Don Nuño when she persuades them to fight Audalla instead of submissively complying with the caliph's demand. The king's acquisition of this dual status brings him close, too, to those brave Asturians who, according to Audalla, come down regularly from the sierras and challenge the authority of their Cordoban overlord. Their "valor" (courage) and "atrevimiento" (daring) epitomize the *brío* King Alfonso identifies with at the end of the comedia, a quality that, according to Don Nuño, Don Laín was also eager to embrace when he, Doña Sancha, and their followers battled Audalla and his men:

NUÑO. Dad algo a Laín de Lara,
Rey, que en aquesta ocasión
Fizo notable matanza
En los cordobeses moros. (act 3, lines 2714–2717)

(NUÑO. Your Majesty, give something to Laín de Lara, who on this occasion killed many Cordoban Moors.)

Don Laín's newly found manhood offers Lope's audience some assurance that King Alfonso will also behave with more *brío* when dealing with the caliph henceforth. The final scene of *Las famosas asturianas* thus replicates what we see dramatized in other national history plays by Lope: a monarch who learns what his duties are as guardian of his kingdom and must align his actions with those of the people he represents. Both goals are inextricably linked in the closing segment of the play to the monarch's ability to address his shortcomings as a man. However, I believe it would be wrong to view *Las famosas asturianas* as a play primarily concerned with the ever-present problem of the education of the monarch in Spanish drama or reflecting the anxiety of Lope's society concerning the question of masculinity.[32] The more aggressive stance against the caliph Alfonso adopts after listening to Don Nuño at the end of the comedia allows him to further the expansion of his kingdom, initiated earlier by his men in the mountains. Behavioral changes associated with gender—the king's assumption of a more masculine role by embracing *brío*, in this case—are therefore closely linked in Lope's play to a shift in attitude toward the territory that privileges conflict and expansion over subjection and enclosure. This change in mindset allows the play to come full circle in terms of the fundamental spatial motif that structures it: Alfonso's decision to finally leave his palace and fight the caliph following the example of Doña Sancha and her fellow *asturianas* explicitly echoes the image of the king emerging from the monastery and facing his enemies on the streets of León that Lope used at the start of the comedia. The enduring presence of this image in the play speaks in no uncertain terms of the expansive geopolitical message that Lope embedded in its plot.

The fact that territorial confinement gives way at the end of *Las famosas asturianas* to war and a future of unbridled expansion also validates the image of the Asturian-Leonese banner stretching down to Andalusia and North Africa, which Nuño presented to the king in act 1 and Alfonso enthusiastically embraced in his speech at the *Alcázar*. Lope's echoing of these expansive images at the close of the comedia confirms their centrality to the political message of a drama whose primary purpose is to imperialize the past by inscribing expansion into a legendary episode of medieval Iberia. This act of inscription rests, as I have argued, on Lope's ability to successfully adapt to the stage the triumph-over-confinement motif that contemporary Spanish historians employed to represent the plan of universal expansion that God had designed for their nation. This plan, echoed often in the dramas of the period, sought to connect, as Antonio Carreño has observed, "el origen fundacional del pasado con el actual vivido por el espectador del siglo XVII" (the founding origin of the past with the present lived by seventeenth-century audiences) through the use of "figuras o tipos, tal como los estudia Erich Auerbach" (*figurae* or types, as studied by Erich Auerbach) ("La fuerza de las historias representadas," 21). Space, very often ignored in studies on the relation between historiography and drama in the Lopian comedia, contributed in a significant way to the functioning of this figural system of understanding and representing history and to the spread of the neo-Gothic ideology it served. Lope was well acquainted with this system through the work of Mariana and other historians and took full advantage of it in *Las famosas asturianas* to spatially connect a small, beleaguered kingdom in eighth-century Iberia with the imperial state governed by the Hapsburgs. The spatial bond he was able to establish between these two distant and vastly different polities helped legitimize the image of Spain as a nation destined from its inception to expand to "the furthest corners of the east and the west," as Mariana put it in his *Historia de España*.

In closing, I suggest that the image of an ever-expanding Spain Lope creates in *Las famosas asturianas* may have also had a significant impact on the audience's perception of the relationship between geography and identity. The strong sense of locality that informed this relationship and the decentralized model of government adopted by the Hapsburg monarchy did little to foster attachments at the supra-regional level among sixteenth- and seventeenth-century Spaniards. As one historian of the period has argued, "the concept of community current in Renaissance Spain reinforced the sense of belonging and obligation towards the locality [e.g., the city] . . . but contributed little to a theory of association between the city and the kingdom, and *a fortiori* between one kingdom and another."[33] In this disjointed political scenario, the articulation of a coherent form of collective sentiment became of paramount importance to fill the ideological gap left by the actual practice of power in the territories governed by the Hapsburgs. Lope's play took a significant step in that direction by promoting an idea of the state that, centered on the unifying theme of expansion, helped bring cohesion to a polity sundered by the local and regional forces that made up its motley political tissue.

CHAPTER 4

Endangered from Within

SPACE AND DIFFERENCE IN *LAS PACES DE LOS REYES Y JUDÍA DE TOLEDO*

Early modern Spanish national history plays, Walter Cohen has written, "tend to emphasize the struggle between Catholic Spain and its infidel external foes" (*Drama of a Nation*, 227). The fight to defend and expand the national territory against external Moorish aggression that Lope dramatizes in *Las famosas asturianas* certainly conforms to the pattern described by Cohen. However, throughout the sixteenth and seventeenth centuries, Spain's fight against the infidel took place as much inside as outside its borders. Despite the conquest of Granada by the Catholic Kings in 1492 and the repression of Islam and Moorish customs that ensued, the presence inside the country of Moorish subjects, the Moriscos, challenged their project of an all-Catholic, imperial nation. This challenge stemmed from the suspicion that the Moriscos were adhering to their prior beliefs and traditions and would attempt to collude with the Turks to expand their dominion in the Mediterranean. Events like the 1568 revolt of the Moriscos in the mountains of La Alpujarras in Granada only served, as historian J. H. Elliott has argued, to reinforce that fear:

> On Christmas night of that terrible year 1568—the year of the danger in Catalonia, of the cutting of the sea-route through the Bay of Biscay, and of the arrest and death of Philip's son and heir, Don Carlos—a band of Morisco outlaws led by a certain Fàrax Abenfàrax broke into the city of Granada, bringing with them the news that the Alpujarras had risen into revolt. Although the rebels failed to seize the city, their incursion signalized the outbreak of rebellion throughout the kingdom of Granada. Spain, which had surrounded itself with such strong defenses against the advance of Protestantism, now found itself endangered from within; and the threat came not, as was expected, from the Protestants, but from its old enemies, the Moors. (*Imperial Spain, 1469–1716*, 235)

The threat posed by this internal enemy did not disappear with the suppression of the Alpujarras uprising in 1570 by Philip II's troops and the subsequent dispersion of the Morisco population throughout Castile he ordered. In 1609, Philip III, the new king, issued a royal edict declaring that the Moriscos were to be expelled from Spain on account of their unwillingness to embrace Catholicism and their seditious activities against the crown. The latter included providing material assistance and intelligence for Muslim raids on Spain's Mediterranean coast and conspiring with the Ottoman Turks and the French Protestants to topple the Spanish monarchy.[1] Even though these treasonous acts could only be substantiated in a few cases, they were conveniently exaggerated in the anti-Morisco literature of the period—quickly, *all* Moriscos became suspect of aiding and abetting the crown's enemies in the popular imagination.[2] The collective psychosis that grew around the fears of a Moorish fifth column acting inside Spain to bring down the monarchy and disrupt its empire was so widespread that even the Moriscos themselves were willing to buy into it. Cervantes echoed this peculiar state of affairs in part two, chapter fifty-four of *Don Quijote* through the character of Ricote, Sancho's Morisco neighbor, whose testimony speaks in no uncertain terms about the dangers for Spain of "nurturing snakes in its bosom" and of "sheltering its enemies at home":

> Y forzábame a creer esta verdad saber yo los ruines y disparatados intentos que los nuestros tenían, y tales, que me parece que fue inspiración divina la que movió a su Majestad a poner en efecto tan gallarda resolución, no porque todos fuésemos culpados, que algunos había cristianos firmes y verdaderos; pero eran tan pocos, que no se podían oponer a los que no lo eran, y no era bien criar la sierpe en el seno, teniendo los enemigos dentro de casa.[3]
>
> (I was forced to believe this truth because I knew the hateful and foolish intentions of our people, and they were such that it seems to me it was divine inspiration that moved His Majesty to put into effect so noble a resolution, not because all of us were guilty, for some were firm and true Christians, though these were so few they could not oppose those who were not, but because it is not a good idea to nurture a snake in your bosom or shelter enemies in your house.)[4]

The deep anxiety regarding infiltration and the possibility of harboring the enemy that Ricote so vividly portrays in this passage is also echoed, I will argue in this chapter, in *Las paces de los reyes y judía de Toledo* [The Reconciliation of the Monarchs and the Jewess of Toledo] (ca. 1610–1612), a play Lope wrote during or immediately before Philip III's edict of expulsion against the Moriscos was enforced.[5] Lope's comedia dramatizes an episode of marital infidelity involving King Alfonso VIII of Castile and a young Jewish woman from Toledo that was first recorded in the *Castigos e documentos para bien vivir ordenados por el rey don Sancho*, a thirteenth-century manual for proper comportment commissioned by King Sancho IV of Castile for his eldest son, Fernando.[6] The episode was later incorporated into the *Tercera Crónica General* of 1390 and in the expanded version of that text that Florián de Ocampo printed in 1541 with the title *Las quatro partes enteras de la Crónica de España*, which provided Lope with the outline for his comedia.[7]

Lope's handling of this controversial chapter of King Alfonso's life in *Las paces* projects into the past the same concerns regarding the relationship between space and difference that informed Spain's attitude toward the Moriscos before and during their Expulsion: a pervasive fear of collective undoing due to the presence inside the nation of individuals whose beliefs and customs undermined the project of a universal, all-Catholic monarchy embraced by the Hapsburgs. This fear is persistently expressed in the comedia, as I will discuss first, through images of infiltration and betrayal that underline the inability of those in power to guard the territories they rule effectively and through the connection some characters establish between the king's relationship with Raquel, his Jewish mistress, and the dissolution of Castile as a kingdom.[8] The prospect of this dissolution, expressed through the frequent references to an imminent Moorish invasion that Alfonso's courtiers and his wife, Queen Leonor, make throughout the play, transfers onto the Jewish woman the same spatial anxiety Lope's Spain felt concerning the Moriscos. As a result, contemporary views regarding the menace posed by the Moriscos, I will finally argue, are highly relevant to understanding the relationship between the play and the historical context of *Las paces*.

The Enemy Within: Infiltration and Betrayal in *Las paces de los reyes*

Much as the frantic scene of pursuit that opens act 1 of *Las famosas asturianas*, *Las paces* begins with the covert arrival of a new king (Alfonso VIII) in the capital of his kingdom (Toledo) to assume the responsibilities of government. A tense dialogue in the Church of San Román between Don Manrique de Lara, one of the nobles who has arranged Alfonso's entry into Toledo, and Fernán Ruiz, a local nobleman, informs the audience about the problems caused by the king's sudden appearance.[9] Alfonso, Ruiz explains, is still under fifteen, and therefore, according to the terms set by his father, King Sancho III, in his testament, cannot assume the crown of Castile. Thus, his place on the throne will continue to be occupied by his uncle, King Fernando II of León, whose attitude toward Alfonso has been far from friendly. The older Leonese king has established an alliance with the powerful clan of the Castros, a high-ranking Castilian-Leonese family, to keep Alfonso from assuming the throne and to attempt several times to murder his nephew. These efforts, however, have been in vain, for, as Don

Manrique states, the young Alfonso has managed to stay alive thanks to the protection provided by the loyal "hidalgos de Ávila" (noblemen of Ávila) and is now inside a city that yearns to give itself over to him:

MANRIQUE. ¡Toledo por Alfonso, rey legítimo
De Castilla! ¡Toledo por Alfonso,
Hijo del rey don Sancho el Deseado
Y del emperador de España nieto!
. . . .
FERNÁN. ¿Quién alborota la ciudad, soldados?
¿Qué es esto de decir viva Alfonso?
¿No sabéis que Toledo se defiende
Por el rey de León, y que yo tengo
Su alcázar por Fernando, y que los muros
No se darán al de Castilla en tanto
Que tenga los quince años que su padre
Mandó en su testamento? ¿Qué dais voces?
MANRIQUE. Fernán Ruiz, aunque Fernando lleva
De Toledo las rentas, y se llama
Injustamente su señor, bien sabes
Que Alfonso su sobrino es rey legítimo.
Bien sabes que ha querido y procurado
Quitarle el reino, y que guardó su vida
La gran lealtad de los hidalgos de Ávila,
Que le han criado y defendido siempre.
Toledo quiere darse a su Rey; deja
Que el rey goce a Toledo.[10]

(MANRIQUE. Toledo for Alfonso, rightful king of Castile! Toledo for Alfonso, son of King Sancho, "The Desired," and grandson of the Emperor of Spain!

FERNÁN. Soldiers, who stirs up the city like this? What is all this "long live Alfonso!" business? Don't you know that Toledo is under the protection of Fernando, king of León, who has charged me with defending its fortress, and that the city will not to be given over to the king of Castile until he is fifteen, as his father ordered in his testament? Why then do you raise your voices?

MANRIQUE. Fernán Ruiz, Fernando may collect taxes in Toledo and unlawfully call himself its lord, but you know very well that Alfonso, his nephew, is the rightful king. You know quite well that Fernando wants and has tried to take the throne away from him and that he is still alive due to the great loyalty shown to him by the noblemen of Ávila, who raised Alfonso and have always protected him. Toledo wants to give itself over to its king. Let the king enjoy his city.)

The short history lesson concerning Alfonso's troubled childhood and the strained relations between twelfth-century León and Castile outlined in this passage introduces two interrelated spatial motifs to which Lope will return throughout the comedia: infiltration and the powerlessness of rulers to maintain control over the lands they rule. These two motifs, presented initially in a positive light through the image of a young and endangered monarch who manages to escape murder and sneak daringly into his capital to claim the throne, will later acquire a somber and ominous tone once Alfonso is crowned king by the Castilian nobility. This becomes evident in the episode of the siege of the castle of Zurita that follows Alfonso's entry into Toledo and his coronation in the city's cathedral, an event that will test the young monarch's readiness to assume the throne and accept the military and political responsibilities of power. In this episode, which occupies most of act 1, Alfonso faces a recalcitrant aristocrat, Don Lope de Arenas, who, despite his initial promise to recognize Alfonso as the rightful king, refuses to relinquish control of the fortress he commands in the small garrison town of Zurita, on the outskirts of Toledo. Don Lope, like Alfonso's uncle before him, feels he has nothing to fear from *el Rey Chico* (the "Child King") because, as he explains to Dominguillo, his trusted servant, Zurita's walls are impregnable and will easily hold at bay the young monarch:

> LOPE. Necio vienes, Dominguillo,
> Pues no has visto en tantos días
> Que no hay humanas porfías
> Contra tan fuerte castillo.
> Reírme quiero de ti
> Y de Alfonso, que los dos
> Parecéis niños, ¡Por Dios!,
> Él en venir contra mí,
> Y tú en decir que me guarde. (act 1, lines 490–501)

> (LOPE. Don't be stupid, Dominguillo. Have you not seen now for many days that no human force will topple this castle? I want to laugh at you and Alfonso. Both of you act like children, for God's sake! He for attacking me, and you for telling me to beware of him.)

Unbeknownst to the unwary and overconfident nobleman, however, Dominguillo has been plotting to let Alfonso inside Zurita and thus facilitate his fall and that of his wife, Doña Costanza. Driven by greed and his desire to cozy up to the new monarch, the devious servant uses a wicket door in the walls of the fortress to parley with Alfonso and present to him a plan to take the castle—a strategy that, as he explains to the audience, will also leave Don Lope dead and Doña Costanza in mourning:

Dominguillo. ¡Oh, cómo parte seguro,
Con su querida Costanza,
En la fuerza de este fuerte,
Porque no sabe que soy
Quien al Rey le ha de dar hoy,
A ella luto, y a él la muerte!
Yo sé en el fuerte un portillo
Por donde pienso salir,
Ir, venir, entrar, huir
A la plaza del castillo.
Presto verá lo que pasa:
Que daña con gran rigor
En el cuerpo mal humor
Y el ladrón dentro de casa. (act 1, lines 528–541)

(Dominguillo. Oh, see how he goes, with his dear Costanza, trusting the strength of this fortress blindly because he does not know that today I will deliver it to the king and bring death to him and mourning to Doña Costanza! There is a wicket door I will use to come in and out of this fortress, to enter it and flee to the courtyard of this castle. He will soon realize how badly it hurts when you have a bad humor in your body or a thief in your house.)

Don Lope's blind trust in Dominguillo allows the latter to easily put into practice his treasonous plan. Thus, while his master shaves, Dominguillo drives a *venablo* (hunting spear) through his chest and kills him. The distraught Doña Costanza surrenders Zurita to Alfonso, who, as promised, pays Dominguillo handsomely for his services but orders his men to have the traitor's eyes removed. The king's behavior toward Dominguillo reproduces, as Frederick de Armas has argued, a common pattern found in texts from antiquity and the early modern period, in which traitors are typically treated harshly by those who benefit from their actions.[11] Considered within the strict textual boundaries of *Las paces*, however, Alfonso's interaction with Dominguillo also revisits the opening scene of the comedia, in which we see the king trying to sneak into an enclosed and heavily fortified environment (Toledo) with the help of those living inside its walls. The king's reaction to Dominguillo's treachery also recalls the advice given to him during his coronation by one of his mentors, Don Nuño, who recommends Alfonso secure complete internal control of his territory before trying to conquer the distant lands occupied in southern Iberia by the Moors:

Alfonso. Yo, niño rey, diez años perseguido,
Sin patria, sin palacio, sin posada,
Por una y otra parte siempre huido,

¿qué puedo dar, pues nunca tuve nada?
Mas ya que hoy tomo el cetro y me he ceñido
Para cobrar mis reinos esta espada,
Busquemos a los moros, porque quiero
Daros lo que ganare con su acero.
ESTEBAN. Bien dice el rey en esto.
MANRIQUE. Tan bien dice
Que le bendice, Esteban, todo el suelo.
NUÑO. Sí, pero no ha de entrar en la conquista
De las tierras extrañas el que tiene
Tantas guerras y engaños en las propias.
Cobre Alfonso las suyas y, cobradas,
Podrá poner la mano en las ajenas. (act 1, lines 339–353)

(ALFONSO. What can I, a child king, persecuted for ten years, always fleeing, without a country, a palace, or a place to stay, give if I never owned anything? But, since today I grabbed the scepter and girded myself with this sword to reclaim my kingdom, let's go find the Moors, for I want to give you whatever I win with my blade.
ESTEBAN. The king speaks well.
MANRIQUE. So well, Esteban, that the whole country blesses him.
NUÑO. True, but he who faces war and deception at home should not embark on the conquest of foreign lands. Let Alfonso regain his kingdom. Once he recovers it, he can lay hands on the lands of others.)

The advice provided by Don Nuño and the negative examples of Don Lope and King Fernando underline the importance of safeguarding one's territory against internal threats, a theme featured throughout *Las paces*. This problem is primarily dramatized in Lope's comedia using two closely connected spatial motifs—infiltration and the inability of rulers to protect their domains—that, as the example of Don Lope's murder demonstrates, take a dark turn in the play after Alfonso is crowned in Toledo. The events that follow Alfonso's conquest of Zurita confirm, as we shall see, this trend and reemphasize the comedia's concern with the vulnerability of monarchs and kingdoms when faced with threats coming from within their territories.

These threats are personified in acts 2 and 3 of the play in the figure of Raquel, with whom the king falls in love after watching her bathe in the Tagus with her sister, Sibila. Alfonso's chance encounter with the Jewish woman in the river while taking a stroll along its banks echoes, as Raymond McCurdy has noted, the tragic Biblical story of David and Bathsheba and spells trouble for a king who has left his childhood and teenage years behind to become one of Europe's most accomplished rulers.[12] In the years that have elapsed since the conquest of Zurita, the Castilian monarch has conquered and unified his kingdom, participated successfully in the Third Crusade alongside Richard the Lionheart, and obtained from this English monarch the hand of his daughter (Leonor) in marriage.[13] All of these accomplishments and the safety of Castile as a kingdom are suddenly jeopardized, however, by Alfonso's decision to start an extramarital relationship with Raquel, whom Belardo, the king's gardener, describes in the following terms when questioned by his master about Raquel's background:

ALFONSO. ¿Sabes su estado y hacienda?
BELARDO. Debajo de ser quien son,
¿qué más queréis saber dellas?
Si alguna os parece bien
Y sois persona de prendas
Como se parece en vos,
Huid de aquí treinta leguas.
ALFONSO. No me quiero yo casar.
BELARDO. ¿Para qué puede ser buena
Una mujer mal nacida,
Si después tenéis un hijo en ella?
ALFONSO. (Miedo me ha puesto el villano.) (act 2, lines 1427–1438)

(ALFONSO. What do you know about their station and wealth?
BELARDO. Besides knowing what they are, what else do you need to know about them? You are, it seems, a man of means and distinction. If one of them pleases you, you should run at least thirty miles from here.
ALFONSO. I do not intend to marry her.
BELARDO. What good is an ill-begotten woman if you end up having a son with her?
ALFONSO. This peasant has frightened me.)

Belardo's characterization of Raquel as ill-begotten or "mal nacida" (literally, "badly born") reflects the impact that, as David Nirenberg has argued, biological ideas about breeding and reproduction had made on the understanding and expression of cultural and religious difference in Spain since the late Middle Ages.[14] According to these ideas, a person's lineage—their "good" or "bad" birth—was inextricably linked to the beliefs and customs they would adopt as an adult.

Belardo's words reflect this amalgamation of birth, religion, and social practices that defined what Antonio Feros has called "the rhetoric of difference"[15] in early modern Spain, but, more importantly, they also establish a clear analogy between Raquel and Dominguillo, whom Don Lope described as an "hombre mal nacido" (ill-begotten man) (act 1, line 825) at the moment of his death.[16] The statement made by the nobleman may signify a Jewish origin for Dominguillo, but the parallel his words establish between his servant and Raquel reflects concerns that go beyond those typically attached to religion and lineage in early modern Spain. Like Don Lope's treacherous servant, Raquel is made to embody in *Las paces* the danger associated with individuals whose presence and actions may jeopardize the well-being and functioning of a polity from within. This danger is verbalized in the comedia by Queen Leonor, Alfonso's wife, who, enraged by her husband's seven-year affair with the Jewish woman, summarizes for the Castilian nobles the political situation their kingdom faces as a result of Raquel's relationship with her husband:

LEONOR. Raquel reina, Raquel tiene
De Castilla la corona,
. . . .
Bajan de la Andalucía,
De Granada y de Archidona
Los moros, y a ése [Alfonso] se atreven
De quien temblaron la sombra;
La Sierra Morena pasan,
Y destruyendo a Almodóvar
Pasan los campos de Utiel,
Y en la Ciudad Real se alojan.
A este paso, castellanos,
Presto del Tajo en las ondas,
Por dicha con sangre vuestra,
Beberán sus yeguas moras;
Presto en estos altos muros,
En vez de banderas rojas,
Verán pendones azules
Que ya tan cerca tremolan;
Presto en esta santa iglesia,
Donde la Reina y Señora
Del cielo puso los pies,
Pondrá los huesos Mahoma. (act 3, lines 1998–2017)

(LEONOR. Raquel governs; Raquel owns Castile's crown . . . From Andalusia, from Granada and Archidona, the Moors are coming down. Before they feared even Alfonso's shadow, now they challenge him. They have crossed Sierra Morena and, after destroying Almodóvar, have passed the fields of Utiel, and camped down in Ciudad Real. At this pace, soon their mares will be drinking from the Tagus, stained with your blood; soon, on these high walls, instead of red flags, people will see their blue banners, which are flapping ever so near; and soon, in this holy church, where our queen and lady from Heaven set down her feet, Muhammad will lay down his bones.)

Although Raquel, unlike Dominguillo, is not shown in the play conversing with the enemy or facilitating their entry into the territory ruled by Alfonso, her presence in Toledo is directly linked, as the queen's words make apparent, with the impending demise of Castile at the hands of the Moors. This association is reinforced by the anonymous voice the king hears one night in the orchard by the Tagus, where he regularly meets his mistress. The voice heard by Alfonso warns him against losing God's favor on account of his adulterous relationship with Raquel and identifies the Jewish woman with La Cava, the woman who, according to a legend disseminated widely since the mid-thirteenth century, caused "the ruin of Spain" by inviting the Moors in after having been raped by King Don Rodrigo, the last of Spain's Visigothic monarchs:[17]

VOZ. Rey Alfonso, rey Alfonso,
No digas que no te aviso,
Mira que pierdes la gracia
De aquel Rey que rey te hizo.
. . . .
Mira, Alfonso, lo que intentas,
Pues desde que fuiste niño
Te ha sacado libre el cielo
Entre tantos enemigos.
No des lugar desta suerte,
Cuando hombre, a tus apetitos:
Advierte que por la Cava
A España perdió Rodrigo. (act 2, lines 1837–1852)

(VOICE. King Alfonso, King Alfonso, do not say I am not warning you: You are losing the favor of that king who made you king. . . . Beware, Alfonso, of what you are doing, for Heaven has saved you from your enemies many times since you were a child. Now that you are a man, do not give free rein to your desires. Remember that it was on account of La Cava that Rodrigo lost Spain.)

The analogy this anonymous voice establishes between Raquel and La Cava recalls the initial encounter between the king and the Jewish woman before the Tagus. As Raymond McCurdy has pointed out, the story of La Cava's rape by Don Rodrigo was also set in a riverside location in Pedro del Corral's *Crónica del Rey don Rodrigo, con la destruyción de España* (ca. 1443), which provided the basis for all subsequent elaborations of the La Cava legend in early modern Spanish literature and historiography.[18] Echoed in this association between Raquel and La Cava is, presumably, the connection that, as José Ramón Martín Largo has noted, some medieval and early modern historians had established between Alfonso's affair with Raquel and the crushing defeat he suffered in the Battle of Alarcos

(1195).[19] This defeat forced Castile to give up control of large swaths of its territory to the Moors and evoked, therefore, the "ruin of Spain" occasioned by Don Rodrigo.[20] Lope may have been prompted to allude to the shameful episode of Alarcos in his play after reading book X of Juan de Mariana's *Historia de España*, which describes Alfonso's relationship with Raquel in the following terms:

> Túvose por cierto que con aquel desastre tan grande [Alarcos] castigó Dios en particular un pecado del rey, y fue que en Toledo, menospreciada su mujer, se enamoró de cierta judía, que fuera de la hermosura ninguna otra cosa tenía de estimar. Era este trato no solo deshonesto, sino también afrentoso a la cristiandad. (330)
>
> (It was believed that God had used that great disaster to punish a specific sin committed by the king: his falling in love in Toledo with a Jewess who made him despise his wife and who had no worthy quality, other than being beautiful. That relationship was not only lecherous; it was offensive to the Christian religion.)

Given Lope's admiration for Mariana and his familiarity with del Corral's *Crónica* and the numerous versions of the La Cava and Don Rodrigo legend it inspired, it would be foolish to ignore the impact some of these texts probably had on the ominous depiction of Raquel as a new La Cava by the voice that Alfonso heard in the orchard. Central to this depiction, whatever its provenance, is the idea, repeatedly expressed in Lope's play, that polities can be unraveled quickly from within by infiltrators—individuals who, like Raquel and Dominguillo, operate inside a community or territory to plot its destruction. This idea is stressed again in the scene of Raquel's murder at the end of *Las paces*. Critics have traditionally focused on the sympathetic picture of Raquel that Lope paints in this segment of the comedia, where she embraces the religion of her murderers—the Castilian nobles—and appears, therefore, "as the Christian mainstream would like to imagine her: a sincere convert"[21]: "Muero en la ley de mi Alfonso, / testigos los cielos sean, / Creo en Cristo, a Cristo adoro" (I die embracing the religion of my Alfonso. Let Heaven be my witness that I believe in and worship Christ) (act 2, lines 2439–2441).[22] This positive image of Raquel as a Christian is problematized, however, by the characterization that Don Blasco makes of her as a new Helen of Troy, the quintessential infiltrator in Homer's *Illiad* and a forerunner of La Cava, as Patricia Grieve has noted (*The Eve of Spain*, 182–183), in many accounts of her story written in medieval and early modern Spain:

> BLASCO. Caballeros, ¿Qué aguardáis,
> Si en la muerte desta Elena
> Vuestro remedio consiste
> Y el de toda España?
> TODOS. ¡Muera! (act 2, lines 2434–2438)

(BLASCO. Sirs, what are you waiting for? The death of this Helen will be your remedy and that of all Spain.

ALL. Death to her!)

The picture of Raquel as a new Helen that Don Blasco paints will endure in the comedia even after her death, for her memory will live on in Alfonso's mind and exert a powerful influence over his behavior. Thus, haunted by the image of his mistress's ghastly death at the hands of the nobles, the king vows to kill all adult males living in Castile to avenge her murder: "Ya pensarás [Raquel] que de tu muerte fiera / no he de tomar venganza; espera un poco, / que no ha de quedar hombre que no muera" (Maybe you will think, Raquel, that I will not avenge your death. Just wait; there will be no man left alive in Castile) (act 2, lines 2598–2600). Alfonso's plan for a bloody vendetta allows Raquel to continue to play through him the role of infiltrator and underlines, as Gustavo Faverón Patriau has argued, "la intrínseca asechanza del mal del judío al subrayar su ubicación *dentro* del cuerpo del estado"[23] (the intrinsic threat posed by Jewish evilness by highlighting its position *within* the body politic). This "mal" or intrinsic evil that operates now from within the person of the king pushes Castile toward self-annihilation and brings back to mind the words uttered by Dominguillo when he plotted the death of Don Lope in Zurita; "que daña con gran rigor / en el cuerpo mal humor / y el ladrón dentro de casa" (how badly it hurts when you have a bad humor in your body or a thief inside your house) (act 1, lines 539–541).[24]

The king and Castile are clearly in need of a powerful remedy to counteract the pernicious effects of Alfonso's undying devotion to his mistress. That remedy will come in the form of divine intervention, a strategy that—in the eyes of some critics—seems unwarranted and unbefitting of a secular play like *Las paces*, but which Lope often employs in his historical dramas to defuse conflict and to prompt drastic changes in the behavior of his characters.[25] The urgency of these changes is explicitly communicated to Alfonso by an angel that visits him at the church of Illescas, a few miles from Toledo, where he has retired to rest and mourn the passing of his mistress.[26] The angel tells the monarch that Raquel's death was part of God's providential plan to safeguard his kingdom and warns him about the punishment that awaits him if he decides to carry out his vendetta:

ÁNGEL. Alfonso, muy ofendido
Está Dios de tus palabras,
De las blasfemias que dices
Y de que tomes venganza.
Vuelve a ti, que si no enmiendas
Lo que has dicho y lo que tratas
Grande castigo te espera,
Notable rigor te aguarda.

Dios quiere, para que entiendas
Lo que a Dios le desagrada
El sentimiento que has hecho,
Que no te herede en tu casa
Hijo varón; morirán
Sin el reino, por desgracia.
Vuelve en ti, no digas cosas
Que aun a las piedras espantan,
Cuantimás al cielo a quien
Debes eterna alabanza.
Vase
ALFONSO. Pequé, Señor, ofendí
Vuestra Majestad. ¡Perdón! (act 2, lines 2620–2639)

(ANGEL. Alfonso, God has been very offended by your words, your blasphemies, and the revenge you are planning. Come back to your senses, for great punishment and hardship await you if you do not rectify your words and actions. To make you understand how displeased he is, God has willed that no son of yours will inherit your kingdom. All your sons will die, unfortunately, without occupying the throne. Come back to your senses. Stop saying things that horrify not just the stones, but also Heaven, to which you owe eternal praise.
[He leaves]
ALFONSO. I sinned, my Lord. I offended Your Majesty. Forgive me!)

Alfonso's repentance and immediate compliance with the angel's demand to come back to his senses will allow him to remove from his mind—and, by extension, from Castile—all traces of Raquel and thus to neutralize the threat she was still able to pose as an infiltrator. The king is now in a position to seek reconciliation with his wife, as announced in the comedia's title, and to spare his kingdom the fate suffered by Zurita under Don Lope. The avoidance of this fate finally dispels the fear of dissolution and collective undoing that Lope associates in *Las paces* with the characters of Raquel and Dominguillo, whose presence and deeds pose an existential threat to the communities that host them. This fear is insistently expressed in the play through images of infiltration that, although initially positive, acquire a negative tone as the comedia progresses and underline the inability of those in power to protect the territories they govern against internal threats.

This aspect of the play highlights the centrality of space in *Las paces* and its departure from the basic infidelity-repentance plot Lope drew from Florián de Ocampo's *Crónica de España*. In Lope's reworking of Ocampo's account, Alfonso's extramarital relationship with Raquel is portrayed not only as a "fecho malo e desaguisado" (a bad and irrational deed) (*Crónica de España* 4:fol. 386 v) in the eyes of God and the monarch's subjects, but also as an act detrimental to the territorial integrity and ambitions of his kingdom. The insertion of this geopolitical element in the play may have been motivated by the link some medieval and early modern historians (Juan de Mariana among them) had established between Alfonso's infidelity and the defeat he suffered at Alarcos. However, the concerns associated with the unsettling presence of the Moriscos in Lope's Spain also played an essential part in the dramatist's decision to project onto the bygone medieval world of *Las paces* the same spatial anxiety his contemporaries felt about the Moriscos. Feeding that anxiety, I will argue next, was the widespread belief that the Moriscos, like Raquel, were intent on plotting from the inside the ruin of Spain and the collapse of its universal monarchy, a belief that prompted the Spanish authorities to consider all members of this minority infiltrators and enemies of the state.

Rethinking Context: *Las paces de los reyes* and the Expulsion of the Moriscos

When writing about the context surrounding the composition of *Las paces*, critics have underlined the significance that Alfonso's betrayal of his marriage vows has for understanding the real-life issues the comedia addresses. According to Felipe Pedraza, one of those problems is the bigamous relationship Lope maintained with Juana de Guardo, his second wife, and the actress Micaela Luján while living in Toledo in the early 1600s.[27] Lope's unconventional marital situation is echoed, according to Felipe Pedraza, in the plot of *Las paces*, where his proverbial inclination to blur the lines between literature and biography is on full display:

> Y, sin duda, esta situación personal se proyecta sobre la obra. Lope, mitómano empedernido, disfruta transmutándose a sí mismo y trasponiendo sus circunstancias al ámbito de la leyenda . . . Alejándose del tópico del amor único y exclusivo, que se vuelve desdén cuando surge otra pasión en el horizonte, echa mano de su experiencia de bígamo y la trasplanta al corazón de sus personajes. ("*La judía de Toledo*: génesis y cristalización," 26–27)
>
> (Without a doubt, this personal situation is projected onto the play. Lope, relentless in his mythomania, takes pleasure in transfiguring himself and in transferring his biographical circumstance to the sphere of legend . . . Rejecting the cliché of a devoted and exclusive love that turns into disdain when another love interest appears on the horizon, he resorts to his experience as a bigamist and grafts it onto the hearts of his characters.)

More interested in what Alfonso's relationship with Raquel and his wife might tell us about the politics of the period, other critics have tried to link *Las paces* to the domestic and foreign policy issues that defined the earlier part of Philip

III's reign. Thus, McKendrick has interpreted Alfonso's unwavering devotion to Raquel as a reflection of Philip's attachment to his *valido* or court favorite, the Duke of Lerma, who, soon after Philip's accession to the throne in 1598, set about establishing himself as the sole authority in the kingdom by securing the king's favor and filling the most important posts in government with his relatives. The parallel between Philip's *valido* and Raquel, according to McKendrick, could not have been lost on Lope's audience, who would have had no trouble interpreting "the beautiful, tragic Jewess as a deliberate, if incongruous, cipher for the greedy and self-serving Duke of Lerma" (*Playing the King*, 46).

A different view, related this time to Queen Leonor and her willingness to reconcile with her husband at the end of the play, has been expressed by Fernando Rodríguez Gallego. He has evaluated *Las paces* as reinforcing the effort undertaken by Lerma and his government to put an end to the decades of military, religious, and economic hostilities that had defined the relations between Protestant England and Catholic Spain since the mid-sixteenth century. This effort, which culminated in a peace treaty that both nations signed in 1604, was, according to Rodríguez Gallego, the political and ideological backdrop against which Lope wrote *Las paces*, a fact reflected in the comedia's title and the choice of Alfonso as its protagonist:[28]

> Al tiempo, el clima de paz con Inglaterra de los inicios del reinado de Felipe III también pudo contribuir a que Lope volviese la mirada a una figura [Alfonso VIII] que, a través de su matrimonio con Leonor Plantagenet, hija de los reyes de Inglaterra Enrique II Plantagenet y Leonor de Aquitania, se asociaba a un clima de amistad y entendimiento con la corona inglesa. ("Alfonso VIII," 159)
>
> (At the same time, the climate of peace with England at the start of Philip III's reign may have also motivated Lope to turn his attention to a historical figure [Alfonso VIII] who, by means of his marriage to Eleanor Plantagenet, daughter of the king of England, Henry II, and Eleanor of Aquitaine, was identified with a spirit of friendship and cooperation with the English Crown.)

All the views summarized above cogently link significant aspects of Lope's comedia to its biographical and political context, but, oddly enough, they remain completely silent about the most important event taking place in Spain when *Las paces* was written: the Expulsion of the Moriscos. The ideological impact of this episode on Lope and his audience cannot be underestimated. As historian Antonio Feros has written, the decision by the Spanish Crown in 1609 to banish all Spaniards of Moorish descent from the Iberian Peninsula was widely advertised throughout the country "as a fundamental step in the sacred history of Spain, as the crowning event of Spain's unification after the Arab conquest, and as of an importance equal to the taking of Granada in 1492" ("Rhetorics of the Expulsion," 76).[29] It would indeed be surprising if Lope, whose dramas are so often concerned with "la construcción de la idea nacional" (Ryjik, *Lope de Vega en la invención*, 29) and with the role of history in that construction, had paid no heed in *Las paces* to the Expulsion of the Moriscos. This event shaped early modern Spain's sense of communal identity and was presented by the authorities as the crystallization of its destiny as a nation. My contention in the pages that follow is that this critical event, coeval with the writing and staging of *Las paces*, did leave a significant mark on the play, one that can be perceived in the unsettling view of space it presents. That view reproduces in a medieval context the fears and concerns that were repeatedly expressed in the early 1600s by those who identified the Moriscos as a threat to the religious, political, and territorial integrity of Spain and the Catholic empire it supported.

The relation that space allows us to establish between Lope's play and the ousting of the Moriscos can be best understood if we consider the prominence that infiltration and betrayal acquired as themes in the literature produced in support of the Expulsion, which was sizable and covered, as scholars have noted, a wide variety of genres.[30] In this body of written material, as Rafael Benítez Sánchez-Blanco has argued, the removal from Spain of over 300,000 Moriscos "raised a serious doctrinal issue since it involved deporting Christians to Islamic lands where it was obvious that they would, voluntarily or otherwise, renege on their Christian beliefs and embrace the Muslim faith."[31] Faced with this unsolvable religious dilemma, many authors endorsing the Expulsion decided to resort to legal and political arguments to justify their position. One such argument, expounded by Juan de Ribera, Archbishop of Valencia, in two influential *memoriales* (written petitions) addressed to Philip III in 1601–1602, was that the Morisco problem was one grounded not simply in religious recalcitrance or an unwillingness to embrace the Christian faith, the two most common charges leveled against the Moriscos by those seeking their banishment. The Moriscos, Ribera maintained, were also guilty of high treason due to their proven record of allegiance to foreign powers.[32] Ribera's associate, the Valencian cleric Jaime de Bleda, claimed in his *Defensio fidei in causa neophytorum* [Defense of the Faith in the Matter of the New Christians or Moriscos] (ca. 1601) that their ambassadors "han procurado y procuran el daño y perturbación de nuestros Reynos" (have caused and continue to cause harm and distress in our kingdoms) (quoted in Feros, "Rhetorics of the Expulsion," 78) by holding council with and seeking aid from the Turks and the Islamic princedoms of North Africa, to whom they were linked by a natural bond. The charge, meant to motivate King Philip and his favorite, the Duke of Lerma, was hardly new when Bleda, under the guidance of Ribera, included it in his *Defensio*.[33] A few years earlier, Baltasar Álamos de Barrientos, a jurist and prominent political thinker, had already made the same allegation in his *Discurso político al rey Felipe III al comienzo de su reinado* [Political Advice for King Philip III at the Start of His Reign] (ca. 1598–1600), where he warned the newly crowned monarch about the disloyalty and natural leanings of his Morisco subjects:

> Los Moros y sus príncipes de Fez y Marruecos están muy cerca de nosotros . . . y España está llena de Moriscos tan devotos y aficionados suyos, a mi juicio, como cuando profesaban su mala ley públicamente. Y, aunque de presente parezca que viven sosegados, siempre, como descontentos y de contraria secta, han de procurar volver a ella y procurar valerse de cualquier ocasión que haya para ello. Y en fin, obedientes mientras hubiera paz, desleales y muy para ser temidos si hay guerras civiles o revueltas extranjeras, que es cuando los oprimidos, como quiera que sean y lo estén, levantan cabezas y muestran su mal ánimo.[34]
>
> (The Moors and their princes from Fez and Morocco live vey near us . . . and Spain is full of Moriscos, who, in my estimation, are so fond and faithful to them as when they publicly professed their evil religion. Although they may seem to live peacefully now, they will always try to return to their faith and find any means to accomplish that goal because they are unhappy and have embraced a hostile creed. In sum, they will be obedient as long as there is peace, but disloyal and to be feared if there is civil strife or uprisings fostered from abroad, for this is when those who feel oppressed—whichever way they feel it—rear their heads and show their evil intentions.)

The purpose of all these texts was to overcome the religious objections that had been raised regarding the doctrinal correctness of the Expulsion by portraying the Moriscos, as Archbishop Ribera wrote in one of his *memoriales*, as "enemigos domésticos" (domestic enemies) (quoted in Benítez Sánchez-Blanco, "The Religious Debate," 114)—infiltrators bent on destroying Spain from the inside. Faced with the prospect of an attack or an invasion instigated by the Moriscos, the king was urged to act in defense of his subjects according to the principles of divine and human law, which, as Ribera was quick to remind him, compelled him to protect his realms from imminent danger: "A Vuestra Magestad le compete, y le obliga el derecho natural y divino, librar sus reynos de evidentes peligros" (It is Your Majesty's responsibility, as commanded by natural and divine law, to rid these kingdoms of manifest dangers) (quoted in Benítez Sánchez-Blanco, 115). The most effective way for Philip to meet this obligation, it was concluded, was to expel the Moriscos from Spain, a solution that, to assuage any lingering moral or religious concerns the king might have, was presented to him as an opportunity to culminate the efforts made by his ancestors to drive the Moors from Iberia.

The emphasis on infiltration these texts make as a result of their defense of the Expulsion on political grounds correlates directly with the importance this spatial motif has in *Las paces*, where it is insistently featured to underscore the vulnerability of polities and those who rule them to internal threats. This vulnerability, apparent in the relationships that King Alfonso and Don Lope maintain respectively with Raquel and Dominguillo, is also stressed in the words of guidance that Alfonso's mentor, Don Nuño, offers the monarch during his coronation. These words are worth recalling here because they call attention to the spatial anxieties expressed simultaneously in Lope's play and in the literature written in defense of the Expulsion:

> NUÑO. . . . no ha de entrar en la conquista
> De las tierras extrañas el que tiene
> Tantas guerras y engaños en las propias.
> Cobre Alfonso las suyas y, cobradas,
> Podrá poner la mano en las ajenas. (act 1, lines 349–353)

> (NUÑO. . . . he who faces war and deception at home should not embark on the conquest of foreign lands. Let Alfonso regain his kingdom. Once he recovers it, he can lay hands on the lands of others.)

The advice Nuño provides Alfonso in this critical passage of the comedia must have sounded familiar to members of Lope's audience who were acquainted with the arguments used to garner support for the Expulsion when *Las paces* was written and staged.

For example, one common claim made during those years by those who championed Philip III's decision to oust the Moriscos was that Spain's recent failures abroad—in particular, its inability to defeat the Protestant rebels in the Netherlands, with whom the Crown had been at war since 1566—were due to its inability to secure control of its own territory first, which was still home to an embarrassing number of unbelievers.[35] Spain, these individuals believed, should get rid of these infidels to fend off the danger of a possible internally supported Turkish invasion and to gain thereby the necessary stability to reembark on "la conquista de las tierras extrañas" (the conquest of foreign lands), as Don Nuño puts it in Lope's play. This idea is clearly expressed in a *memorial* addressed by Fray Jaime de Bleda to Philip III and his government in 1605 in which the friar, elaborating on some of the arguments he included previously in his *Defensio*, links the expulsion of the Jews and the capture of Granada by the Catholic Monarchs in 1492 to Spain's subsequent success as a colonial power in the Americas. Bleda, as Antonio Feros has noted, urges King Philip to follow the example of Ferdinand and Isabella, his great-grandparents, when dealing with the Moriscos in order to usher in another "golden age" for the Spanish monarchy:

> Fray Jaime Bleda reminded them [Philip III and his government] that in return for taking Granada back from the Muslims in 1492 the Catholic Monarchs had received the divine gift of the New World, whereas in return for the Spanish Crown's inability to solve the Morisco problem, God had punished it with innumerable crises and defeats. Therefore, he asked God to persuade the king to send the Moriscos into exile, just as he had led the Catholic Monarchs to expel 400,000 Jews in 1492; that act had not caused the Spanish kingdoms any

loss, and had led to a strengthened and newly resplendent monarchy. ("Rhetorics of Expulsion," 75)

The not-so-distant days of triumph and expansion that, according to Bleda, would return after the Expulsion of the Moriscos are also yearned for in *Las paces*. As soon as Alfonso returns to Toledo after participating in the Crusades, he is urged to drive the Moors out of his kingdom by his faithful right-hand man, Garcerán Manrique, who, like Bleda, reminds the monarch of the exploits of his ancestors in an effort to switch his focus from matters of the heart to matters of state:

GARCERÁN. Aquí cierra
La puerta Amor, que abrieron tus pasados;
Mas no te excusas de seguir la guerra
Porque la fe, señor, más se dilate
Y salga el moro de tu misma tierra. (act 2, lines 1223–1225)

(GARCERÁN. Love closes here the door that your ancestors opened. Do not refrain from continuing the war, Sire, to spread the Christian faith and make the Moors leave your land.)

Garcerán's call for a push against the Moors in Castile could not have gone unnoticed by Lope's audience, who, by the time *Las paces* was performed, were well aware of the Spanish monarchy's decision regarding the Moriscos. For those audience members who were better informed about the arguments used to support the Expulsion, the words Alfonso mutters to himself a few verses later in response to Garcerán's exhortation would have sounded quite familiar. In them, we hear again the idea, expressed by Bleda in his 1605 *memorial*, that conquest and expansion are only possible when the internal problems of a polity have been addressed:

ALFONSO. (A lindo tiempo guerra,
Cuando con mis sentidos,
Ya reinos divididos
Sobre ganar la tierra,
La traigo yo en el alma,
Donde siempre el amor lleva la palma.) (act 2, lines 1645–1650)

(ALFONSO. [What a perfect time to bring up war, now that my senses, like opposing kingdoms, are fighting for control of the territory within my soul, where love always ends up victorious].)

Lilia Dapaz Strout has interpreted this passage as echoing the old medieval allegorical theme of the *psychomachia*, the battle for the soul, adding that the state of internal conflict Alfonso experiences in *Las paces* reflects the political turmoil his kingdom faces as a result of the external menace posed by the Moors: "[Alfonso] Está muy preocupado en su interior y ese estado íntimo de su alma se refleja en el peligro exterior de los moros"[36] (Alfonso is very conflicted inside and that mood of his soul is reflected in the external danger posed by the Moors). I would add to this interpretation that, in addition to reflecting the commotion that the prospect of a Moorish invasion raises in Castile, Alfonso's mental and emotional distress also echoes that of Lope's Spain as depicted in the numerous *memoriales* and treatises that addressed the Morisco problem when *Las paces* was written and staged. The weak, vulnerable, and self-divided country to which the king likens himself in these lines bears a striking resemblance to the declining, exposed, and endangered nation that, according to Bleda, Ribera, and others, Spain had become as a result of the continued presence of a treasonous minority that refused to embrace Catholicism and conspired with its enemies to bring down its universal monarchy.

That Lope should have resorted to characters like Dominguillo and, above all, Raquel to echo the fears and geopolitical anxieties expressed by supporters of the Morisco Expulsion in *Las paces* is not something that should surprise us. Past events and historical and legendary personages were often employed in early modern Spanish drama, as scholars have frequently noted, to facilitate observations about contemporary Spain. To this, it must be added that Jews and Moors were routinely conflated in the mind of early modern Spaniards. The features and customs of one group were often used to describe the other; so much so, as John Beusterien has noted, that circumcision, a rite much more widespread among followers of Islam than of Judaism, was taken to be "a quintessentially Jewish practice"[37] in sixteenth- and seventeenth-century Spain.[38] This conflation of Moors and Jews was purposely exploited in the literature written to support the Expulsion, which often described the ousting of the Moriscos as either a repetition or a continuation of the eviction of the Jews ordered by the Catholic Monarchs in 1492.

Bleda's exhortation to Philip III to do unto the Moriscos what his great-grandparents had done unto the Jews clearly underlines the prevalence of a practice that can be identified first in a *memorial* that Francisco de Ribas, a Minim friar, addressed to Philip II in 1582 to provide the monarch with guidance on how to deal with the Morisco problem: "Lo mejor de todo sería lo que Abraham dixo al rico avariento: *chaos magnum formatum est inter vos et nos*; y que huviese mar en medio dellos y de nosotros, como se hizo con los judíos de España, con lo cual se remediaron los daños que dellos venían" (It would be best to say what Abraham said to the rich miser, "between you and us there is a great chasm," and to put an ocean between them and us, as it was done with the Jews) (quoted in Benítez Sánchez-Blanco, "The Religious Debate," 107). The reference Ribas makes to the Expulsion of the Moriscos in this premonitory document as being no different from the Expulsion of the Jews caters to a desire to reinforce the identification between these two groups, which was far from exceptional in early modern Spanish society and which Lope himself tried to echo in *Las paces*. Consider, for instance, the statement Raquel makes in act 2 boasting of her Spanishness after she hears her sister Sibila praise Queen Leonor for her beauty and dignified demeanor:

> RAQUEL. ¿Es posible que te agrada
> Aquella nieve del norte?
> ¿Qué cosa habrá que reporte,
> Con una hermosura helada,
> El gusto de quien la mira?
> ¡Oh talle, oh brío español!
> . . . .
> Yo, Sibila, aunque no soy
> Cristiana, soy española,
> Que basta esta gracia sola. (act 2, lines 1125–1143)

> (RAQUEL. How can you like that northern snow? How can a frozen beauty please anyone who looks at it? Praised be the Spanish vigor and shape! . . . I, Sibila, though I am not a Christian, am Spanish; and this grace is good enough.)

Raquel's proud defense of her Spanish *talle* (shape, appearance) and *brío* (vigor) in this passage has often attracted the attention of critics, who have interpreted her words as an example of Lope's efforts to override the rabid anti-Semitism of his society in *Las paces*. Read in the context of the debates surrounding the Morisco Expulsion that were publicized when the play was written, Raquel's self-description acquires a different meaning. Instead, it bears a striking resemblance to what some texts of the period said about the outward appearance and temperament of the Moriscos, which, as the humanist Pedro de Valencia wrote in his lengthy *Tratado acerca de los moriscos de España* [Treatise on the Spanish Moriscos] (1606), was no different from those of their fellow Spaniards:

> En cuanto a la complexión natural, y por el consiguiente en cuanto al ingenio, condición y brío [los moriscos] son españoles como los demás que habitan en España, pues ha casi novecientos años que nacen y se crían en ella y se echa de ver en la semejanza o uniformidad de los talles con los demás moradores de ella.[39]

> (Concerning their temperament, and therefore their resourcefulness, nature, and vigor, the Moriscos are as Spanish as the rest of the people who live in Spain, for they have been born and have been living here for the past nine hundred years. This can be seen in their appearance, which is similar and comparable to that of all other Spaniards.)

The echo of Valencia's views and language in Raquel's depiction of herself as a true-blue Spaniard illustrates the readiness to conflate Moors and Jews in Lope's society and underscores the impact that the literature of the Expulsion had on the representation of difference in *Las paces*. That impact goes beyond the simple transfer of attributes from one minority to another that we witness in this passage and touches directly on the fears and concerns commonly expressed in this body of texts regarding the true allegiance of the Moriscos to the Spanish Crown. Lope echoes those concerns in his play through the use of spatial motifs that focus on the problem of infiltration and associate the figure of Raquel—and, to a lesser extent, Dominguillo—with the perceived threat to national security posed by the Moriscos.

The presence of these motifs in in *Las paces* shows that, as Thomas Case has argued in relation to other dramas written by Lope, the dramatist "approached the theme of the Moriscos in indirect ways,"[40] embodying in a member of the medieval Jewish community the anxiety and misgivings that people of Moorish descent raised among his contemporaries. By choosing this strategy, Lope used the past, once more, as an extension of the present, creating the impression for his audience that the drastic solution adopted by Philip III's government to address the problem of difference in early seventeenth-century Spain was in line with events taking place centuries earlier in the history of Castile. The past is thus imperialized in *Las paces* to legitimate the present, making true the assertion made by Mariana in his *Historia de España* that "los tiempos pasados y los presentes semejables son" (the past and the present are similar) (lii). This imperial refashioning of legendary and historical events is also at work, I will argue in the final chapter, in *Los guanches de Tenerife y conquista de Canaria* [The Guanches from Tenerife and the Conquest of the Canary Islands], a play that, although set in premodern times, deals with an issue still resonant for Lope and his audience: transatlantic conquest. Lope's account of the late fifteenth-century Spanish occupation of the island kingdom of Tenerife in *Los guanches* projects onto the past, as we shall see, some of the spatial ideas and motifs that early modern cosmography and historiography developed to assert European supremacy in the New World and to articulate Europe's ambivalent response to the new foodstuffs and realia arriving from the Americas.

CHAPTER 5

Atlantic Conquests, Transatlantic Echoes

SPACE, GENDER, AND DIETETICS IN *LOS GUANCHES DE TENERIFE Y CONQUISTA DE CANARIA*

The imperialized image of medieval otherness that Lope presents in *Las paces de los reyes* by embodying in Raquel the fears and concerns his culture associated with the Moriscos underscores what Alberto Sandoval Sánchez has called "la transposición geográfica, racial y étnica de prácticas imperialistas" (the geographical, racial, and ethnic transposition of imperialist practices) ("Moros por indios," 540) that often takes place in the literature of early modern Spain. This strategy, which assigned to members of a subjugated group the attributes of another despite marked differences between them, has often been understood as a phenomenon involving the importation into early modern scenarios of religious and ethnic stereotypes inherited from the past. Thus, as scholars have pointed out, the views on Jews and Moors collected in the ballads and epic poems of the Reconquest provided sixteenth- and seventeenth-century Spanish writers and historians with "a template for describing their cultural encounter with the New World."[1] An example of how this process worked in the literature of the period is the unmanly picture of Native American men that Lope paints in acts 2 and 3 of *El nuevo mundo descubierto por Cristóbal Colón*, which reproduces, as José Cartagena Calderón has argued, the image of the Moor as lustful, sentimental, and unable to control his passions, which we find in many of Lope's *comedias de moros y cristianos* (plays about Christians and Moors):

> Lope entrelazará, conectará y hará contigua dicha desmasculinización del moro con la representación de los nativos del Nuevo Mundo, quienes aparecen como Tarfe, el rey Boabdil, Zelindo, Abindarráez y otros héroes musulmanes consumidos y derrotados por la volatilidad emocional, la entrega a la pasión de una mujer, la lujuria, la lascivia o el desenfreno sexual. Mediante dicha estrategia

desvirilizadora de la alteridad americana moldeada sobre la musulmana Lope pone al descubierto la construcción de una mitología cultural que se ofrece a la repetición y a la reactivación. (*Masculinidades en obras*, 128–29)

(Lope will weave, link, and make continuous the emasculation of the Moor with the representation of Native Americans, who, like Tarfe, King Boabdil, Zelindo, and other Muslim heroes, appear consumed, defeated by their emotional instability and their surrender to lust, lechery, debauchery, or their passionate love for a woman. By applying this emasculating strategy he used with the Moors to American alterity, Lope lays bare the construction of a cultural mythology that lends itself to repetition and reactivation.)

Alongside the repetition and reactivation of historical ethnic and racial paradigms, the Lopian comedia also exported to the past new ideas and formulations of difference that reflected Spain's unique experience as a modern-day imperial power. Thus, commenting specifically on the way indigenous women are represented in *El nuevo mundo*, Allen Carey-Webb has argued that in this play, Lope "incorporates and modifies the Malinche model, projecting it backward in time to the very earliest encounter of Spaniards and Native Americans."[2] The application to the past of this contemporary imperial model that describes the behavior of the Nahua woman who helped Cortés conquer the Aztec Empire by acting as his interpreter, mistress, and advisor, is best exemplified, according to this critic, by the character of Tacuana. "Like Malinche," Carey-Webb has written, "Tacuana has been taken from her family by a rival tribe, turns to the Spanish because of divisions among the Native Americans, gives up her Indian husband in order to become a mistress to a conquistador, and, finally, leaves her own people to join the camp of the invaders" (50–51).

As in *El nuevo mundo*, I will argue in this chapter, the dramatized rendering of the fifteenth-century conquest of Tenerife, the largest of the Canary Islands, by the crown of Castile, which Lope presents in *Los guanches de Tenerife y conquista de Canaria* [The Guanches from Tenerife and the Conquest of the Canary Islands] (ca. 1604–1606), is permeated by images and notions of difference that postdate the events dramatized in the play.[3] These are woven into the plot of *Los guanches* (a play whose title reflects the name given to the indigenous inhabitants of the Canary Islands) to describe the connection Spanish conquistadors establish with the territory, which they readily identify with the female inhabitants of the island and formulate in terms of penetration and ingestion.[4] The geopolitical significance that these two spatial motifs have in the play reflects, I will contend, their centrality in the cosmographical and historiographical literature of early modern Europe, where they are frequently deployed to signify both the attraction and fear that the newly discovered territories in the Americas inspired among European explorers. Lope's adaptation of these motifs to an episode of conquest that predated Spain's large-scale efforts to colonize the

New World confirms his continued commitment to imperializing Spanish history in his drama and mirroring the past in the present. A careful analysis of this commitment in *Los guanches* reveals, I will conclude, that although Lope posed "destabilizing questions about the Spanish [imperial] enterprise in the Americas via the Canary Islands" (Merediz, *Refracted Images*, 157), he also critically reinforced that enterprise by projecting backward in time some of the spatial premises on which it rested.

Conquest as Penetration: Gendering the Canaries

Lope's dramatized version of the Spanish conquest of Tenerife in *Los guanches* reflects important changes in the relationship between Europe and the Canary Islands that took place at the onset of the early modern period. Although the Canaries had loomed large in Western political and geographical thought since the time of Hesiod and Plato, their discovery—or rather rediscovery—in the fourteenth century by Genoese navigators marked a landmark event in the history of the archipelago's perception in Europe. It was then, as historians have argued, that the islands were forced to shed the mythic halo they had enjoyed as an earthly paradise in ancient and medieval literature, transforming into an object within the imperial plots and ventures of European nations.[5] This transformation was completed in 1496 when a group of conquistadors commanded by the Andalusian Alonso Fernández de Lugo was able to conquer the island kingdom of Tenerife and add the last of the Canaries to the dominion of the crown of Castile.[6] Lugo's conquest sealed the fate of the archipelago, which became thereafter linked, as Gonzalo Fernández de Oviedo noted in his *Sumario de la natural historia de las Indias* [Summary of the Natural History of the Indies] (1526), to the network of sea routes connecting Spain to the Americas:

> La navegación desde España que comúnmente se hace para las Indias, es desde Sevilla . . . y se embarcan en Sant Lúcar de Barrameda, donde el río de Guadelquevir entra en el mar Océano, y de allí siguen su derrota para las islas de Canaria, y comúnmente tocan en una de dos de aquellas siete que son, y es en Gran Canaria o en la Gomera; y allí los navíos toman refresco de agua y leña y quesos y carnes frescas y otras cosas, las que les parece que deben añadir sobre el principal bastimento que ya desde España llevan.[7]
>
> (Usually, the navigation from Spain to the Indies starts in Seville . . . people board the ships in San Lúcar de Barrameda, where the Guadalquivir River flows into the ocean, and from there they continue their journey to the Canary Islands. They usually stop in either one of these two islands of the seven that make up the archipelago: Gran Canaria or Gomera. There the ships get restocked with water, firewood, cheese, fresh meat, and other supplies they think they should add to the ones they carry from Spain.)

The relationship with the New World would only intensify in the years following Oviedo's account. As a result, the Canaries became not only a mandatory stop for Spaniards to restock supplies on their way to the Americas, but also, as Peter Mason has noted, "un filtro . . . para 'aclimatar' la información que llegaba del Nuevo Mundo y para facilitar su consumo por parte del Viejo Mundo"[8] (a filter . . . to "assimilate" the information that arrived from the New World and to facilitate its consumption by the Old World).

The "filtering role" the Canaries played in relation to the Americas is fully on display in the gendered view of Tenerife Lope presents in *Los guanches*. This view, which identifies the island as a woman and its conquest as an act of penetration, reinforces "the typical reference to the female body as a metaphor of the land to be conquered" that we find in seventeenth-century comedias featuring Amerindian women.[9] It is closely related, in this context, to the playwright's creation of what Isabel Castells has called "la bárbara" (the female barbarian), a non-European female type living in a faraway Arcadia who, despite her adherence to the strictures of *honra* or sexual decorum, shows "permeabilidad e incluso simpatía"[10] (permeability and even friendliness) toward the Spanish invaders. In *Los guanches*, Castells identifies this type with the character of Dacil—a *guanche* princess who falls madly in love with Captain Castillo, one of the conquistadors who accompanied Lugo to Tenerife—and links her to depictions of female behavior often found in Lopian drama:[11]

> Las bárbaras que combinan la desnudez con la posesión de la honra y los arcos y flechas con la asimilación de un lenguaje petrarquista, por un lado, y el hecho de que se desarrollen intervenciones sobrenaturales y dramas de capa y espada en un entorno selvático, por otro, son pruebas palmarias que Lope de Vega no está haciendo otra cosa que trasladar a nuevos escenarios las exitosas fórmulas de la Comedia Nueva. ("'Suele amor,'" 95–96)

> (Female barbarians combining nudity with honor and bows and arrows with the use of Petrarchan language, on the one hand, and the presence of supernatural interventions and cloak and dagger plots in jungle environments, on the other, clearly demonstrate that Lope is transferring the successful formulas of the *comedia nueva* to new settings.)

Despite echoing the behaviors and well-known conventions of Lope's *comedia nueva*, the friendly and permeable attitude Dacil exemplifies in *Los guanches* can be more productively related to what Louis Montrose has called "the work of gender" in the European discourse of discovery in the sixteenth century, namely, "the projection into the New World of European representations of gender" that codify exploration as a "manly" and phallic activity and classify the explored territory as female and penetrable.[12] The effect that this "work of gender" had on European cosmography in the early modern period surfaces in the allegorical depictions of America that appeared regularly on the cover and front pages of some of the best-known atlases of the age.[13] Thus, on the title page of Abraham Ortelius's *Theatrum Orbis Terrarum* [Theater of the Orb of the World] (1570), the most authoritative and widely disseminated cosmographic work published during Lope's lifetime, Europe appears at the top as a fully clothed, seated female figure, while America is shown naked and lying on the floor, hinting clearly at the possibility of copulation or penetration (figure 5.1).

That possibility is presented as an actual historical event in the *explicatio* that accompanies the images of the continents on the frontispiece of Ortelius's *Theatrum*, which describes the discovery and exploration of America by the Florentine Amerigo Vespucci in explicitly sexual terms:

Inferiore solo quam cernis America dicta est:
Quam nuper vectus pelago Vespucius audax
Vi rapuit, tenero nympham complexus amore.
Illa oblita fui, castique oblita pudoris
Nuda sedet totum corpus, nisi vista capillos
Plumea vinceret, frontem nisi gemma notaret,
Ambirent teretes nisi tintinnabula surat.[14]

(The one you see at the bottom is called America.
Bold Vespucci, voyaging recently across the sea,
took her by force, embracing the nymph with tender love.
Oblivious to herself and to her pure modesty,
she sits entirely naked, except for a feathered headdress
that binds her hair, a jewel that adorns her forehead,
and the bells that encircle her shapely calves.)

Indirectly, this Ortelian passage significantly impacted the opening scene of Lope's comedia, which describes the arrival of the Spanish in Tenerife using the following stage direction: "Dando una vuelta un monte, por la otra parte será una media nave con muchos estandartes"[15] (A mountain turns and its back side will show half a ship with many military banners).[16] This phallic image of the prow—the front end of a ship—crossing into the background of a coastal landscape appears in many sixteenth-century drawings and engravings that, inspired by the account included in the frontispiece of Ortelius's *Theatrum*, illustrated the encounter between Vespucci and America. Thus, in a widely disseminated drawing by the Flemish artist Jan van der Straet that depicts the arrival of Vespucci in the New World (figure 5.2), we see the prows of two ships entering the pictorial space at the left and opening a path of penetration into the virgin landscape shown in the foreground. Presiding over this landscape is an allegorical figure of America represented, once again, as a naked, recumbent woman.

Figure 5.1. Title page, Abraham Ortelius, *Theatrum Orbis Terrarum* (1570). Library of Congress.

Figure 5.2. Engraving, "Allegory of America," by Theodoor Galle, from *Nova Reperta* (ca. 1600), plate 1. The Metropolitan Museum of Art.

I would suggest that Lope was familiar with some of these broadly circulated images, which explains the phallic scenario that opens his play.[17]

That scenario is expanded and given dramatic form in the encounter between Castillo and Dacil that occupies most of act 1 of *Los guanches*. Lope's rendition of the meeting between the Spanish conquistador and the *guanche* princess both adheres to and departs from his source, Antonio de Viana's *Las Antigüedades de las Islas Afortunadas de la Gran Canaria* (Seville, 1604), an epic poem written in response to the critical account of the conquest of the Canaries presented a few years earlier by the Dominican Alonso de Espinosa in *Del Origen y Milagros de la Santa Imagen de Nuestra Señora de la Candelaria* (Seville, 1594).[18] As Eyda Merediz has argued, Espinosa's text echoes many of the views expressed by Bartolomé de las Casas regarding the unlawful and violent nature of the Spanish conquest of the Americas.[19] Lope, like Viana, attempts to turn the encounter between Dacil and Castillo into a symbol of the harmonious *mestizaje* between the *guanche* and Spanish societies that Espinosa had denounced as false or nonexistent in his treatise. The dramatist's description of this episode is, however, much more detailed and eroticized than Viana's.[20]

Though both Castillo and Dacil are fully clothed in Viana's poem, in Lope's play, the conquistador, charged by his generals with reconnoitering Tenerife, happens upon the *guanche* princess while she is bathing naked in a pond close to the spot where the Spanish have dropped anchor.[21] Although she initially retreats behind the branch of a tree at the sight of Castillo, Dacil's friendly attitude toward the invader and her willingness to be immediately seduced by him—"Dacil me llamo, y ya puedo / llamarme cautiva tuya" (My name is Dacil, but I can already call myself your captive) (act 1, lines 664–665)—make her the perfect embodiment of the *bárbara* or female barbarian, as Castells has observed ("'Suele amor,'" 89), and bring her close, once again, to the "extremely eroticized" female Amerindians who "actively attempt to seduce the conquerors" and act "as instruments for the assimilation and acculturation of their people" (Robalino, "The Role of Amerindian Women," 14) in other seventeenth-century comedias.[22] Moreover, this naked and alluring depiction of Dacil adheres to the sexualized images of America found in early modern atlases and in the drawings and engravings they inspired. Dacil's resemblance to these images is made apparent by the symbolic gift she receives from Castillo—a few feathers to adorn her hair—before their meeting is abruptly interrupted by the *guanche* warriors who have escorted the princess to the pond:

DACIL. Parte, español, y si acaso
    Allá te acuerdas de mí, . . .
CASTILLO. Que me acordaré de ti
    Ten por sin duda.
DACIL. Habla paso,
    Y toma aqueste cordón
    En señal de que me pesa
    De no ir contigo presa,
    Quedando en mayor prisión.
CASTILLO. Pues yo, ¿qué te puedo dar?
    Mas estas plumas te doy,
    Porque si ya tuyo soy,
    No tengo más que volar. (act 1, lines 799–810)

(DACIL. Leave, Spaniard, and if by chance you remember me there, . . .
CASTILLO. You can be sure I'll remember you.
DACIL. Lower your voice and take this string that signifies how much I regret not leaving with you as your captive, feeling more imprisoned by remaining here.
CASTILLO. What can I give you in return? I'll give you these feathers, for, being yours already, I have no need to fly anymore.)

Castillo's gift, meant to signify his decision to put down roots in Tenerife, also brings to mind the image of America "entirely naked, except for a feathered headdress that binds her hair" that appears in the frontispiece of Ortelius's *Theatrum*. This Ortelian image of the plumed and naked Dacil underlines the impact that the gendered codes of sixteenth-century cosmography had on the iconography and representation of colonial space in *Los guanches* and possibly in other plays featuring transatlantic territories.[23] Like Ortelius and other early modern cosmographers, Lope identifies a newly discovered territory with the naked body of its women and equates its exploration and conquest with the possibility of sexual intercourse with the female inhabitants.[24]

That possibility, it may be argued, was already suggested in the medieval ballads and epics Lope made frequent use of to write his comedias. These texts, as Louise Mirrer has argued, "tell of Muslim towns, transformed into women through personification, that powerful Christian men surround and penetrate with artillery fire" and "call the cities held by Muslim rulers potential 'brides' of Christian Kings" ("Representing 'Other' Men," 172).[25] The presentation of the analogy between women and territory, conquest and penetration, in *Los guanches* differs substantially, however, from what we find in the medieval literary tradition Lope exploited in his theater. In *Los guanches*, the iconographic elements that define Dacil's physical appearance (her nudity and the feathers she receives from Castillo) explicitly underline the significance that cosmographic representations of America as a plumed and naked woman had, either directly or indirectly, on the construction of that analogy. The impact of those representations on the gendered and sexualized view of the territory Lope presents in the comedia bears witness, once again, to the close relationship that existed between the Canaries and the New World in the minds of the dramatist and his contemporaries, highlighting the filtering role the former often played in relation to the latter.

Lope's effort to depict Dacil according to the codes of early modern cosmography did not imply, however, a blind or uncritical acceptance on his part of the phallic rhetoric that informed this discipline. Penetration is indeed one of the key tropes Lope used to conceptualize and represent conquest in *Los guanches*, but, as opposed to what we read, for instance, in the incipit of Ortelius's *Theatrum*, its physical or sexual dimension has been deliberately erased or transformed into something else in Lope's play. This is made apparent by the fact that the relationship between Dacil and Castillo is presented in terms that always exclude or omit physical consummation in *Los guanches*—a significant detail, given that, as pointed out before, Lope's description of the meeting between the conquistador and the princess contains a strong erotic component that is lacking in Viana's text.

A telling example of how Lope erases or sublimates penetration in the play can be seen in the dialogue that takes place in act 2 between Dacil and one of her guards, Manil, after Castillo returns to the Spanish camp to inform his superiors about the landscape of Tenerife and his meeting with the princess. The dialogue alludes to the fact that Dacil has been penetrated or "entered" by Castillo, but, as Manil's words make clear, the penetration is simply of a spiritual kind, for it involves only the soul of Castillo, which Dacil feels burning inside her breast:[26]

DACIL. Tal estoy desde ayer tarde,
Que me muero y no sosiego;
Todo el pecho es vivo fuego.
MANIL. A la fe, que yo me guarde
De que ningún español
Me meta el alma en el pecho.
Dilo a tu padre. (act 2, lines 1195–1201)

(DACIL. I feel like dying and cannot rest since yesterday. My chest is a raging fire.
MANIL. By God, I'll be sure not to let any Spaniard put his soul inside my chest. Go tell your father.)

Similar attempts to sublimate penetration abound in the play, especially in the first two acts, where we frequently see the *guanche* women perform the role of human maps. These women are still closely related to the naked and alluring figures that Ortelius, van der Straet, and other early modern cosmographers and artists used to represent America in their works. However, their ability to entice European invaders and explorers is presented exclusively in geographical terms.

The clearest representation of this strategy in *Los guanches* is an erotic scene in act 2 in which two *guanche* women, Palmira and Erbasia, spend the night in a cave with two stranded conquistadors, Trujillo and Valcázar. The setting of the scene, reminiscent of the grotto where Dido and Aeneas make love in Virgil's *Aeneid* (book 4, lines 160–172), and the regrets expressed by Palmira the morning after—"perdí el honesto recato, y la libertad perdí" (I lost my honest modesty and my freedom) (act 2, lines 1261–1262)—clearly suggest sexual intercourse to the audience. Nevertheless, Lope sublimates penetration by presenting it as a strictly topographic activity set in motion by the information collected from the women:

PALMIRA. Si por este monte abajo
Quieres [Trujillo] llegar a las cuevas,
Entre esas olivas nuevas
Hallarás un verde atajo;
Luego una fuente pequeña
Que forma en el prado un charco,
Y cuanto un tiro de arco,
Enfrente una blanca peña.
Allí, español capitán,
Comienza la habitación
De aquesta nuestra nación,
Donde ya juntos están
Todos los más importantes,
Los más valientes y diestros

De los nobles Guanches nuestros,
En que hay algunos gigantes. (act 2, lines 1231–1246)

(PALMIRA. Take the green shortcut that goes through those newly grown olive trees when you go down this mountain, Trujillo, if you want to reach the caves where we live. Then you will see a small spring that makes a pond in the field and a white rock in front of it, about the distance of an arrow shot. There, captain, begins our people's settlement, where our mightiest, bravest, and ablest nobles have gathered, with a few giants among them.)

While Palmira's role as seductress is explicitly linked to penetration in this episode, the act has been transposed from her body onto the local terrain. The scene of sexual intercourse that Lope insinuates to his audience here turns thus into a scene of topographic charting, with Palmira posing as a sublimated version of the naked America that Ortelius described embraced "with tender love" by Vespucci in the incipit of his *Theatrum*. The use of this strategy, which Lope extends to all *guanche* women who come into contact with the Spanish in the play, minimizes aggression and presents conquest as a much less violent affair than what we see in the work of early modern cosmographers, artists, and engravers.

Turning women into maps and penetration into an act of charting also allows Lope to lend more legitimacy to the Spanish project of colonization in the Canaries. The colonial map, as Anne McClintock has observed, "is a document that professes to convey the truth about a place in pure rational form, and promises at the same time that those with the technology to make such perfect representations are best entitled to possession."[27] By making themselves available as human maps to the Spanish, the *guanche* women grant that technology to the invaders and rob their people of their right to possess the territory. The transfer of that right to the conquistadors is implicit in the wishes for a successful invasion that Palmira expresses to Trujillo as he leaves her cave in the morning:

PALMIRA. Ya me pesa que te vayas,
Y ¡plega a Dios que tengáis
La tierra que deseáis
En estas desiertas playas,
Y que no os maten aquí,
Como otras veces, los nuestros! (act 2, lines 1263–1268)

(PALMIRA. I am sorry to see you leave. Pray God you get the land you covet in these deserted beaches and that our people do not kill you, as they have done before.)

Although Palmira will have to wait until the end of act 3 to see her wishes fulfilled, her farewell to Trujillo signals the end of Tenerife as a *guanche* possession. The process of imagining, constructing, and claiming control over the island as a colonial space that began in act 1 with the depiction of Dacil in Ortelian fashion as a naked and plumed seductress culminates here—a *guanche* woman wishes for the final seizure of her island by the invading Spaniards.

Clearly, the key to this process in *Los guanches* is the role that women play as alluring and penetrable guardians of the territory, a role that parallels that of female Amerindians in other plays and that is largely determined by the sexualized codes of early modern cosmography. These codes impose on the play a gendered view of space, the legitimacy of which is only enhanced by the efforts Lope makes to desexualize their content. By sublimating penetration and presenting it in either spiritual or topographic terms, Lope depicts the conquest of Tenerife as an act of male imperial possession rooted not in sexual aggression, but rather in the power and authority of love and cartography. The map and the soul thus replace war and sexual violence as the preferred means used by the Spanish invaders to access the feminized land and body of the other, which validates their occupation of the territory.

Similarly, as I will argue next, the conversion of the *guanches* to Catholicism in act 3 and the idealized pastoral lifestyle they are associated with in the play help legitimize the incorporation of their island into the crown of Castile's territory. These two features of *guanche* society are presented as necessary preconditions for the integration of Tenerife into the universal, Catholic monarchy of Spain, a phenomenon Lope identifies with ingestion or the intake of food in his comedia. Such identification and the ambivalent feelings it triggers—particularly in Castillo—echo the references to the Americas as a delectable but potentially noxious fruit that occasionally appear in the contemporary *crónicas de Indias* that Lope read. By using the material contained in these *crónicas* to represent the fate of Tenerife as a colonial space, Lope again imperializes the episode of Spanish history he dramatizes in *Los guanches*.

Conquest as Ingestion: The Edible Canaries

If the representation of Tenerife as female, penetrable, and chartable plays a central role in the tropes of conquest and land acquisition in *Los guanches*, so does the depiction of the island and its people as edible items ready to be consumed by the Spaniards. This digestive view of conquest is directly related to the use of food as a vehicle to express the expansive designs of the Spanish Crown that we occasionally see in the *crónicas de Indias*, a historiographical subgenre Lope knew well and frequently made use of in his comedias.[28] These *crónicas* provide an account not only of the battles, military exploits, and efforts to convert the Amerindians undertaken by the Spanish in the New World, but also valuable information about the ethnography, geography, and natural resources of the Americas, including detailed descriptions of plants and animals unknown to most European readers of the time.

The importance of these descriptions in conjuring a mental picture of the Americas and whet the "colonial appetite" of the metropolitan public was such that chroniclers usually endowed them with a starring role in their narratives and devoted significant portions of their writing to extol the traits and virtues of the new American realia. The best example of this, perhaps, is the description of the pineapple that Gonzalo Fernández de Oviedo, royal chronicler and colonial governor of Santo Domingo, included in his *Historia general y natural de las Indias* (1535), a text that paved the way for later zoological and botanical accounts of the Americas written in the sixteenth and seventeenth centuries. Oviedo's description of the pineapple is especially remarkable for its vividness and detail, as it strives to capture the materiality of the fruit for the reader by making constant reference to the senses:

> Mirando el hombre la hermosura desta fructa, goza de ver la composiçión é adornamento con que la natura la pintó é hizo tan agradable á la vista para recreaçión de tal sentido; oliéndola goza el otro sentido de un olor mixto con membrillos é duraznos ó melocotones, y muy finos melones, y demás exçelençias que todas esas fructas juntas y separadas, sin alguna pesadumbre; y no solamente la mesa en que se pone, mas mucha parte de la casa en que está, seyendo madura é de perfecta saçón, huele muy bien y conhorta este sentido del oler maravillosa é aventajadamente sobre todas las otras fructas. Gustarla es una cosa tan apetitosa é suave que faltan palabras en este caso para dar al propio su loor en esto . . . Palparla, no es á la verdad tan blanda ni doméstica, porque ella misma pareșçe que quiere ser tomada con acatamiento de alguna toalla ó pañiçuelo; pero puesta en la mano ninguna otra da tal contentamiento. Y medidas todas estas cosas y particularidades, no hay ningún mediano juiçio que deje de dar á estas piñas ó carchophas el principado de todas las fructas.[29]
>
> (Contemplating the beauty of this fruit, man takes pleasure in seeing the composition and adornment with which nature has endowed it and made so pleasurable to his sight, for the delight of this sense. Smelling it, the other sense enjoys a mixed sense of quince, peaches, very fine melons, and other delightful sensations, which all these fruits, together or alone, with no unpleasantness possess; not only the table onto which they are put, but a large part of the house in which a pineapple is found, if it is ripe and in perfect condition, smells very good and, above all other fruits, comforts the sense of smell in a marvelous and surpassing manner. To taste it is something so appetizing and sweet that in this case words fail me properly to praise the object itself . . . To touch it, if truth be told, is not all that soft or gentle, for it seems that the fruit itself wants to be picked up respectfully, with a towel or handkerchief, but once in your hand no other gives such contentment. And, weighing all these attributes and individual features, there is no person of

middling judgement who would not give these pineapples or artichokes preeminence over all fruits.)[30]

José Rabasa has suggested evaluating this passage beyond its scientific or pseudoscientific context and considers Oviedo's description of the pineapple "an allegory of the invention of the exotic as America."[31] More recently, Juan José Daneri has expanded upon Rabasa's view by reading Oviedo's text "as the Spanish Crown's desire to digest symbolically the new colonies for its subjects."[32] More than a metaphor for exuberance and strangeness, the pineapple is, according to Daneri, a symbol of consumption that underlines the semiotic richness of colonial writing and its complicity in the project of geographical, epistemological, and political absorption of the Americas spearheaded by writers and crown officials like Oviedo.

Considered from this perspective, it is crucial to realize that Oviedo identifies the pineapple in his chronicle as a Pan-American fruit: "en estas islas todas es fructa qual tengo dicho y muy común, porque en todas ellas y en la Tierra-Firme las hay" (in all these islands this fruit is as I have described, and very common, for it can be found in all of them and in Tierra Firme as well) (*Historia general y natural*, 281; *Fernández de Oviedo's Chronicle*, 161). For the chronicler, the pineapple becomes an emblem of all transatlantic territories and the consumptive desires they stimulated back on metropolitan soil.[33] This aspect of the text, unnoticed by Daneri, was not ignored, I would suggest, by Lope de Vega, who also uses fruit in *Los guanches* to emblematize the appeal of Tenerife as a soon-to-be colonial possession, noting the desire for consumption the island stirs among the Spanish conquistadors. Lope does not specifically use the pineapple as a symbol in his play, but the reference to Dacil as a "fruta de tierras extrañas" (fruit from strange lands) that Castillo makes in act 1 while speaking with the princess at the pond is clearly related to the way the pineapple is employed in Oviedo's text:

DACIL. Por lo que en tu trato advierto,
O tú eres el más honrado
Del mundo, o yo no te agrado,
Que debe de ser lo cierto.
CASTILLO. En lo postrero te engañas;
Mas contigo me sucede
Lo que a un hombre que ver puede
Frutas de tierras extrañas,
Que viéndolas tan hermosas,
Bien las desea comer,
Mas teme que puedan ser
Por ventura venenosas.
Confiésote que no sé
Comer, Dacil, tu hermosura;

Que temo que en tu blandura
Mi muerte y veneno esté. (act 1, lines 751–766)

(DACIL. Judging from your behavior, you are either the most respectful man in the world or you don't like me, which must be true.

CASTILLO. You are wrong about the latter. What happens to me when I am with you is what happens to a man who contemplates fruits from strange lands: seeing their beauty, he wishes to eat them, but fears they can be poisonous. I must admit, Dacil, I do not know how to eat your beauty, for I fear poison and my death in your softness.)

The relationship between conquest and food consumption that Castillo establishes here by comparing Dacil to a soft exotic fruit takes place in a romantic context, but it would be wrong, in my view, to read the captain's simile only in terms of eroticism or sexual attraction. The figure of Dacil, as we have seen before, is closely related in Lope's play to the sexualized and allegorized images of the continents found in the atlases and drawings of early modern cosmographers and artists. It can be understood, therefore, as representing the island kingdom of Tenerife. Castillo's urge to eat Dacil's beauty has thus not only sexual but also geopolitical connotations and expresses the desire of the Spanish Crown to digest or incorporate the Canaries as a colonial territory.

This desire, emblematized, as in Oviedo's text, in the figure of an exotic fruit, is constantly reiterated throughout the play in the many references to food and ingestion the Spanish make after landing in Tenerife. Thus, at the close of act 1, we hear Castillo comparing a hypothetical victory over the *guanches* to eating baskets full of eggs: "¡Vive Dios, que sólo baste / a sorberme, como huevos / frescos, canastas de guanches!" (By God, I will suck in, like fresh eggs, baskets full of guanches!) (act 1, lines 1008–1010). Similarly, in act 3, Alonso de Lugo and the field marshal Lope Fernández de Guerra order their men to sit down and enjoy a picnic right before the final battle against the islanders: "Tended sobre esa hierba los manteles. / Comamos, capitanes, un bocado" (Lay the tablecloths over that grass and let us have, captains, a bite) (act 3, lines 2548–2549). Taken together, all these scenes suggest that eating satisfies more than a biological need in *Los guanches*. The act of ingesting food in Lope's play is a vehicle to express the political and territorial ambitions of the Spanish monarchy and its view of colonial space as readily available for consumption.

That view, however, awakens uneasy and ambivalent feelings among the Spanish. This becomes apparent in the way their desire to ingest food is portrayed in the play as hampered by caution and fear. Thus, the "fruits from strange lands" to which Castillo likens Dacil in act 1 cannot be ingested due to their suspected poisonous nature: "Confiésote que no sé / comer, Dacil, tu hermosura; / que temo que en tu blandura / mi muerte y veneno esté" (I must admit, Dacil, I do not know how to eat your beauty, for I fear poison and my death in your softness) (act 1, lines

763–766). Castillo's misgivings in this scene may be related to the overall view of women as both seductive and dangerous that pervaded the moral and emblematic literature of early modern Europe. This view is clearly conveyed, for instance, in an emblem that the royal accountant Hernando de Soto—a friend of Lope's—included in his *Emblemas moralizadas* [Moral Emblems] of 1599 (figure 5.3).
The emblem likens women to the flower that grows on the oleander plant, which, as the poem that accompanies the emblem explains, is pleasant to the eye but deadly if eaten:[34]

De la Adelfa y de su rosa
Es el engaño increíble
Que a la vista es apacible
Pero al gusto venenosa.
Mata a cualquiera animal
Que la come descuidado.
Y esto en la mujer he hallado
Deshonesta y sensual.

(Incredible is the deception in the oleander and its rose. They look pleasant to the eye but are poisonous when tasted. This plant will kill any animal who eats it unawares. I found the same to be true of immodest and sensual women.)

Despite its connection to the misogynistic discourse of contemporary emblematic literature, Castillo's ambivalent response toward Dacil's fruit-like presence in Lope's play reflects more accurately the general attitude toward exotic foods prevalent in early modern Europe, where, as Ken Albala has noted, "dieticians . . . were stridently defending their native food habits from foreign corruption."[35] In Spain, this tendency seems to have been triggered by the influx of new fruits and agricultural products from the Americas, which, as Rebecca Earle has explained, were received with a mixture of fear and skepticism by early modern Spaniards. Their consumption, it was generally believed, "might alter not only the customs but also the very bodies of the [Spanish] settlers" (*The Body of the Conquistador*, 3) and in some cases even cause illness or death.[36] Given this widespread belief, it is not surprising, as Fabio López-Lázaro has argued, that Spain decided early on in the process of colonization to protect its identity and economic interests by refusing to import and incorporate into the national diet new ingredients from the New World.[37] Echoes of this defensive attitude can be found throughout the literature of the period, including in the work of Fernández de Oviedo, whose description of the pineapple contains praise as well as critical and cautionary remarks about the fruit:

También digo que la carnosidad desta fructa tiene sotiles briznas, como las pencas de los cardos que se comen en España . . . y por esto no son útiles á

MORALIZADAS. 88

Meretricum fallacia.

El engaño en la muger.

De la Adelfa y de ſu roſa
Es el engaño increyble,
Que a la viſta es apacible,
Pero al guſto venenoſa.
Mata a qualquiera animal
Que la come deſcuydado:
Y eſto en la muger he hallado
Deshoneſta y ſenſual.

Siendo

Figure 5.3. Emblem, "Meretricum fallacia. El engaño en la mujer." Hernando de Soto, *Emblemas moralizadas* (1599). Bibliothèque Nationale de France.

las ençías é dentadura, quando se continúan á comer muy á menudo. (*Historia general y natural*, 283)

(I also want to mention that the fleshy texture of this fruit has subtle fibers, much like the leaves of the thistles [i.e., artichokes] eaten in Spain . . . and because of this they are not good for gums and teeth if you continue to eat them very frequently.) (*Fernández de Oviedo's Chronicle*, 163)

The humanist Francisco de Medina, in his prologue to Fernando de Herrera's famous *Anotaciones* [Commentaries] (1580) to the poetry of Garcilaso de la Vega, also warned specifically about the danger of incorporating into the Spanish diet exotic fruits, which in his view were "tan dañosas a la salud cuan varias y desconocidas"[38] (as harmful to one's health as they are varied and unfamiliar).

Underneath all these manifestations of suspicion and concern about exotic foods (fruits, in particular) lies a fear of becoming tainted, contaminated, or infected that is often countered in Western imperial discourse by an effort to domesticate or Europeanize food in order to purge it of its threatening qualities.[39] This is particularly true, as Rebecca Weaver-Hightower has observed, in island narratives that relate the trials of castaways and colonizers, where the compulsion to Westernize the food supply is often manifested through the colonist's attempt "to project himself onto the island before he can, in a literal sense, incorporate it."[40] Lope's play—an island narrative in dramatic form—exemplifies this strategy of self-projection, as Tenerife and its native dwellers are subjected to a thorough process of hispanization before they are finally consumed or *incorporated* into the body politic of the Spanish monarchy at the end of act 3. The details of this process involve three critical elements: the *guanches*' use of the Spanish language, their lifestyle and political organization, and their religious conversion in the final segment of the play.

Concerning language, the initial communication problems that exist between *guanches* and Spaniards when Dacil and Castillo meet for the first time by the pond have already disappeared by the end of act 1.[41] Furthermore, the report that Manil, Dacil's guard, gives to King Bencomo in act 2 about the conversation he had at the close of the previous act with the field marshal Lope Fernández de Guerra leads Lope's audience to believe that the *guanches* have acquired native-like competence in the language of the invaders:

MANIL. Yo fui con un capitán [Castillo] . . .
Y sirviéndole de guía,
Por mandado de la Infanta [Dacil],
Vi que su fuerza no es tanta
Como su loca osadía.
Hablé con su general,
Y él de ti me preguntó;

Respondíle, y pienso yo
Que a propósito y no mal. (act 2, lines 1079–1090)

(MANIL. I accompanied one of their captains [Castillo] . . . and, serving him as a guide, as ordered by the princess [Dacil], I saw that their army is not as big as their mad daring. I spoke with their general and he asked me about you. I answered him well, I think, and in a suitable manner.)

The phrase Manil uses in this passage to assess his own response to Fernández de Guerra—"a propósito y no mal" (well and in a suitable manner)—underlines his dexterity in the use of Spanish. The fact that his countrymen do not consider this an extraordinary or unusual achievement suggests that being able to communicate efficiently in Spanish is something almost every *guanche* could accomplish.

This advanced level of linguistic competence is also highlighted in the speech of King Bencomo at the start of act 2 that describes his dwelling, diet, and way of life. Bencomo's depiction of his rustic abode, eating regime, and daily habits mirrors the language and conventions of early modern Spanish pastoral poetry and echoes the idealized picture of country life included in works such as Fray Antonio de Guevara's best-selling *Menosprecio de corte y alabanza de aldea* [Contempt of the Court and Praise of Village Life] (1539):[42]

BENCOMO. Yo soy un rey que el primero
Salgo a guardar mi ganado;
Es mi palacio dorado
La cueva de un risco entero.
De una vez Naturaleza
Mis aposentos labró;
En ellos no encierro yo
La codiciada riqueza.
Sobre pieles de animales
Duermo hasta que sale el día,
Desde que la noche fría
Baña sus umbrales.
Es harina de cebada,
En un guanigo molida,
Mi sustento y mi comida,
Sobre unas brasas tostada;
Alguna silvestre fruta
A aquellos árboles debo,
Agua con las manos bebo
De aquella enriscada gruta. (act 2, lines 1023–1042)

(BENCOMO. Though king, I am the first outside to watch my cattle; my golden palace is a cave that occupies a whole cliff. Nature built in one go my rooms. I do not hoard in them coveted riches. I sleep on animal hides from the moment the cold night bathes my threshold until sunrise. My sustenance is barley flour ground in an earthen pot and toasted on embers. The wild fruit I eat, I owe to those trees. My water comes from that craggy cave and I drink with my hands.)

In addition to showcasing his literary and linguistic skills as an improvising pastoral poet, Bencomo is also endorsing here the revered biblical image of the shepherd king that sixteenth- and seventeenth-century Spanish writers celebrated in poems like Hernando de Acuña's "Al Rey nuestro señor" [To the King Our Lord], in which the emperor Charles V is represented as a shepherd governing a diverse flock of peoples.[43] From a linguistic and political perspective, the *guanches* thus appear as an idealized mirror image of their invaders and not as a strange and fierce group of devil-worshiping barbarians, as the *adelantado* (admiral and future governor) Alonso Fernández de Lugo characterizes them at the beginning of the play:

ALONSO. Bárbara es esta nación
Y desnuda de riqueza,
Mas nuestra justa intención
Es reducir su fiereza
A piadosa religión.
Eche [Tenerife] al demonio de sí
Como salió de Canaria
Por vosotros y por mí,
Que es cosa a razón contraria
Sufrir tal vecino aquí. (act 1, lines 21–30)

(ALONSO. This is a barbarian people, lacking in wealth, but our legitimate intent is to make their fierceness submit to pious religion. Let us expel the devil from Tenerife like we expelled it from Gran Canaria, for it does not stand to reason to tolerate such a neighbor here.)

The Tenerife Fernández de Lugo depicts in this opening passage seems to have cleansed itself of some of what to the Spaniards are its most disturbing features and has become a much more familiar place for the invaders by the time they decide to conquer the island. This process of hispanization that precedes the political ingestion of Tenerife culminates with the conversion of the *guanches* to Catholicism. The experience was sparked, on the one hand, by the apparition of the Virgin of *La Candelaria* to Manil in a cave at the start of act 3, and, on the other, by the visit that the archangel Saint Michael pays to King Bencomo at the end of the same act to persuade him to surrender peacefully to the Spanish.[44] The transformative effect these two events have on Tenerife and on *guanche* society as a whole is described in the closing lines of the play, which list the changes, both physical and spiritual, the island will undergo as a result of the *guanches*' conversion to the new religion:

CASTILLO. Esta es la Madre de Dios,
La que en sus entrañas santas
Le trajo y parió, quedando
Virgen.
BENCOMO. ¡Hermosura rara!
Por ella todos queremos
De vuestro bautismo el agua.
CASTILLO. Y yo casarme con Dacil,
En siendo Dacil cristiana.
TRUJILLO. Yo, señores, con Palmira.
VALCÁZAR. Y yo con la bella Erbasia.
ALONSO. Por lo menos, comenzamos,
La población con tres casas
Y con tan sagrado templo
De la Virgen Candelaria,
Que ha de ser nuestra Patrona. (act 3, lines 2992–3006)

(CASTILLO. This is the mother of God, who bore him inside her holy body and gave birth to him while remaining a virgin.
BENCOMO. Strange beauty! Because of her we all want to receive the water of your baptism.
CASTILLO. And I want to marry Dacil as soon as she becomes a Christian.
TRUJILLO. And I, sirs, want to marry Palmira.
VALCÁZAR. And I the beautiful Erbasia.
ALONSO. We have at least three houses to start our settlement and a temple, so sacred, consecrated to the Virgin of La Candelaria, who will become our patroness.)

The dramatic cultural and geographical transformation Tenerife will go through due to the religious conversion of its inhabitants is contrasted by the lack of significant changes experienced by the Spanish as a result of their contact with the *guanches*. The example of Castillo is particularly revealing in this respect. Left on the island for months after the Spanish suffered a resounding defeat in act 2, he reappears in act 3 wearing a ragged *hábito de bárbaro* (barbarian attire) in the company of Dacil. In his case, however, clothes do not make the man, and he quickly returns to the Spanish camp to dress like a conquistador and prepare for war as soon as his comrades reappear on the beaches of Tenerife for a final showdown against King Bencomo.[45] Castillo is therefore allowed to "play native," but not to "go native" in *Los guanches*, a luxury Lope's comedia does not afford the inhabitants of Tenerife. In contrast, the process of hispanization they are forced to undergo in the drama is critical for cleansing their island kingdom of its original strangeness and bringing it within the compass of a Spanish sensibility that will make it available for consumption to both the invading conquistadors and the play's audience.

The cleansing and consumptive impulse that guides *Los guanches*, especially in act 3, muffles and ultimately muzzles the subversive and anti-imperial message some critics have identified in its plot. Lope's comedia does contain, as Merediz has argued, "a destabilizing questioning of the Spanish enterprise in the New World, via the Canary Islands" (*Refracted Images*, 157) through its criticism of the conquistadors' appetite for gold and its echoes of Lascasian and Erasmian thought. However, that questioning is eventually blunted and silenced by the play's reiteration of themes of consumption and its use of digestive images to represent the relationship between the Spanish and the island. Those images, common in the *crónicas de Indias* Lope read prior to or during his writing of *Los guanches* to describe the alluring and exuberant realia of the New World, complement the picture of the island as a space destined for possession that emanates from the playwright's gendered view of the territory in the first two acts of the comedia. This view relies on the sexualized codes employed by early modern cosmographers to portray the Americas as a penetrable and chartable space.

To the colonial master trope of penetration, Lope adds that of ingestion to signify and legitimize the Spanish claims over Tenerife and the Canaries as a whole, a territory that, although mostly forgotten by writers and historians by the end of the sixteenth century, still occupied a central place in the history of Spain's expansion across the Atlantic. The set of discourses (cosmographic, sexual, and dietetic) that make possible the functioning of these two master tropes in Lope's play generates a view of the past that reflects ideas of space deeply rooted in the imperial present. These ideas determine the overall ideological message of *Los guanches* that, despite challenging at times the moral legitimacy of Spain's transatlantic conquests, underpins the processes of cultural, political, and geographical appropriation we associate with them. The impact of these ideas on the representation of personal relationships and on the depiction of military and political events in the play also serves to remind us that space was one of the central means by which Lopian drama strove to "map" or make sense of history at a time when theater—due in considerable measure to Lope's efforts—had become, in the words of the famous nineteenth-century scholar Marcelino Menéndez Pelayo, a "crónica dialogada" (dramatized chronicle) ("Observaciones preliminares," xii) of the past. The extent to which this chronicle relied on space to promote an imperialized understanding of history under the influence of Lope is something I have highlighted in this and previous chapters. The lessons that can be drawn from the relationship they trace among space, history, and empire are briefly summarized in the remarks that conclude this study.

Conclusion

Audiences attending a performance of *Los guanches* in 1604 must have felt struck with wonder as, in the opening scene of the play, a ship crowned with pennants emerged onstage from behind a mountain. For many early modern Spaniards, ships were almost as unfamiliar a sight as the remote and strange territory Alonso de Lugo and his men were about to invade. Moreover, the experience of long-distance travel evoked by the vessel was one far removed from the heavily localized existence most of them led. In this society, defined primarily by relations established within the parish and the municipality, the new type of theater espoused by Lope de Vega significantly altered the way individuals perceived their relationship to space.

Audiences gathered inside the corrales of early modern Iberia could move in one instant, as Cervantes wrote in *El rufián dichoso*, from Valladolid to Gante and feel thus empowered to reach in no time a variety of "tiempos, teatros, lugares" (times, settings, and places) (*El rufián dichoso*, act 2, lines 1223–1224). This freedom and ease of movement underline the close relationship between the optical regime of cartography and Lopian drama and the adherence of the comedia to the type of spatiality exemplified by the map. Like the cosmographers and cartographers of his time, Lope minimized the problem of distance in his theater and therefore promoted an idea of the world in which audiences were given immediate, unimpeded access to the places represented. As David Woodward has written of maps, this was a world "over which systematic dominance was possible" because it allowed the viewer to grasp space synchronically or quasi-synchronically.[1]

This conception of space and the feeling of dominance it engendered were not limited in Lope's comedias to the depiction of settings and locales situated in the present—Chile, Brazil, or Flanders, for instance. More often than not, the places Lope referred to and depicted in his drama hosted events that occurred in the past, a past that stretched from eighth-century Iberia to the not-so-distant reign of the Catholic Kings. In these old settings, where "los sucesos, guerras, paces, consejos, diferentes estados de la fortuna, mudanzas, prosperidades, declinaciones de reinos y períodos de imperios y monarquías grandes"[2] (events, wars, peace agreements, councils, various states of fortune, changes in destiny, prosperous times, the decline of kingdoms, and the rise of empires and great monarchies) took place, Lope deployed the synchronous, *distanceless* view of space characteristic of maps that some of his predecessors began to embrace in the late 1580s. They did so by dramatizing events "no en relación, como de antes, / sino en hecho" (not in words, like before, but in deeds) (act 2, lines 1246–1247), as the character Comedia explains in Cervantes's *El rufián dichoso*.

A clear example of how this conception of space impacted Lope's national history theater is, as I discussed in chapter two, the swift journey from his court in León to a remote village in Galicia that King Alfonso VII takes in *El mejor alcalde, el rey*, a journey that mirrors the dominance over space Lope's audiences were allowed to enjoy in the corrales. Another case in point, using *Los guanches* as a frame of reference, is the ability of the "brave Spaniards" who accompany Alonso Fernández de Lugo to Tenerife to fly over the oceans in their "winged" vessels to conquer lands far away from their home—an ability King Bencomo bitterly complains about in his address to the sun at the beginning of the comedia:

BENCOMO. ¡Oh poderoso y ínclito planeta
Que con tu resplandor el mundo ilustras!
¿Cómo permites que las claras ondas
En que se miran tus divinos rayos
Enturbien estos pájaros de España
Que con alas de cuerda y de lienzo
Vuelan encima de la mar, furiosos,
Trayendo en sus entrañas esta gente
Que nos molesta con tan varias armas
Y nos quiere arrojar injustamente
De aquella patria que nos diste propia
Desde que nos hiciste entre estos montes? (act 1, lines 232–243)

(BENCOMO. Oh, powerful and illustrious planet that shines on the world with your brightness! Why do you allow these Spanish birds that fly raging over the sea with wings made of canvass and rope to darken the clear waves where your divine rays contemplate themselves? They bring in their insides people who harass us with various weapons and want to oust us unfairly from this homeland you gave us when you created our people among these mountains.)

Audiences listening to Bencomo's message would have seen something of themselves reflected in Fernández de Lugo's men. Huddled similarly in a wooden structure that took them in an instant to distant locations, they would have naturally identified with men who could easily transport themselves across "the clear waves" and travel wherever they wished.

The association of this synchronous view of space with a twelfth-century king and a group of fifteenth-century conquistadors speaks to Lope's effort to imperialize the past in his national history theater and underlines the critical role that space played in that endeavor. No less important in this context than allowing premodern characters to overcome distance and materialize in far-off locations was the objective Lope pursued in some of his *comedias historiales* of making the kingdoms of medieval Iberia prefigure the expansive, universal monarchy ruled by the Hapsburgs. This goal, clearly discernible in the depiction of eighth-century Asturias as a territory destined to expand that Lope constructs in *Las famosas asturianas*, echoes the figural reading of history espoused by early modern Spanish historians, who often searched the national past for signs or prefigurations of the vast imperial polity they praised in their works. The expanding image of tiny and beleaguered Asturias that Lope conjures up in *Las famosas asturianas* constitutes, in this sense, a clear reflection of the proto-imperial view of this territory articulated by historians like Ambrosio de Morales and Juan de Mariana, who repeatedly identified this narrow stretch of territory in northern Iberia with "los principios y medios por donde [España] se encaminó a la grandeza que hoy tiene" (the beginnings and middles by which [Spain] arrived at its present greatness) (Mariana, *Historia de España*, li).

Excluded from this "greatness" in Lope's comedias are Spain's internal others, the Jews and the Moors, whose identities were often conflated in the literature and culture of the period. Their role as traitors, infiltrators, and fifth columnists in plays like *Las paces de los reyes y judía de Toledo* runs counter to the expansive ethos Asturias embodies and prefigures in *Las famosas asturianas*. Moreover, this depiction projects back into the past the same anxiety regarding space and difference that informed Spain's attitude toward the Moriscos in the early modern period: an omnipresent fear that the presence of this minority inside the nation would bring about its collapse and end the dream of a universal, all-Catholic monarchy espoused by the Hapsburgs. The association of this fear with the characters of Raquel, the king's Jewish mistress, and Dominguillo in *Las paces* highlights, as I argued in chapter four, the dramatist's ability to purposefully reinterpret the past through the use of space in his theater and to use legendary and historical events to reflect the political concerns of the present.

That ability is also on display in *Los guanches de Tenerife y conquista de Canaria*, which revisits one of the great watersheds of Spain's geopolitical history—the annexation of the Canary Islands to the crown of Castile in the fifteenth century—through the lens of early modern cosmography. The work also reflects contemporary perceptions of the realia and new foodstuffs coming from the Americas that were embedded in historiographical and anthropological accounts written in the wake of Spain's conquest and settlement of the New World. Lope's use of these extraliterary sources to dramatize the Castilian annexation of Tenerife in *Los guanches* produces an image of the past that is heavily influenced by ideas of space that were employed to take stock of and legitimize Spain's imperial ventures across the Atlantic in the sixteenth and seventeenth centuries. These ideas, which include the representation of Tenerife as a young maiden willing to be penetrated by the conquistadors and the depiction of the island and its inhabitants as edible, inform the overall imperialistic message of the play and neutralize its questioning of Spain's evangelizing and civilizing mission in the New World.

This bolstering role that *Los guanches* and the other comedias I have analyzed in this book play in relation to Spain's imperial mission comes to light only through a form of reading that focuses on space in the texts under consideration. This approach reflects the prominence that space has recently gained as an object of inquiry in literary and cultural studies. However, its pertinence to the study of the Lopian comedia is perfectly justified in historical terms by the proverbial ability of this type of theater to represent, as Francisco Ruiz Ramón has written, "cualquier espacio físico o metafísico, exterior o interior, único o múltiple, tanto a nivel textual como escénico" (any space, physical or metaphysical, exterior or interior, singular or multiple, both within the text and on the stage) (*Celebración y catharsis*, 91). The ability to evoke, symbolize, and denote space allowed the Lopian comedia to perform a role quite similar to that of cartography in the dramatist's society, an activity with the primary aim of representing, signifying, and rendering space visible to the viewer.

The parallel between these two spheres of practice rested, as mentioned above, on the synchronous, distanceless view of space they both shared and promoted, but also on their ability to provide audiences with a sense of place by presenting them with a coherent and broad picture of the world they inhabited. For Lope, that picture included—increasingly since the late 1590s—the past; so much so, in fact, that, as Stephen Gilman has argued, most of his comedias can be understood as an unceasing "vivificación oral de lo pretérito"[3] (oral vivification of the past). Behind this relentless vivification may have been, as some scholars have suggested, the mandate issued by the crown in 1599 to only allow the staging of historical plays in the Madrid corrales—a measure designed to counter "el escándalo y mal ejemplo"[4] (the turmoil and bad example) that, according to historian Luis Cabrera de Córdoba, theatrical representations provoked in Spain's capital—or it may have been the playwright's decades-long aspiration to be appointed *cronista real* (royal chronicler) by his sovereign. Be that as it may, what is certain is that Lope's national history theater provided audiences with a unique opportunity to plot, as on a map, Spain's imperial trajectory through the centuries and to feel part of that journey due to the spatial bonds Lope established between past and present. Bringing awareness to the political significance of those bonds has been the primary objective of this book, and in its pages, the reader is invited to consider anew the relationship between history and empire in Lopian drama.

Acknowledgments

A graduate and undergraduate seminar I taught in the fall of 2019 under the title "Geographies of Power: Space and Empire in Early Modern Spanish Drama" formed the seed from which this book grew. I am indebted to all the students who took that class for the enthusiasm with which they embraced the topic and for unwittingly helping me envision the overall structure of this project.

I am also extremely grateful to the chair of the Department of Foreign Languages and Literatures at East Carolina University, Dr. Katherine Ford, and to the members of the department's Administrative Committee for providing me with the time and financial backing necessary to complete this project.

On a more personal note, I thank my wife, Jung-Ja, and my two sons, Diego and Mateo, for their ongoing support, encouragement, and willingness to be deprived of time and attention when they needed it. Busy writers, as they can well attest, do not make the best dads and husbands.

Finally, I am grateful to Bucknell University Press's anonymous readers for their valuable feedback on the manuscript, as well as to Suzanne Guiod, Pam Dailey, and Anne Jones for their assistance with the editorial process. Anonymous reviewers for the journals *Bulletin of the Comediantes* and *Letras Hispanas* also helped me hone my arguments in chapters 2, 3, and 5. Portions of chapter 2 originally appeared as "'Que los reyes nunca están lejos para castigar los malos': Space and the Imperialization of History in Lope de Vega's *El mejor alcalde el rey*" in *Bulletin of the Comediantes* 72, no. 1 (2020): 35–51. An earlier version of chapter 5 was also published in *Bulletin of the Comediantes* 64, no. 1 (2012): 1–18 as "Lope's Imperial Geography: Cosmography, Gender, and Dietetics in *Los guanches de Tenerife y conquista de Canaria*." A brief section of chapter 3 was previously published as "Imperial Asturias: The Politics of Space in Lope de Vega's *Las famosas asturianas*" in *Letras Hispanas* 11 (2015): 78–87. I thank both journals for granting me permission to reprint these materials here.

Acknowledgments

Notes

INTRODUCTION

1. Lisa Skwirblies, "Theaters of Colonialism: Theatricality, Coloniality, and Performance in the German Empire, 1894–1914" (PhD diss., University of Warwick, 2017), 4, http://wrap.warwick.ac.uk/106458/.

2. Skwirblies, "Theaters of Colonialism," 5.

3. Within the field of Hispanism, see, for instance, Robert Shannon, *Visions of the New World in the Drama of Lope de Vega* (New York: Peter Lang, 1989); Iván Cañadas, "Nation, Empire, and Local Community in Lope de Vega's Peasant Drama and *El nuevo mundo descubierto por Cristóbal Colón*," *Journal of Iberian and Latin American Studies* 8, no. 2 (2002): 81–92; Barbara Simerka, *Discourses of Empire: Counter-Epic Literature in Early Modern Spain* (University Park: Pennsylvania State University Press, 2003), 39–128; Susan Castillo, "Performing Encounters: Lope's *El nuevo mundo descubierto por Cristóbal Colón*," *Bulletin of the Comediantes* 58, no. 1 (2006): 57–72; Moisés Castillo, *Indios en escena: la representación del amerindio en el teatro del Siglo de Oro* [Indians on Stage: The Representation of Amerindians in Golden Age Theater] (West Lafayette, IN: Purdue University Press, 2009); Chad M. Gasta, *Imperial Stagings: Empire and Ideology in Transatlantic Theater of Early Modern Spain and the New World* (Chapel Hill: University of North Carolina Press, 2012); Madera Allan, "Shouting Distance: Local History and a Global Empire in Lope de Vega's *Famosa comedia del nuevo mundo descubierto por Cristóbal Colón*," in *Imagining Early Modern Histories*, ed. Allison Kavey and Elizabeth Ketner (Farnham, UK: Ashgate, 2016), 13–26; and Matthew Goldmark, "Settling Down: Itinerant Empire and the Ends of Conquest in *El burlador de Sevilla*," *Bulletin of Hispanic Studies* 96, no. 8 (2019): 799–814. Spain and its imperial possessions have also become an object of study for scholars of English drama working on the intersection between theater and empire. See in this respect Eric J. Griffin, *English Renaissance Drama and the Specter of Spain: Ethnopoetics and Empire* (Philadelphia: University of Pennsylvania Press, 2009); Barbara Fuchs, *The Poetics of Piracy: Emulating Spain in English Literature* (Philadelphia: University of Pennsylvania Press, 2013), 55–78; Saugata Bhaduri, "Polycolonial Angst: Representations of Spain in Early Modern English Drama," in *Theater Cultures within Globalising Empires: Looking at Early Modern*

England and Spain, ed. Joachim Küpper and Leonie Pawlita (Berlin: De Gruyter, 2018), 150–159.

4. The interest in transatlantic approaches to the comedia has grown exponentially in the last two decades, covering both textual and cultural analyses of texts and critical editions of plays dealing with the subject of the Americas. For a useful summary of this critical and editorial output, see José R. Cartagena Calderón, "Lope and the Matter of America: Approaching the *Comedia* from a Trans-Atlantic Perspective," in *Approaches to Teaching Early Modern Spanish Drama*, ed. Margaret R. Greer and Laura R. Bass (New York: Modern Language Association of America, 2006), 152–158; Mindy Badía and Bonnie L. Gasior, eds., *Crosscurrents: Transatlantic Perspectives on Early Modern Spanish Drama* (Lewisburg, PA: Bucknell University Press, 2006).

5. Edward Said, "Representing the Colonized: Anthropology's Interlocutors," *Critical Inquiry* 15, no. 2 (1989): 218.

6. By examining the political role of space in Lope's historical drama, this book heeds the recent call by David Castillo and Bradley Nelson to use the study of space, landscape, and place to open a path of inquiry into early modern, modern, and postmodern Hispanic culture in their introduction to *Spectacle and Topophilia: Reading Early Modern and Postmodern Hispanic Cultures* (Nashville: Vanderbilt University Press, 2011), ix–xxiv. Castillo also includes some important reflections on the representation of the Castilian landscape "as the moral and social reservoir of monarchical Spain" (14) in the chapter he devotes to Lope's *Fuenteovejuna* and the poetry of García Lorca, "Monumental Landscapes in the Society of the Spectacle: From *Fuenteovejuna* to New York," *Spectacle and Topophilia*, 3–18.

7. José María Ruano de la Haza, "The World as a Stage: Politics, Imperialism, and Spain's Seventeenth-Century Theater," in *A History of Theater in Spain*, ed. María M. Delgado and David T. Gies (Cambridge: Cambridge University Press, 2012), 60.

8. Fernando Wulff, *Las esencias patrias. Historiografía e historia antigua en la construcción de la identidad española (siglos XVI–XX)* [The Spirit of the Nation: Historiography and Ancient History in the Construction of Spanish Identity (Sixteenth and Seventeenth Centuries)] (Barcelona: Crítica, 2003), 34.

9. Alan K. G. Paterson, "Stages of History and History on Stage: On Lope de Vega and Historical Drama," in *Spanish Theatre: Studies in Honour of Victor F. Dixon*, ed. Kenneth Adams, Ciaran Cosgrove, and James Whiston (London: Tamesis, 2001), 154.

10. Javier Rubiera Fernández, *La construcción del espacio en la comedia española del Siglo de Oro* [The Construction of Space in the Spanish Golden Age Comedia] (Madrid: Arco Libros, 2005), 58. The predominance of scenography in spatial studies on the comedia has been established by John J. Allen and José María Ruano de la Haza in *Los teatros comerciales del siglo XVII y la escenificación de la comedia* [Seventeenth-Century Commercial Theaters and the Staging of the *Comedia*] (Madrid: Castalia, 1994); also important in this respect are José Amezcua's "El espacio simbólico: el caso del teatro español del Siglo de Oro" [Symbolic Space: The Case of Spanish Golden Age Theater], *Signos* 1 (1987): 291–301 and "Hacia el centro: espacio e ideología en la *Comedia nueva*" [Toward the Center: Space and Ideology in the *Comedia Nueva*], in *Espectáculo, texto y fiesta. Juan Ruiz de Alarcón y el teatro de su tiempo* [Spectacle, Text, and Festival. Juan Ruiz de Alarcón and the Theater of His Times], ed. José Amezcua and Serafín González (Iztapalapa, México: Universidad Autónoma Metropolitana Iztapalapa, 1990), 159–172. Equally impactful has been Marc Vitse's "Sobre los espacios en *La dama duende*: el

cuarto de don Manuel" [Space in *La dama duende*: Don Manuel's Room], *Notas y Estudios Filológicos* 2 (1985): 7–32. Two collections of essays published in the early 2000s—Françoise Cazal, Christophe González, and Marc Vitse, eds., *Homenaje a Frédéric Serralta. El espacio y sus representaciones en el teatro español del Siglo de Oro* [Hommage to Frédéric Serralta. Space and Its Representations in Spanish Golden Age Theater] (Madrid and Frankfurt: Iberoamericana/Vervuert, 2002), and Francisco Saéz Raposo, ed., *Monstruos de apariencias llenos. Espacios de representación y espacios representados en el teatro áureo español* [Monsters Chock-Full of Appearances: Spaces for Representation and Represented Spaces in Spanish Golden Age Theater] (Barcelona: Bellaterra, 2011)—have contributed to reinforcing the prominence of this approach.

11. Ricardo Padrón, *The Spacious Word: Cartography, Literature, and Empire in Early Modern Spain* (Chicago: University of Chicago Press, 2004), 58.

12. José M. Regueiro, *Espacios dramáticos en el teatro español medieval, renacentista y barroco* [Dramatic Spaces in Medieval, Renaissance, and Baroque Spanish Theater] (Kassel, Germany: Edition Reichenberger, 1996); Rubiera Fernández, *La construcción del espacio*; Sáez Raposo, *Monstruos de apariencias llenos*.

13. The semiotic approach adopted in these studies is informed by the works of Michael Issacharoff, *Discourse as Performance* (Stanford: Stanford University Press, 1989); Patrice Pavis, *Languages of the Stage: Essays in the Semiology of the Theater* (New York: Performing Arts Journal Publications, 1982) and *Dictionary of the Theater: Terms, Concepts, and Analysis* (Toronto: University of Toronto Press, 1998); and Keir Elam, *The Semiotics of Theater and Drama* (London: Methuen, 1980).

14. Anthony Pagden, *Lords of All the World: Ideologies of Empire in Spain, Britain, and France, c. 1500–1800* (New Haven: Yale University Press, 1995), 15.

15. For more on the distinction between these two types of space, see Rubiera Fernández, *La construcción del espacio*, 81–94, and Javier Huerta Calvo, "Espacios poéticos en el primer teatro clásico" [Poetic Spaces in the First Classical Theater], in Sáez Raposo, *Monstruos de apariencias llenos*, 17–21.

16. For the importance of scenography in spatial analyses of the comedia, see the bibliography cited in note 3. For the relation between costumes and space, see Robert Shannon, "The Staging of America in Golden Age Theater: Scenery, Costumes, Special Effects," in *Looking at the Comedia in the Year of the Quincentennial*, ed. Bárbara Mújica and Sharon D. Voros (Lanham, MD: University Press of America, 1993), 53–66; Aurora Biedma Torrecillas, "Influencia del vestuario en el teatro del Siglo de Oro" [The Impact of Wardrobe in Golden Age Theater], in *Moda y sociedad. Estudios sobre educación, lenguaje e historia del vestido* [Fashion and Society: Studies on the Education, Language, and History of Costume], ed. Emilio J. García Wiedemann and María Isabel Montoya Ramírez (Granada: Universidad de Granada, 1998), 125–134; María M. Carrión, "The Balcony of the *Chapín*, or the Vain Architecture of Shoes in Early Modern Spain," *Journal of Spanish Cultural Studies* 14, no. 2 (2013): 143–158; and Javier Irigoyen García, *Moors Dressed as Moors: Clothing, Social Distinction, and Ethnicity in Early Modern Iberia* (Toronto: University of Toronto Press, 2017), 161–181. The spatial dimension of music in the comedia has been partially examined, among others, by Carmelo Caballero Fernández-Rufete, "La música en el teatro clásico" [Music in Spanish Classical Theater], in *Historia del teatro español* [History of Spanish Theater], ed. Javier García Calvo (Madrid: Gredos, 2003), 1:677–716; Antonio Martín Moreno, "Música, pasión y razón: la teoría de los afectos en el teatro y la música del Siglo de Oro" [Music, Passion, and Reason:

The Theory of the Affects in Golden Age Drama and Music], *Edad de Oro* 22 (2003): 321–360; María Asunción Flórez Asensio, "'Cantaron desta suerte . . .': funciones de la música en el auto *Bodas entre el alma y el amor divino* de Lope de Vega, trasposición a lo divino de las Bodas Reales de 1599" ["Thus They Sang . . .": The Role of Music in Lope de Vega's *The Marriage between the Soul and Divine Love*, the Divinization of the Royal Wedding of 1599], *Anuario Lope de Vega* 18 (2012): 233–255; and Amparo Izquierdo Domingo, "La importancia de la música y el baile en los autos lopianos" [The Importance of Music and Dance in Lope's Religious Plays], in *Fiesta y teatro en el Siglo de Oro: ámbito hispánico* [Festival and Theater in the Golden Age: The Hispanic World], ed. Miguel Zugasti and Joseba Andoni Cuñado (Toulouse: Presses Universitaires du Midi, 2019), 205–213.

17. Barbara Fuchs, "Imperium Studies: Theorizing Early Modern Expansion," in *Postcolonial Moves: Medieval through Modern*, ed. Patricia Clare Ingham and Michelle R. Warren (New York: Palgrave Macmillan, 2003), 73.

18. For a summary of how the term *empire* has been applied to Spain's early modern monarchy in contemporary historiographical discourse, see Christian Hausser and Horst Pietschmann, "Empire. The Concept and Its Problems in the Historiography on the Iberian Empires in the Early Modern Age," *Culture and History Digital Journal* 3, no. 1 (2014): 1–10, http://dx.doi.org/10.3989/chdj.2014.002. For the relation of this term to sixteenth- and seventeenth-century political theory, see Pagden, *Lords of All the World*, 29–63; and Manuel Herrero Sánchez, "Spanish Theories of Empire: A Catholic and Polycentric Monarchy," in *A Companion to Early Modern Spanish Imperial Political and Social Thought*, ed. Jörg Tellkamp (Leiden: Brill, 2020), 17–52.

19. Joan Ramón Resina, "The Role of Discontinuity in the Formation of National Culture," in *Cultural Authority in Golden Age Spain*, ed. Marina S. Brownlee and Hans S. Gumbrecht (Baltimore: Johns Hopkins University Press, 1995), 293.

20. For the way national consciousness is manifested in Lopian drama, see Joan Oleza, "Del primer Lope al *Arte Nuevo*" [From the First Lope to the *Arte Nuevo*], in *Lope de Vega. Peribáñez y el comendador de Ocaña* [Lope de Vega. Peribáñez and the Commander of Ocaña], ed. Donald McGrady (Barcelona: Crítica, 1997), ix–lv; Anthony Cascardi, *Ideologies of History in the Spanish Golden Age* (University Park: Penn State University Press, 1997), 17–74; Paterson, "Stages of History," 147–156; Veronika Ryjik, *Lope de Vega en la invención de España. El drama histórico y la formación de la conciencia nacional* [Lope de Vega and the Invention of Spain. Historical Drama and the Formation of National Consciousness] (Woodbridge, UK: Tamesis, 2011); and Guillem Usandizaga, *La representación de la historia contemporánea en el teatro de Lope de Vega* [The Representation of Contemporary History in the Theater of Lope de Vega] (Madrid and Frankfurt: Iberoamericana/Vervuert, 2014).

21. Antonio Carreño, "La fuerza de las historias representadas: Lope de Vega y las alegorías del poder" [The Power of Represented History: Lope de Vega and the Allegories of Power], in *El teatro del Siglo de Oro ante los espacios de la crítica: encuentros y revisiones* [Golden Age Theater and the Spaces of Criticism: Encounters and Revisions], ed. Enrique García Santo-Tomás (Madrid and Frankfurt: Iberoamericana/Vervuert, 2002), 227.

22. All the dates provided for the composition of Lope's plays follow the canonical study on the chronology of his comedias written by S. Griswold Morley and Courtney Bruerton, *Cronología de las comedias de Lope de Vega* [The Chronology of Lope de

Vega's Comedias] (Madrid: Gredos, 1968). I provide further information on the dating of the plays in the notes that accompany each chapter.

23. Lope de Vega, *El premio de la hermosura*, ed. Florence D'Artois and Héctor Ruiz, vol. 1 of *Comedias de Lope de Vega. Parte XVI*, ed. Florence D'Artois and Luigi Giuliani (Madrid: Gredos, 2017), act 2, lines 1829–1830.

24. What Oleza refers to as *dramas de hechos famosos públicos* (dramas on famous public events) have long been identified by critics as a central genre within Lope's theater. Critics have traditionally used the term *dramas históricos* to designate these dramas and have subsumed within this category what Oleza calls *dramas de hechos particulares* (dramas about private events). For Oleza, however, the latter constitute a separate genre because they combine "historia y acontecimientos de índole privada" (history and events of a private nature). "Los dramas históricos de hechos particulares, de Lope de Vega: una exigencia de sujetos" [Lope de Vega's Historical Dramas on Private Events: The Demands of the Subject], *Revista sobre teatro áureo* 7 (2013): 106. Oleza identifies the personal conflicts portrayed in Lope's *dramas de hechos particulares* with the emergence of a modern sense of the private, which he, following the ideas of Canadian philosopher Charles Taylor, defines as "una nueva percepción de la vida individual que crece hacia dentro y crea una dimensión de interioridad, al tiempo que se inserta en el marco de la vida corriente, no de una vida idealizada o heroica" (a new way of perceiving the life of individuals that grows inward and produces a sense of interiority while immersing itself in the realm of ordinary—not idealized or heroic—life). "Variaciones del drama historial en Lope de Vega" [Variations on Lope de Vega's Historical Drama], *Anuario Lope de Vega* 19 (2013): 9.

25. Oleza notes that critics have still not been able to determine the exact number of plays he ascribes to the two genres he identifies: "La bibliografía sobre los dramas históricos de Lope es bastante abundante, dada la importancia estética de muchos de ellos, pero en cambio es escasa la que se plantea una visión de conjunto, y más escaso todavía el corpus de obras que se manejan" (the number of studies on Lope's historical dramas is quite extensive given the aesthetic significance of many of them, but there are few that provide an overall view of the whole. The number of plays being examined is even smaller). "Los dramas históricos," 107. Oleza estimates that the number of *dramas de hechos particulares* and *dramas de hechos famosos públicos* that Lope wrote was eighty-one, a number that surpasses the seventy-five *comedias urbanas* (urban plays) and fifty-two *comedias palatinas* (courtly plays) that we can safely attribute to him.

26. José Miguel Martínez Torrejón, prologue to *Los guanches de Tenerife*, by Lope de Vega, ed. José Miguel Martínez Torrejón, in vol. 2 of *Comedias de Lope de Vega. Parte X*, ed. Ramón Valdés and María Morrás (Barcelona: Editorial Milenio, 2010), 771.

27. Lope's preeminence as a writer of historical dramas does not merely reflect the number of plays inspired by historical events that he wrote. It also reflects his ability to creatively engage with the popular and historiographical materials he used to write his *comedias historiales*. As Geraldine Coates has recently noted, "due to his sensitivity to his sources, and his creative use of them, Lope became the best-known dramatist of Spain's history." "Lope de Vega, the Chronicle-Legend Plays and Collective Memory," in *A Companion to Lope de Vega*, edited by Alexander Samson and Jonathan Thacker (Woodbridge, UK: Tamesis, 2008), 132–133.

28. Speaking for instance about the comedias that dramatize contemporary conflicts in Flanders, Ryjik has observed that "el tipo de relación que se establece entre las flamencas

y los españoles . . . parece un calco directo de las relaciones entre las moras y los cristianos de las comedias sobre la Reconquista" (the type of relationship Flemish women establish with Spanish men . . . looks like a carbon copy of the relationships between Moorish women and Christian men we find in Lope's comedias about the Reconquest), *Lope de Vega en la invención*, 179. For the depiction of the Americas and its inhabitants according to patterns found in comedias dealing with the struggle between Christians and Moors in medieval Iberia, see Thomas E. Case, "El indio y el moro en las comedias de Lope de Vega" [The Indian and the Moor in Lope de Vega's Comedias], in *Looking at the Comedia in the Year of the Quincentennial: Proceedings of the 1992 Symposium on Golden Age Drama at the University of Texas*, ed. Barbara Mújica and Sharon D. Voros (Lanham, MD: University Press of America, 1992), 13–21; Alberto Sandoval Sánchez, "Moros por indios: ensayando una lectura ex-céntrica del discurso colonial en *La Manguilla de Melilla* de Juan Ruiz de Alarcón" [Moors for Indians: Toward an Excentric Reading of Colonial Discourse in Juan Ruiz de Alarcón's *La Manguilla de Melilla*], *Revista Iberoamericana* 67, no. 172–173 (1995): 535–553; José R. Cartagena Calderón, *Masculinidades en obras: el drama de la hombría en la España imperial* [Masculinities at Work: The Drama of Manhood in Imperial Spain] (Newark, DE: Juan de la Cuesta 2008), 114–189; Castillo, *Indios en escena*, 63–66; and Ryjik, *Lope de Vega en la invención*, 190–200.

29. For a detailed description of the "spatial turn" and its theoretical foundations, see Robert Tally Jr., *Spatiality* (New York: Routledge, 2013), 11–43; and Alexander Beaumont, "Literary Studies after the Spatial Turn," *Journal of Urban Cultural Studies* 3, no. 3 (2016): 395–405, https://doi.org/10.1386/jucs.3.3.395_1.

30. Denis Cosgrove, "Spectacle and Society: Landscape and Theater in Premodern and Postmodern Cities," in *Understanding Ordinary Landscapes*, ed. Paul Groth and Todd W. Bressi (New Haven: Yale University Press, 1997), 101.

31. *Dramas de corte* should not be confused with *comedias palatinas*. Whereas the former were performed in palaces and noble houses, the latter were performed in the corrales. The term *palatinas* refers to the royal or noble extraction of the main characters, who are usually involved in love relationships with other characters from a lower social stratum. *Comedias palatinas* usually take place in foreign or faraway locations and involve the concealment of identity through the use of masks and disguises.

32. José María Ruano de la Haza, "Lope de Vega and the Theater in Madrid," in *A Companion to Lope de Vega*, ed. Alexander Samson and Jonathan Parker (Woodbridge, UK: Tamesis, 2008), 49.

CHAPTER 1 — SPACE AND THE IMPERIAL APPROPRIATION OF THE PAST IN THE LOPIAN COMEDIA

1. A comprehensive history of how this feature of the comedia has been perceived by critics has not yet been written. As Rubiera has noted, the spatial mobility that characterizes Lopian drama was perceived by Lope and his contemporaries as a major break with the dramatic tradition of antiquity: "La dispersión del lugar se veía de este modo, como un atentado contra la comedia antigua no porque así se defendiera en las poéticas de la antigüedad sino porque el ejemplo de los poetas del pasado servía como modelo preceptivo" (geographical dispersion was thus seen as an attack on classical theater; not because ancient poetics warned against it, but because the example of ancient dramatists functioned as a prescriptive model) (*La construcción del espacio*, 45). Modern critics like Francisco Ruiz Ramón have hailed this mobility as "una de las grandes maravillas

de nuestro teatro clásico" (one of the great wonders of our classical theater). *Celebración y catarsis (leer el teatro español)* [Celebration and Catharsis (Reading Spanish Theater)] (Murcia: Universidad de Murcia, 1988), 19.

2. Margaret R. Greer, "Espacios teatrales: su significación dramática y social" [Theatrical Spaces: Their Social and Dramatic Meaning], in *Espacios de representación y espacios representados en el teatro áureo español* [Spaces for Representation and Represented Spaces in Golden Age Spanish Theater], ed. Francisco Sáez Raposo (Barcelona: Bellaterra, 2011), 306–307. The reference to English urban drama in Greer's quote is from Jean E. Howard's *Theater of a City: The Places of London Comedy, 1598–1642* (Philadelphia: University of Pennsylvania Press, 2009). For a review of this and other scholarly works devoted to the study of space in early modern English drama, see Sarah Dustagheer, "Shakespeare and the Spatial Turn," *Literature Compass* 10, no. 7 (2013): 570–581.

3. See Benedict Anderson, *Imagined Communities: Reflections on the Origin and Spread of Nationalism* (London: Verso, 2006), 37–46.

4. Greer's reference to "el espacio concebido" (conceived space) and "el espacio percibido" (perceived space) echoes Henri Lefebvre's triadic division of space (perceived-conceived-lived) in *The Production of Space*, trans. Donald Nicholson-Smith (London: Blackwell, 1991). Perceived space is the sum of all the stimuli and activities that facilitate the human perception of the outside world. It is materialized through the agency of the body and the sensory organs. Conceived space dominates Western societies. It comprises the space designed by "scientists, planners, urbanists, technocratic subdividers and social engineers, and of a certain type of artist with a scientific bent" (*The Production of Space*, 38). The last term completing the triad, lived space, is "space as directly lived through its associated images and symbols, and hence the space of 'inhabitants' and 'users,' but also of some artists and perhaps of those, such as a few writers and philosophers, who describe and aspire to do no more than describe" (39).

5. Marcelino Menéndez Pelayo, "Observaciones preliminares (I)," in *Obras de Lope de Vega publicadas por la Real Academia Española* (Madrid: Sucesores de Ribadeneyra, 1892), 1:xii.

6. Most of the comedias belonging to this corpus were written between 1599 and 1614 and mark, according to Oleza, "el cambio más profundo experimentado en la trayectoria dramática del Fénix" (the most substantial change Lope's drama experienced) ("Del primer Lope," xxviii). Paterson's view that these plays reveal an acute sense of historical consciousness on the part of Lope and his audience contrasts with the opinion expressed by Fernando Lázaro Carreter, who has written that "para Lope España fue siempre como era entonces" (for Lope Spain had always been as it was back then). *Lope de Vega: introducción a su vida y obra* [Lope de Vega: An Introduction to His Life and Works] (Madrid: Anaya, 1966), 215. For a summary of these and other critical positions surrounding this topic, see Guillem Usandizaga, *La representación de la historia*, 13–36.

7. David Roas, "Lope y la manipulación de la historia: realidad, leyenda e invención en la *Comedia de Bamba*" [Lope and the Manipulation of History: Reality, Legend, and Invention in the *Comedia de Bamba*], *Anuario Lope de Vega* 1 (1995): 189.

8. Geoffrey Parker, *The Army of Flanders and the Spanish Road, 1567–1659*, 2nd ed. (Cambridge: Cambridge University Press, 2004), 42.

9. Before Parker, French historian Fernand Braudel had already made this point explicit: "To understand the importance of distance is to see in a new light the problems of governing an empire in the sixteenth century. Above all, the immense Spanish empire."

The Mediterranean and the Mediterranean World in the Age of Philip II, trans. Siân Reynolds (New York: Harper & Row, 1972), 1:341.

10. Fontana worked in Rome for Popes Sixtus V and Clement VIII and then moved to Naples to work for the Spanish Viceroy, Juan de Zúñiga Avellaneda y Bazán, count of Miranda. The mausoleum he designed for Philip II, "Mausolei Typus Neapoli in Funere Philippi II," was built in the middle of Naples Cathedral by the city authorities. A copy of its design was included in *Descriptio honorum qui Neapoli habiti sunt in funere Philippi II. Catholici Regis* (Ms. Latin 6175, Bibliothèque Nationale de France).

11. John A. Marino, *Becoming Neapolitan: Citizen Culture in Baroque Naples* (Baltimore: Johns Hopkins University Press, 2011), 158.

12. Miguel de Cervantes Saavedra, *El rufián dichoso*, ed. Valentín Núñez Rivera, in *Miguel de Cervantes. Comedias y tragedias*, ed. Luis Gómez Canseco (Madrid: Real Academia Española, 2015), act 2, lines 1206–1264. Text references are to the acts and lines of this edition.

13. The classical loci where Cervantes's views on theater are expressed are the discussion on the writing and staging of plays that take place in *Don Quijote* I.38 (1605) between the priest and the Canon of Toledo and the short interlude *El retablo de las maravillas* [The Stage of Wonders], included in his *Ocho comedias y ocho entremeses nuevos* [Eight Plays and Eight New Interludes] (1615). For detailed commentary on these texts and their relation to Lope's comedia, see Jean Canavaggio, *Cervantes dramaturge. Un théâtre à naître* [Cervantes, Playwright: A Drama in the Making] (Paris: Presses Universitaires de France, 1977), 31–47; Jesús Maestro, *La escena imaginaria. Poética del teatro de Miguel de Cervantes* [The Imaginary Scene: Miguel de Cervantes's Poetics of Drama] (Madrid and Frankfurt: Iberoamericana/Vervuert, 2000), 55–94; Michael Gerli, "*El retablo de las maravillas*: Cervantes' 'Arte nuevo de deshacer comedias,'" [*The Stage of Wonders*: Cervantes's New Art of Subverting Plays] *Hispanic Review* 57, no. 4 (1989): 477–492; and William Childers, "'Ese tan borrado escrito': The Deconstruction of Lope's Religious Theater in *El retablo de las maravillas* and *El rufián dichoso*," *Bulletin of the Comediantes* 56, no. 2 (2004): 241–268, https://doi.org/10.1353/boc.2004.0000. Childers, developing a point made earlier by Nicholas Spadaccini and Jenaro Talens in *Through the Shattering Glass: Cervantes and the Self-Made World* (Minneapolis: University of Minnesota Press, 1993), 89–91, has identified *El rufián* as an attempt to deconstruct hagiographic plays and Lope's *comedias de santos* in particular.

14. Aurelio González has explained the presence of distant geographical settings in *El rufián* in relation to Cervantes's commitment to verisimilitude in the following terms: "Sin embargo, a nuestro parecer, lo que pretende Cervantes es dramatizar, dentro de lo que permite su concepción de fidelidad a la verdad, la vida del hombre y su proceso de santidad, y no solo la piedad del dominico, y por lo tanto se vuelve de gran importancia representar también su transformación y conversión. . . . Esto obliga a Cervantes a manejar dos lugares muy alejados geográficamente: el primero de ellos muy conocido por él (Sevilla), y el otro (la Nueva España) desconocido y que no pasaba de ser una referencia determinada por su fuente cronística." (However, in our view, what Cervantes tries to do is dramatize—as much as his ideas about verisimilitude allow it—the life of Lugo and the process by which he became a saint, not just the piety of the Dominican. Representing his conversion and transformation become therefore very important. . . . This forces Cervantes to handle two very distant locations: Seville, which he knew very well, and New Spain, unknown to him and a mere geographical reference

in the chronicle he used as his source.) "Espacio y dramaturgia cervantina" [Space and Cervantine Drama], in *Memoria de la palabra. Actas del VI Congreso de la Asociación Internacional Siglo de Oro* [Memory of the Word: Proceedings of the Fourth Meeting of the International Association of Golden Age Studies], ed. Francisco Domínguez Matito and María Luisa Lobato López (Madrid and Frankfurt: Iberoamericana/Vervuert, 2004), 900–901. It should be noted, however, that the dialogue between *Curiosidad* and *Comedia* makes no mention of the concept of verisimilitude and that the comments contained in it are a reflection on contemporary dramatic practice in general and not on *El rufián* specifically.

15. The impact of Lope de Vega's *Arte nuevo* on Cervantes's reference to "the changing times" as a factor contributing to the transformation of ancient dramatic practice in *El rufián dichoso* was first noted by Jörg Dünne, who has also related *Comedia*'s views on the neo-Aristotelian notion of unity of place to the influence of Lope's treatise: "La comedia justifica esa transformación de manera muy semejante al *Arte nuevo* de Lope de Vega, con el argumento de que 'los tiempos mudan las cosas / y perficionan las artes.' Más adelante, su respuesta enfoca la cuestión de la unidad de lugar, ya discutida por Lope de Vega en su *Arte nuevo*." (Cervantes's play justifies that transformation in a manner very similar to that employed by Lope in the *Arte nuevo*: by stating that "time changes things / and perfects the arts." Later, his response to Curiosity focuses on the question of unity of place, which Lope had already discussed in his *Arte nuevo*). "'Ya la comedia es un mapa.' Cervantes y la teatralización del espacio geográfico ["Theater Has Now Become a Map." Cervantes and the Dramatization of Geographical Space], *Olivar* 13, no. 17 (2012): 36.

16. Cristóbal de Virués, *Elisa Dido*, in *La gran Semíramis. Elisa Dido*, ed. Alfredo Hermenegildo (Madrid: Castalia, 2003), act 1, lines 228–247.

17. Alfredo Hermenegildo, introduction to *La gran Semíramis. Elisa Dido*, 65.

18. Farnese's visit to his mother in Naples at the outset of *Los españoles en Flandes* is interrupted by a missive from King Philip, who orders him to join the *tercios* gathered in Milan by the Marquis of Ayamonte. When Farnese arrives in Milan, the Spanish troops have already left for Flanders, where the rebels have broken the truce signed with the Spanish authorities and are planning an attack on the imperial forces under the command of Don Juan de Austria, the king's brother. Farnese will have to play catch-up with the *tercios* throughout act 1, allowing Lope to constantly switch the action between different geographical locations in this initial segment of the play.

19. For the civic role assigned to history by Renaissance humanism, see Hans Baron, *In Search of Florentine Civic Humanism: Essays in the Transition from Medieval to Modern Thought* (Princeton: Princeton University Press, 1988), 1:94–134; and Eric Cochrane, *Historians and Historiography in the Italian Renaissance* (Chicago: University of Chicago Press, 1981), 15–20.

20. Timothy Hampton has studied in detail the process by which Renaissance humanists extracted models of ethical conduct from ancient history in *Writing from History: The Rhetoric of Exemplarity in Renaissance Literature* (Ithaca: Cornell University Press, 1990), 1–30.

21. For a thorough discussion of the notion of *figura* and its place in the Western exegetical tradition, see David Dawson, *Christian Figural Reading and the Fashioning of Identity* (Berkeley: University of California Press, 2004), 83–137; and James I. Porter, "Disfigurations: Erich Auerbach's Theory of *Figura*," *Critical Inquiry* 44, no. 1 (2017): 80–113.

22. See in this regard Harald E. Braun, *Juan de Mariana and Early Modern Spanish Political Thought* (Aldershot, UK: Ashgate, 2007), 32–33.

23. The relation between Lope and Mariana, as Joan Oleza has noted, transcends their mutual bond with their patron, the Duke of Sessa, and deserves to be considered in more depth by Lope scholars: "No se trata solo de que Lope utilizara tal o cual relato de Mariana para sus dramas, ni de las relaciones personales que hubo entre ambos y el duque de Sessa, sino de que la concepción de la historia en ambos proporciona indicios de ser lo suficientemente pareja como para reclamar una investigación más particularizada." (It is not just that Lope used this or that story by Mariana for his dramas or that there was a personal relationship between both and the duke of Sessa. The idea of history that both Lope and Mariana embraced looks similar enough to warrant more focused research.) "Del primer Lope," xxxiv.

24. Lope de Vega, *El primer rey de Castilla*, ed. Adrián J. Sáez, vol. 1 of *Comedias de Lope de Vega. Parte XVII*, ed. Daniele Crivellari and Eugenio Maggi (Madrid: Gredos, 2018), act 1, lines 2682–2695.

25. See Coates, "The 1541 *Crónica general.*" Coates has offered as proof of Lope's fascination with space in the chronicles that inspired his dramas the "language of space" (26) he uses in *Las almenas de Toro*. This language, which focuses on the opposition between entrance and expulsion, reproduces, in her view, the spatial dichotomies that inform Florián de Ocampo's account in *La crónica de España* (1541) of King Sancho II of León and Castile's siege of Zamora in 1072.

26. Florián de Ocampo, *Las quatro partes enteras de la Crónica de España que mandó componer el serenissimo rey don Alonso llamado el Sabio: vista y emendada mucha parte de su impresión por el maestro Florián Docampo* [The four complete parts of the Chronicle of Spain that the most serene King Alfonso, "The Wise," ordered to be written: Reviewed and emended for printing by master Florián Docampo] (Zamora: Agustín de Paz y Juan Picardo, 1541), fol. 773r. I have modernized for ease of reading the Spanish spelling of all citations from Ocampo's chronicle included in this book. I will henceforward refer to this text as *Crónica de España*.

27. Ambrosio de Morales, *Corónica general de España* (Madrid: Oficina de Don Benito Cano, 1791), 7:60. I will henceforward refer to this text as *Crónica general*.

28. Herbert Lindenberger, *Historical Drama. The Relation of Literature and Reality* (Chicago: University of Chicago Press, 1975), 5.

29. Following Lindenberger's assertion, Carol Bingham Kirby has stated that the aim of Lope's historical comedias is "establecer alguna analogía entre el momento-espacio histórico que se representa en el escenario y el del espectador" (to establish some analogy between the historical time/space represented onstage and that of the audience.) "Observaciones preliminares sobre el teatro histórico de Lope de Vega" [Preliminary Observations on Lope de Vega's Historical Theater], in *Lope de Vega y los orígenes del teatro español. Actas del I Congreso Internacional sobre Lope de Vega* [Lope de Vega and the Origins of Spanish Theater. Proceedings of the First International Conference on Lope de Vega], ed. Manuel Criado de Val (Madrid: Edi-6, 1981), 329). By underlining the comedia's reliance on space and figural patterns of reading to connect past and present, my study significantly expands the critical framework proposed by Kirby.

30. Walter Cohen, *Drama of a Nation: Public Theater in Renaissance England and Spain* (Ithaca: Cornell University Press, 1985), 227.

31. See also in this respect the bibliography cited in note 28 of the introduction.

32. On Cazalla, Ponce de la Fuente, and the finding of Protestant cells in Seville and Valladolid, see José Nieto, "Herejía en la capilla imperial: Constantino Ponce de la Fuente y la imagen del diablo" [Heresy in the Imperial Chapel: Constantino Ponce de la Fuente and the Image of the Devil], in *Carlos V y la quiebra del humanismo político en Europa (1530–1558)* [Charles V and the Collapse of Political Humanism in Europe (1530–1558)], ed. José Martínez Millán (Madrid: Sociedad Estatal para la Conmemoración de los Centenarios de Felipe II y Carlos V, 2001), 4:213–226; Salvador Fernández Cava, *Constantino de la Fuente (1505–1559). El camino de la verdad)* [Constantino de la Fuente (1505–1559). The Road to Truth] (Ciudad Real: Almud, 2007); Christine Giesen, "Audacia y precaución: Constantino Ponce de la Fuente, defensor del protestantismo," [Daring and Caution: Constantino Ponce de la Fuente, Defender of Protestantism] *Res Publica. Revista de Historia de las Ideas Políticas* 20, no. 2 (2017): 227–241.

33. J. H. Elliott, *Imperial Spain, 1469–1716*, 3rd ed. (London: Penguin, 1990), 212.

34. The rumors of Turkish support for the Granada Moriscos were motivated in part by the fact that the leader of the revolt, Farax Abenfarax, appeared in Granada dressed in Turkish garb in order to convince the inhabitants of the city that the uprising had the support of the Ottoman Empire. Abenfarax's plan, however, was not successful. For more details on this episode, see Irigoyen García, *Moors Dressed as Moors*, 99–105.

35. As Miguel Ángel Bunes Ibarra has pointed out, after the death of Suleyman the Magnificent in 1566, "the Ottoman sultans concentrated their efforts on holding their possessions and forgot the great foreign adventures in support of other nations which had been carried out in the period of Süleyman." "The Expulsion of the Moriscos in the Context of Philp III's Mediterranean Policy," in *The Expulsion of the Moriscos from Spain: A Mediterranean Diaspora*, ed. Mercedes García Arenal and Gerard A. Wiegers (Leiden: Brill, 2014), 39; Antonio Feros, "Rhetorics of the Expulsion," in *The Expulsion of the Moriscos from Spain*, 70.

36. This view of the Canaries has been contested by Felipe Fernández Armesto in *The Canary Islands after the Conquest: The Making of a Colonial Society in the Early Sixteenth Century* (Oxford: Clarendon Press, 1982). Fernández Armesto has rejected the idea that "the Canarian experience [had] any formative influence on the institutions of government in the Hispanic World" (209). The islands, in his view, "were not a 'laboratory' of colonial government, in which controlled experiments were carried out" but rather "a crucible into which ingredients were flung at random" (209).

37. Eyda M. Merediz, "Traveling Icons: The Virgin of Candelaria's Transatlantic Journeys," *Arizona Journal of Hispanic Cultural Studies* 5 (2001): 120–121.

38. The vanishing of the Canaries from historical consciousness in the early modern period paralleled, as Felipe Fernández Armesto has argued, the subsidiary role they came to acquire in the economy of the period: "As the New World grew in importance, the Canaries declined in their own right, and became of value only or largely for the sake of the New World trade" (*The Canary Islands after the Conquest*, 205).

CHAPTER 2 — "QUE LOS REYES NUNCA ESTÁN LEJOS"

1. Juan de Zabaleta, *Errores celebrados*, ed. David Hershberg (Madrid: Espasa-Calpe, 1972), 56.

2. As Morley and Bruerton note, *El mejor alcalde* is one of Lope's shortest comedias (*Cronología de las comedias de Lope de Vega*, 359). The text used in most modern editions of the play—the one included in Parte XXI of Lope's *Comedias* (1635)—contains

only 2,410 lines. Other plays written by Lope between 1620 and 1625 contain on average 350 lines more. This has led some scholars to conclude that "*El mejor alcalde* was cut, possibly by actors who performed it." Donald McGrady, "Lope de Vega's *El mejor alcalde, el rey*: Its Italian *Novella* Sources and Its Influence Upon Manzoni's *I promessi sposi*," *Modern Language Review* 80, no. 3 (1985): 604. The review of three extant manuscripts of the play—one from the library of the Hispanic Society of America and two from the Biblioteca Histórica Municipal de Madrid—that Fausta Antonucci has recently conducted seem to corroborate this opinion. Commenting on the editorial and documentary value of these manuscripts, Antonucci points out that they most likely came from "el mundo del teatro, y es improcedente comparar la actitud hacia el texto del hombre de teatro con la del editor . . . porque responden a criterios totalmente diferentes" (the world of the theater, and it is unfair to compare the attitude of a man of the theater toward the text to the attitude of an editor . . . because they reflect totally different criteria). "La tradición manuscrita e impresa de *El mejor alcalde, el rey*, desde finales del siglo XVII hasta finales del siglo XVIII" [The Print and Manuscript Traditions of *El mejor alcalde, el rey*, from the End of the Seventeenth Century to the End of the Eighteenth], *Anuario Lope de Vega* 27 (2022): 284, https://doi.org/10.5565/rev/anuariolopedevega.446. Antonucci, nevertheless, takes into account the different textual nuances offered by these manuscripts in the critical edition of the *El mejor alcalde* she is preparing for Parte XXI of Lope's comedias with the editors of Prolope/Gredos.

3. The notion of "peasant honor drama" as a category was advanced more than half a century ago by Noël Salomon in *Recherches sur le thème paysan dans la "Comedia" au temps de Lope de Vega* [Peasant Lifestyle in the "Comedia" in the Time of Lope de Vega] (Bordeaux: Institut d'Études Ibériques et Ibéro-Américaines, 1965), 747–779 and 805–842. For a revision of the concept and the way it applies to *Fuenteovejuna*, *Peribáñez*, and *El mejor alcalde*, see Melveena McKendrick, *Playing the King: Lope de Vega and the Limits of Conformity* (Woodbridge, UK: Tamesis, 2000), 167–199. McKendrick has summarized in the following terms the themes that link these three comedias: "The works in question—*Peribáñez y el comendador de Ocaña*, *Fuenteovejuna*, and *El mejor alcalde el rey*—do not form a narrative triad nor are they the constituent parts of a single dramatic structure or vision. They are strikingly different dramatic and poetic creations. But they are related in that they represent a continuing preoccupation over some eighteen years with the same set of interconnected issues—rank, power, and individual worth—dramatically activated and elaborated through recourse to the *comedia* staples of love and honour, in a rural setting where the stark contrast and certainties of a feudal culture are shown beginning to yield to a more complex and nuanced view of society" (*Playing the King*, 167). Antonio Sánchez Jiménez has recently underlined the key significance that *hidalguía* has in *El mejor alcalde* in relation to the male protagonist, Sancho: "[*El mejor alcalde*] comparte con *Fuenteovejuna* y *Peribáñez* la situación histórica, el entrelazamiento de acciones públicas y privadas, y la presencia de un abuso de poder simbolizado por un desafuero sexual. . . . Sin embargo, tiene una diferencia fundamental con respecto a las dos anteriores: el protagonista, Sancho, es hidalgo, y no un simple campesino enriquecido" ([*El mejor alcalde*]shares with *Fuenteovejuna* and *Peribáñez* the historical contextualization, the interlacing of public and private actions, and the presence in it of abuse of power embodied in sexual excess. . . . However, there is a fundamental difference between *El mejor alcalde* and the two previous

plays: in *El mejor alcalde* Sancho is a petty nobleman, not just a rich peasant.) *Lope. El verso y la vida* [Lope: Poetry and Life] (Madrid: Cátedra, 2018), 209.

4. Robin Carter, "History and Poetry: A Re-Examination of Lope de Vega's *El mejor alcalde, el rey*," *Forum for Modern Language Studies* 16 (1980): 193–233, and Melveena McKendrick (*Playing the King*) have also emphasized the central role of the king in Lope's comedia, but they have argued that his authority is covertly called into question by the dramatist. Carter ("History and Poetry," 198–199) has referred in this respect to the constant violation of established legal procedures in Alfonso's dealing with Don Tello, which raises doubts about the king's sense of justice. McKendrick, for her part, has concentrated on the narrow moral scope of Alfonso's behavior in the comedia, which, in her view, is dictated by selfish political concerns: "In *El mejor alcalde, el rey* a more comfortable and less threatening route for justice is discovered, a route whereby the state itself becomes the guarantor of right. Even here, however, the lingering implications are disturbing, in that the state finally acts because its own authority has been ignored and not because a peasant woman has been raped—it reacts to *lèse-majesté*, not to wrong-doing" (*Playing the King*, 171).

5. Donald R. Larson, "Rape, Redress, and Reintegration: Ritualized Social Drama in *El mejor alcalde, el rey*," in *La violencia en el mundo hispánico en el Siglo de Oro* [Violence in the Hispanic World in the Golden Age], ed. Juan Manuel Escudero Baztán and Victoriano Roncero López (Madrid: Visor, 2010), 125–126.

6. Elliott, *Imperial Spain, 1469–1716*, 176.

7. Juan de Solórzano y Pereira, *Política indiana* (Madrid: Diego Díaz de la Carrera, 1648), 671, http://bdh-rd.bne.es/viewer.vm?id=0000134097&page=1. Although Solórzano y Pereira speaks primarily about the Americas, his view, as Anthony Pagden has noted, "was taken word for word from a discussion of the Italian dominions of the Castilian Crown by the Milanese Camillo Borello" (*Lords of All the World*, 140). The same view was echoed, Pagden has added, by the Spanish jurists and theologians Domingo Soto and Francisco Suárez "and applied to the [Spanish] monarchy as a whole" (140).

8. For a detailed overview of how this image manifests in classical literature, geography, and ethnography, see John Gillies, *Shakespeare and the Geography of Difference* (Cambridge: Cambridge University Press, 1994), 1–25.

9. See chapter 1 for a definition and discussion of the "optical regime."

10. The events on which Lope's play is based are also recounted, as Xulio Pardo de Neyra has observed in "El juego literario de la colonización en *El mejor alcalde, el rey*" [The Literary Game of Colonization in *El mejor alcalde, el rey*], *Anuario de Estudios Filológicos* 27 (2004): 237–258), in the *Sumario de los Reyes de España* [Compendium of Spanish Kings] written at the beginning of the fifteenth century by Juan Rodríguez de Cuenca, housekeeper for princess Leonor of Castile, queen consort of Navarre. However, the very limited circulation of this work makes it unlikely that Lope consulted it for the composition of his comedia. The fifteenth-century diplomat and historian Diego de Valera also briefly referenced the events dramatized by Lope, as Rafael Ramos has noted in "De Heródoto a Lope: Nota a *El mejor alcalde, el rey*" [From Herodotus to Lope: A Note on *El mejor alcalde, el rey*], *Anuario Lope de Vega* 1 (1995): 235–240), in his *Doctrinal de príncipes* [Instruction for Princes] (ca. 1474–1477). As Donald McGrady has argued in "Lope de Vega's *El mejor alcalde, el rey*." Lope likely consulted the tales of various Italian *novellieri* (Masuccio, Bandello, and others) to supplement his dramatization of the events recorded in Ocampo's chronicle.

11. Lope de Vega, *El mejor alcalde, el rey*, ed. Frank P. Casa and Berislav Primorac (Madrid: Cátedra, 1993), act 3, lines 2406–2410. Text references are to the acts and lines of this edition.

12. Lope de Vega, *Arte nuevo de hacer comedias. Edición crítica. Fuentes y ecos latinos* [New Art of Writing Plays. Critical Edition. Sources and Latin Echoes], ed. Felipe Pedraza Jiménez and Pedro Conde Parrado (Cuenca: Ediciones de la Universidad de Castilla-La Mancha, 2016), 327–328. John Varey made explicit the connection between *El arte nuevo* and the concern with *honra* in *El mejor alcalde* in a footnote appended to his critical study of the play in *Cosmovisión y escenografía. El teatro español en el Siglo de Oro* [Worldview and Scenography. Spanish Theater in the Golden Age] (Madrid: Castalia, 1987), 161. Paterson, for his part, has attributed Lope's decision to focus his drama on the abduction of a woman to his professional instincts as a dramatist: "Lope changed the original subject of dispute [in the chronicle], a land inheritance, into a stolen bride. No doubt the level of human interest and audience attention are raised by this change, for Lope, like any dramatist of his age, knew that love and sex form a staple ingredient of all *comedias*" ("Stages of History," 151).

13. The type of transgressive behavior Gillies has identified as occurring more frequently in classical representations of the barbarian is incest. Physical contact with the barbarian through miscegenation is therefore strongly discouraged in the classical sources this critic has examined. For more details, see Gillies, *Shakespeare and the Geography of Difference*, 15–25.

14. The plays for which Gillies has explored the threatening presence of these "exotics" include *Titus Andronicus*, *Antony and Cleopatra*, *The Merchant of Venice*, *Othello*, and *The Tempest*.

15. Harrison Meadows, "Disruptive Marginality: The Representation of Wildness in Lope de Vega's Baroque Dramatic Art," *Romance Quarterly* 65, no. 4 (2018): 182. According to Meadows, "the wild figure is the Baroque's marginal monster par excellence" (181). Its disruptive presence in the drama of Lope, Calderón, and other dramatists revolved around "the problem of *ser/parecer*" that defined the culture of the Baroque and often triggered "the axiomatic inclination toward *desengaño*" (182) that is characteristic of the literature of the period.

16. Camilo Fernández Cortizo, "El señorío rural gallego en tiempos de Felipe II" [The Galician Rural Fiefdom in the Time of Philip II]," in *El reino de Galicia en la monarquía de Felipe II* [The Kingdom of Galicia in Philip II's Monarchy], ed. Antonio Eiras Roel (Santiago de Compostela: Xunta de Galicia, 1998), 381.

17. José Luis de las Heras Santos, *La justicia penal de los Austrias en la corona de Castilla* [Hapsburg Penal Justice in the Crown of Castile] (Salamanca: Ediciones Universidad de Salamanca, 1991), 76. For more details on the creation, history, and functioning of the Galician *Audiencia*, see Baudilio Barreiro Mallón, "La Audiencia de Galicia en la época de Felipe II [The Galician High Court in the Age of Philip II]," in *El reino de Galicia en la monarquía de Felipe II*, 191–213.

18. María del Carmen Saavedra Vázquez, "Política imperial y élites locales: la evolución del concejo coruñés en los siglos XVI y XVII" [Imperial Policy and Local Elites: The Evolution of Corunna's Town Council in the Sixteenth and Seventeenth Centuries], in *Monarquía, imperio y pueblos en la España moderna. Actas de la IV reunión científica de la Asociación Española de Historia Moderna* [Monarchy, Empire, and Municipalities in Modern Spain. Proceedings of the Fourth Meeting of the Spanish Association of

Modern History], ed. Pablo Fernández Albaladejo (Alicante: Caja de Ahorros del Mediterráneo and Universidad de Alicante, 1997), 280.

19. For the impact on Galicia of Philip II's annexation of Portugal, see Isidro Dubert, "Galicia en la incorporación de Portugal, 1579–1581" [Galicia and the Annexation of Portugal, 1579–1581], in *El reino de Galicia en la monarquía de Felipe II*, ed. Eiras Roel, 139–168. For the impact on this region of Philip's fight against Protestantism and piracy, see María del Carmen Saavedra Vázquez's "Galicia en la política atlántica de Felipe II: la Gran Armada y sus efectos" [Galicia in Philip II's Atlantic Policy: The Great Armada and Its Effects], in *El reino de Galicia en la monarquía de Felipe II*, ed. Eiras Roel, 89–113, and "El corsarismo inglés en Galicia: los ataques a Vigo y Coruña y la militarización del reino" [English Privateering in Galicia: The Attacks on Vigo and Corunna and the Militarization of the Kingdom], in *El reino de Galicia en la monarquía de Felipe II*, 115–137. It should be noted that the idea of Galicia's singularity or "marginal position" in relation to the rest of Spain was also a source of pride for the nobility of that territory. As Elizabeth Wright has noted in her edition of Lope's *Los ramilletes de Madrid* [The Bouquets of Madrid] (ed. Elizabeth Wright, in *Comedias de Lope de Vega. Parte XI*, ed. Laura Fernández and Gonzalo Pontón [Madrid: Gredos, 2012], 1:604), the powerful count of Gondomar, Spanish ambassador to England, took a strong stance against the Portuguese chronicler Fray Bernardo de Brito for suggesting in his *Segunda parte da monarquía Lusitana* [Second Part of the Lusitanian Monarchy] (Lisbon, 1609) that Galicia, like the rest of Spain, had been conquered by the Moors. Gondomar's view could be the target of Lope's humor in *El mejor alcalde*—for example, when he makes Don Tello state in act 2, lines 1582–1586, that he owes nothing to King Alfonso because his ancestors took Galicia from the Moors.

20. Tomás Mantecón Movellán and Susana Truchuelo García, "La(s) frontera(s) exteriores e interiores de la Monarquía Hispánica: perspectivas historiográficas" [The Interior and Exterior Border(s) of the Spanish Monarchy: Historiographical Perspectives], *Historia Crítica* 59 (2016): 23.

21. Sofía Eiroa, "Galicia y los gallegos, tópicos y contrastes en Tirso de Molina: *Mari Hernández, la Gallega*" [Galicia and Galicians: Stereotypes and Contrasts in Tirso de Molina's *Mari Hernández, la Gallega*], *Hesperia: Anuario de Filología Hispánica* 5 (2002): 59.

22. Miguel Ángel Teijeiro Fuentes, "Galicia y los gallegos en la literatura española del Siglo de Oro" [Galicia and Galicians in Golden Age Spanish Literature], *Scriptura* 11, no. 1 (1996): 203–246.

23. The plays examined by Teijeiro Fuentes include *La llave de la honra* [The Key to Honor] (ca. 1614–1619), *El casamiento en la muerte* [Married after Death] (ca. 1595–1597), and *Más valéis, vos, Antona, que la corte toda* [You Are Worth More, Antona, Than the Entire Court] (ca. 1620–1623).

24. "De Heródoto a Lope," Rafael Ramos has provided a detailed account of the classical and medieval models Lope may have followed to depict Sancho's conduct in the woods, which hearken back to Herodotus and the Bible.

25. Gillies, *Shakespeare and the Geography of Difference*, 2–12.

26. For the play's role in praising the figure of Hurtado de Mendoza, see Victor Dixon, "Lope de Vega and America: *The New World* and *Arauco Tamed*," *Renaissance Studies* 6, no. 3/4 (1992): 249–269; and Guillem Usandizaga, *La representación de la historia*, 103–111. Moisés Castillo has also discussed *Arauco* and its portrayal of Mendoza in

relation to contemporary debates over the conquest of the New World that took place in early modern Spain in *Indios en escena*, 79–96.

27. Lope de Vega, *Arauco domado por el excelentísimo señor don García Hurtado de Mendoza*, in *América en el teatro clásico español: estudio y textos* [America in Spanish Classical Theater: Study and Texts], ed. Francisco Ruiz Ramón (Pamplona: Universidad de Navarra, 1993), 75–140.

28. Lope de Vega, *El nuevo mundo descubierto por Cristóbal Colón*, ed. Luigi Giuliani, in *Comedias de Lope de Vega. Parte IV*, ed. Luigi Giuiani and Ramón Valdés (Lérida: Editorial Milenio, 1997), act 1, scene 2, line 1905.

29. The ideological and dramatic congruity between *El mejor alcalde* and Lope's "American" plays is also manifested at the levels of plot and vocabulary. It should be noted, for instance, that both Tacuana and Elvira are kidnapped by local strongmen who separate them from their husbands. Also, both women resort to the word *tirano* (tyrant) to address and revile their respective abductors.

30. Ernst Kantorowicz, *The King's Two Bodies: A Study in Medieval Political Theory* (Princeton: Princeton University Press, 1997), 7–23.

31. José A. Rodríguez Garrido, "El ingenio en la mujer: *La traición en la amistad* de María de Zayas entre Lope de Vega y Huarte de San Juan" [Ingenuity in women: María de Zayas's *La traición en la amistad* between Lope de Vega and Huarte de San Juan], *Bulletin of the Comediantes* 49, no. 2 (1997): 364.

32. For McKendrick the desire for a more involved form of rule carries with it an implicit criticism of "the increasing distance between monarch and people that characterized Hapsburg rule" (*Playing the King*, 37). Similarly, Varey identified such desire with the yearning felt by "many serious Spaniards" to limit the power of the *privado* or court favorite over the king: "Aunque puede argumentarse que el papel de privado evolucionaba de manera gradual hacia el de primer ministro de la Corona, no cabe duda de que muchos españoles serios pensaban que el rey debiera tomar parte más directa y personal en la administración de su reino y el ejercicio de la justicia" (Although one could argue that the role of the favorite was gradually evolving to become like that of prime minister, there were undoubtedly many Spaniards who felt that the king should become more personally and directly involved in the administration of justice and in managing the affairs of the kingdom) (*Cosmovisión y escenografía*, 158).

33. Page 33. I include here the page number where the letter appears in the edition of *El mejor alcalde* I use throughout this chapter. The letter has not been included in the verse count by the editor.

34. The conflict between Alfonso and Ramiro, "The Monk," resulted from the dynastic tensions caused by the second marriage of Alfonso's mother, Queen Urraca, to Ramiro's brother, Alfonso, "The Battler." For more details on Alfonso's coronation and his rivalry with Aragón, see Bernard F. Reilly, *The Kingdom of León-Castilla under King Alfonso VII, 1126–1157* (Philadelphia: University of Pennsylvania Press, 1998), 15–52.

35. Peter Linehan notes in this context the difficulty that the meaning of Alfonso's coronation has posed to historians: "In the twentieth century, something of a cottage industry has developed around the question of what the imperial coronation was all about. Was it just on account of his personal hegemony and the quantity and quality of his vassals that Alfonso was intent on having himself called emperor? Or did he think of himself as emperor of a real *imperium*? And if so, what did he imagine it was? The old Visigothic kingdom plumped up? Or something European-style, the empire of a twelfth-

century Spanish Charlemagne with a touch of the Roman? There is no evidence that these interesting questions were asked at the time." *History and the Historians of Medieval Spain* (Oxford: Clarendon Press, 1993), 236.

36. Carlos Ayala Martínez, "The Episcopate and Reconquest in the Times of Alfonso VII of Castile and León," in *Between Sword and Prayer: Warfare and Medieval Clergy in Cultural Perspective*, ed. Radoslaw Kotecki, Jacek Maciejewski, and John S. Ottet (Leiden: Brill, 2018), 207–232.

37. As Ayala Martínez points out, this crusade idea was widely embraced throughout Europe during Alfonso's reign: "The Iberian Peninsula and more specifically the lands ruled by Alfonso VII were by no means separated from this intensified fulfilment of the crusade idea, in which Christian Europe was involved in the quarter-century between the First Lateran Council in 1123 and the failed attempt at conquering Damascus in 1148" (207).

38. Paul Carranza, "Garcilaso's Third Eclogue, Verses 65–68: The Tagus River, Exile, and Caesar's Campaign in Gaul," *Revista Canadiense de Estudios Hispánicos* 41, no. 3 (2017): 500, https://www.jstor.org/stable/26393651. Carranza notes in this respect that "the ability of a Roman emperor to cross rivers and, symbolically, to conquer them, was considered important—hence Caesar's fame for crossing the Rhine, as well as the appearance of rivers in triumphal processions, a practice adopted by Charles V, for example, after the victory [over the Turks] in Tunis [in 1535]" (504). See also in this context Santiago Montero, *El emperador y los ríos. Religión, ingeniería y política en el Imperio Romano* [The Emperor and Rivers. Religion, Engineering, and Politics in the Roman Empire] (Madrid: UNED, 2012), 165–251; and Brian Campbell, *Rivers and the Power of Ancient Rome* (Chapel Hill: University of North Carolina Press, 2012), 372–373.

39. Garcilaso de la Vega, "Égloga II," in *Obra poética y textos en prosa* [Poetic Works and Texts in Prose], ed. Bienvenido Morros (Barcelona: Crítica, 1995), lines 1471–1474.

40. In her recent electronic edition of the play for the *Biblioteca Virtual Cervantes*, Teresa Ferrer Valls has drawn attention to the obvious erotic allusions contained in the lines "que el Sil entre verdes cañas / llevar las faldas codicia" (which under the shade of these skirt-shaped mountains, coveted by the reedy Sil) by replacing *llevar* (to wear; to covet in my translation) with *besar* (to kiss). *El mejor alcalde, el rey*, ed. Teresa Ferrer Valls (Alicante: Biblioteca Virtual Miguel de Cervantes, 2002), act 1, scene 1, lines 3–4. Surprisingly, María del Carmen Artigas has made no reference to these verses in her article "Erotismo en *El mejor alcalde, el rey*" [Eroticism in *The Best Judge, the King*], *Bulletin of Hispanic Studies* 71, no. 2 (1994): 185–196, https://doi.org/10.1080/14753829420003711185.

41. Robin Carter has also pointed out that Lope's play does not show the same concern with legal procedure as Ocampo's chronicle: "The Alfonso of the *Crónica* was able to adduce first-hand and ostensibly impartial testimony against the *infanzón*, and drew up charges accordingly. In Lope's play, these judicial formalities are either absent or pointedly distorted" ("History and Poetry," 199).

42. Touching also upon the issue of metatheatricality, Varey (*Cosmovisión y escenografía*, 175) argued that Alfonso's role as *alcalde* or chief justice in the comedia lends legitimacy to the figure of the *alcalde de Casa y Corte* in the Madrid corrales, who was charged by the city authorities with guaranteeing public order during theatrical performances. For additional details regarding the role and figure of the *alcalde de Casa*

y Corte, see Varey, 172–174; and N. D. Shergold, *A History of the Spanish Stage from Medieval Times until the End of the Seventeenth Century* (Oxford: Clarendon Press, 1967), 390–398.

43. The source of Tragedy's speech is, as Luigi Giuliani points out, "Consideraciones preliminares sobre la tragedia de los años de 1580" (Preliminary considerations on tragedy in 1580s). Lupercio Leonardo de Argensola. *Tragedias* [Lupercio Leonardo de Argensola. Tragedies], ed. Luigi Giuliani (Zaragoza: Prensas Universitarias de Zaragoza, 2009), lxv, the prologue of Giraldi Cinthio's tragedy *Orbecche* (1541). Lope's familiarity with Lupercio Leonardo de Argensola's dramatic output is attested in a letter written to his patron, the Duke of Sessa, on October 9, 1611: "De Lupercio hubo algunas tragedias, pienso que buenas, lo que permitió aquel siglo, en que ni los ingenios eran tantos ni los ignorantes tan atrevidos." (Lupercio wrote a few tragedies, which were good, I think, considering the times. Back then there were fewer wits and ignorant people were not so daring.) Lope de Vega, *Epistolario de Lope de Vega Carpio* [Lope de Vega's Letters], ed. Agustín González Amezúa (Madrid: Artes Gráficas Aldus, 1941), 66.

44. Lupercio Leonardo de Argensola, "La Alejandra," in *Tragedias*, ed. Luigi Giuliani (Zaragoza: Prensas Universitarias de Zaragoza, 2009), 54–79.

CHAPTER 3 — BORN TO EXPAND

1. Historian Claudio Sánchez Albornoz first referred to this narrative using the term *neogoticismo* in his popular *España, un enigma histórico* [Spain, a Historical Enigma] (Buenos Aires: Editorial Sudamericana, 1962), 1:135. The earliest major written manifestations of this narrative date back to the early thirteenth-century Latin chronicles of Lucas de Tuy (*Chronicon mundi*) and Rodrigo Jiménez de Rada (*De rebus hispanie*), and to the *Estoria de Espanna* [History of Spain], begun around 1260 by the Castilian King Alfonso X. For the impact of *neogoticismo* in medieval and early modern Spanish historiography, see Carlos Clavería, "Reflejos del goticismo español en la fraseología del Siglo de Oro" [The Impact of Spanish Neogothicism on Golden Age Phraseology], in *Studia Philologica: Homenaje a Dámaso Alonso* [Studia Philologica: An Homage to Dámaso Alonso] (Madrid: Gredos, 1960), 1:357–372, and "Notas generales sobre los godos y su proyección histórica" [General Notes on the Goths and Their Historical Projection], *Cuadernos hispanoamericanos* 280–282 (1973): 541–556; José Antonio Maravall, *El concepto de España en la Edad Media* [The Idea of Spain in the Middle Ages] (Madrid: Instituto de Estudios Políticos, 1964), 299–335; Robert Tate, *Ensayos sobre la historiografía peninsular del siglo XV* [Essays on Fifteenth-Century Peninsular Historiography], trans. Jesús Díaz (Madrid: Gredos, 1970), 68–73; Diego Catalán, "España en su historiografía: de objeto a sujeto de la historia" [Spain in Its Historiography: From Object to Subject of History], introduction to *Los españoles en su historia* [The Spaniards in Their History], by Ramón Menéndez Pidal (Madrid: Espasa-Calpe, 1982), 16–49; Alan S. Deyermond, "The Death and Rebirth of Visigothic Spain in the *Estoria de España*," *Revista Canadiense de Estudios Hispánicos* 9, no. 3 (1985): 345–367; J. N. Hillgarth, *The Visigoths in History and Legend* (Toronto: Pontifical Institute of Mediaeval Studies, 2009), 82–160; Manuel de la Fuente Merás, "La 'España imperial' y los distintos modos de pensar su identidad" [Imperial Spain and the Different Ways to Think About Its Identity], *El Catoblepas* 38 (2005): 12–49; Martín Ríos Saloma, "De la Restauración a la Reconquista: la construcción de un mito nacional (Una revisión historiográfica. Siglos XVI–XIX)" [From Restoration to Reconquest: The Construction of a National Myth (A Historio-

graphical Review. From the Sixteenth to the Nineteenth Centuries)], *La España Medieval* 28 (2005): 379–414; Fernando Wulff, *Las esencias patrias*, 36–60; and Adrián J. Sáez, *Godos de papel. Identidad nacional y reescritura en el siglo de oro* [Paper Goths. National Identity and Rewriting in the Golden Age] (Madrid: Cátedra, 2019), 83–142.

2. Lucia Binotti, "*Restauratio imperii, restitutio linguae*: The Sixteenth-Century Spanish Historiographical Tradition and the Linguistic Definition of the Middle Ages," in *Recuerde el alma dormida: Medieval and Early Modern Spanish Essays in Honor of Frank Dominguez*, ed. John K. Moore Jr., and Adriano Duque (Newark, DE: Juan de la Cuesta, 2009), 43.

3. For the Roman ancestry of Spanish monarchs, see the studies by Marie Tanner, *The Last Descendant of Aeneas: The Hapsburgs and the Mythic Image of the Emperor* (New Haven: Yale University Press, 1993) and Thomas Dandelet, *The Renaissance of Empire in Early Modern Europe* (New York: Cambridge University Press, 2014), 74–199. The coexistence of this ancestry with a desire to identify with the Visigoths as the true founders of Spain led, as Adrián J. Sáez has observed, to "una especie de 'posición esquizofrénica' que trata de enmascarar y reducir la influencia romana sobre todo mediante la apuesta de genealogías nórdicas en un ejercicio de *translatio imperii, translatio studii*, pero se compensa en parte con el interés por su arte y monumentos que domina que en la coleccionística coetánea" (a type of "schizophrenic position" that tried to mask and diminish the Roman influence, especially by relying on Nordic genealogies that reflected the idea of *translatio imperii, translatio studii*. This was counterbalanced by the interest in Roman art and monuments that pervaded the efforts of contemporary collectors] (*Godos de papel*, 67).

4. The reason for this, as Baltasar Cuart Moner observes, is that "La *Hispania Romana*, por brillante que hubiera sido su trayectoria, no había pasado de ser una parte del Imperio, una provincia sometida . . . La *Hispania Gothica*, en cambio, había sido un reino unido e independiente que había sobrevivido al mismo Imperio" (Despite its brilliant trajectory, Roman Spain had been no more than a part of the empire, a conquered province . . . Gothic Spain, by contrast, had been a unified and independent kingdom that had outlasted the empire itself). "La larga marcha hacia las historias de España en el siglo XVI" [The Long Road toward the Histories of Spain in the Sixteenth Century], in *La construcción de las historias de España* [The Construction of Spain's Histories], ed. Ricardo García Cárcel (Madrid: Marcial Pons, 2004), 65.

5. Pedro de Mexía, *Historia del Emperador Carlos V*, ed. Juan de Mata Carriazo (Madrid: Espasa Calpe, 1945), 8.

6. Gonzalo Fernández de Oviedo, *Historia general y natural de las Indias, islas y tierra-firme del mar océano* [General and Natural History of the Indies, Islands and Mainland of the Ocean Sea], ed. José Amador de los Ríos (Madrid: Real Academia de la Historia, 1851), 1:4. On Oviedo's neogothic views as they pertained to the Americas, see David A. Lupher, *Romans in a New World: Classical Models in Sixteenth-Century Spanish America* (Ann Arbor: University of Michigan Press, 2009), 209–220.

7. Hillgarth, *The Visigoths*, 146.

8. As David Arbesú has pointed out in the prologue to his recent edition of the play (*Comedias de Lope de Vega. Parte XVIII*, ed. Adrián J. Sáez and Antonio Sánchez Jiménez, vol. 2, *Las famosas asturianas*, ed. David Arbesú [Madrid: Gredos, 2019], 159), the existence of a manuscript contract from June 1612 attesting to the performance of a play titled *Las famosas asturianas y rey don Alfonso* in the town of Ajofrín, near Toledo,

make it likely that Lope composed *Las famosas asturianas* in or a little before 1612. The contract does not mention Lope as author of the comedia, but it identifies the text with the company of Domingo Balbín, which represented other plays written by Lope during the same period.

9. For the treatment of this episode in medieval and early modern Castilian chronicles and genealogical works, see Marcelino Menéndez Pelayo, *Estudios literarios sobre el teatro de Lope de Vega* [Literary Studies on Lope de Vega's Theater] (Madrid: Librería General de Victoriano Suárez, 1925), 5:lxvi–lxxix; Manuela Manzanares de Cirre, "Las cien doncellas: trayectoria de una leyenda" [The One Hundred Maidens: Trajectory of a Legend], *PMLA* 81, no. 3 (1966): 179–184; Constantino Cabal, *Alfonso II, El Casto* [Alfonso II, the Chaste] (Madrid: Ediciones GEA, 1991), 104–138; Emily Francomano, "The Legend of the *Tributo de las cien doncellas*: Women as Warweavers and the Coin of Salvation," *Revista Canadiense de Estudios Hispánicos* 32, no. 1 (2007): 9–25; and David Arbesú, "*Las famosas asturianas* y los tratados de nobleza: otra comedia histórico-genealógica de Lope de Vega" [*Las famosas asturianas* and Lineage Treatises: Another Historical and Genealogical Play by Lope de Vega], *Hispanófila* 183 (2018): 215–229, https://doi.org/10.1353/hsf.2018.0027.

10. Griswold S. Morley and Courtney Bruerton were not able to provide a date of composition for *Las doncellas de Simancas* and did not consider it likely that Lope wrote it: "Nos inclinamos a creer que esta comedia no es de Lope, pero no podemos probarlo por el texto actual, que, tal y como se encuentra, no puede fecharse" [We are inclined to believe that this comedia was not written by Lope, but we cannot prove it using the current text, which cannot be dated in its present state] (*Cronología de las comedias*, 449). Given their reservations, I have decided not to include it in my study.

11. Arbesú, "*Las famosas asturianas*," 216.

12. Lope de Vega, *La campana de Aragón*, ed. Diego Símini, vol. 2 of *Comedias de Lope de Vega. Parte XVIII*, ed. Adrián J. Sáez and Antonio Sánchez Jiménez (Madrid: Gredos, 2019), 328.

13. Lope, as Melveena McKendrick has noted, "enjoyed something akin to a professional relationship with Mariana," whom he viewed as "another victim of the system, like himself honored in other countries but unappreciated by an 'ingrata patria'" (*Playing the King*, 200). Lope wrote to Mariana on behalf of the Duke of Sessa to obtain advice on how to curry the favor of King Philip III and dedicated to him his historiographical prose work *El triunfo de la fe en los Reinos de Japón* [The Triumph of Faith in the Kingdom of Japan] (1618).

14. Juan de Mariana, *Historia de España* [History of Spain] (Madrid: Real Academia Española, 1950), 188.

15. For a detailed account of this policy, see Paul C. Allen, *Philip III and the Pax Hispanica, 1598–1621: The Failure of Grand Strategy* (New Haven: Yale University Press, 2000).

16. Gender has been the prevailing concern for critics interested in the play. See in this regard Harriet P. Boyer, "*Las famosas asturianas* y la mujer heroica" [*Las famosas asturianas* and the Female Heroine], in *Lope de Vega y los orígenes del teatro español* [Lope de Vega and the Origins of Spanish Theater], ed. Manuel Criado de Val (Madrid: EDI-6, 1981), 479–484; Bruce Burningham, "Beleaguered Hegemony and Triangular Desire in Lope de Vega's *Las famosas asturianas* and John Ford's *Stagecoach*," *Bulletin of the Comediantes* 56, no. 1 (2004): 115–142; and Luzmila Camacho Platero, "*Las famosas asturi-*

anas: celebración de la castidad y la mujer varonil" [*Las famosas asturianas*: Celebrating Chastity and the Virile Woman], in *Cuatro triunfos áureos y otros dramaturgos del Siglo de Oro* [Four Golden Triumphs and Other Golden Age Playwrights], ed. Serafín González García and Lillian von der Walde Moheno (Ciudad de México, DF: Colegio de México, 2010), 497–510. Other scholars have also discussed the political message attached to gender in the play by examining its political context. See Thomas E. Case, "A Time for Heroines in Lope," in *The Perception of Women in Spanish Theater of the Golden Age*, ed. Anita K. Stoll and Dawn L. Smith (Cranbury, NJ: Associated University Presses, 1991), 202–219; Matthew D. Stroud, "Taking Matters Into Their Own Hands: Heroic Women of the Early Reconquest in the Spanish *Comedia*," *Bulletin of the Comediantes* 66, no. 2 (2014): 55–66; and Veronika Ryjik, *Lope de Vega en la invención*, 205–206. Lastly, David Arbesú, in "*Las famosas asturianas*," has reexamined the play's intertextuality considering its connection to genealogical documents related to the noble clan of the Osorios.

17. The reference to Mauregato, who occupied the throne of Asturias between 783 and 789 and was the person responsible for the shameful payment of one hundred maidens to the caliph of Córdoba, appears for the first time in the *Codex Albendensis* [Chronicle of Albelda] and the *Chronica Adefonsi tertii regis* [Chronicle of Alfonso III], which were written in ninth-century Asturias. These two chronicles also refer to him as an illegitimate, bastard king—the natural son of King Alfonso I of Asturias and a Moorish servant—in an effort to cast upon him an extensive *damnatio memoriae*. For more details on the figure of Mauregato and his representation in the Asturian chronicles, see Armando Besga Marroquín, *Orígenes Hispano-godos del Reino de Asturias* [The Hispano-Gothic Origins of the Kingdom of Asturias] (Oviedo: Real Instituto de Estudios Asturianos, 2000), 389–404; and Juan Ignacio Ruiz de la Peña Solar, *La monarquía astur-leonesa. De Pelayo a Alfonso VI (718–1109)* [The Asturian-Leonese Monarchy. From Pelayo to Alfonso VI (718–1109)], vol. 3 of *El reino de León en la alta Edad Media* [The Kingdom of Leon in the Early Middle Ages], ed. José María Fernández Catón (León: Centro de Estudios e Investigación San Isidoro, 1995), 56–71.

18. Lope de Vega, *Las famosas asturianas*, ed. David Arbesú, act 2, lines 107–126. Text references are to the acts and lines of this edition.

19. The religious and political significance of the holy chasuble of Saint Ildephonsus was emphasized by Mariana, who listed it first among the relics Archbishop Urbano took with him to Asturias when the Arabs threatened to occupy Toledo: "El arzobispo Urbano . . . se había retirado a las Asturias y llevado consigo las sagradas reliquias porque no fuesen profanadas por los enemigos del nombre cristiano, en particular llevó la vestidura traída a san Ilefonso del cielo, y un arca llena de reliquias, que por diversos casos fuera llevada a Jerusalem, y después parar en Toledo" (Archbishop Urbano had withdrawn to Asturias and taken with him the holy relics so that they would not be desecrated by the enemies of Christ. Specifically, he took with him the vestment brought from Heaven to Saint Ildephonsus, and a chest full of relics that had been brought to Jerusalem due to various circumstances and that had ended up in Toledo) (*Historia de España*, 183).

20. Antonio de la Torre y del Cerro, ed., *Testamentaría de Isabel la Católica* (Barcelona: Vda. Fidel Rodriguez Ferrán, 1974), 47.

21. As historian J. H. Elliott has remarked, North Africa remained during the early modern period "the cinderella of Spain's overseas possessions—a land unsuited to the particular characteristics of the conquistador" (*Imperial Spain, 1469–1716*, 56). For an

extended reflection on Spain's imperial footprint in North Africa, see Mercedes García Arenal and Miguel Ángel Bunes Ibarra, *Los españoles y el norte de África: siglos XVI-XVIII* [The Spanish and North Africa: Sixteenth and Seventeenth Centuries] (Madrid: Mapfre, 1992); Beatriz Alonso Acero, *Orán-Mazalquivir, 1589–1639: una sociedad española en la frontera de Berbería* [Oran-Mazalquivir, 1589–1639: A Spanish Society on the Border of the Barbary Coast] (Madrid: Consejo Superior de Investigaciones Científicas, 2000); and Barbara Fuchs and Yuen-Gen Liang, "A Forgotten Empire: The Spanish-North African Borderlands," *Journal of Spanish Cultural Studies* 12, no. 3 (2012): 261–273.

22. Richard Kagan, *Clio and the Crown: The Politics of History in Medieval and Early Modern Spain* (Baltimore: Johns Hopkins University Press, 2009), 119.

23. Melveena McKendrick, *Woman and Society in the Spanish Drama of the Golden Age: A Study of the mujer varonil* (Cambridge: Cambridge University Press, 1974), 207–208.

24. The "montera de caza, vaquero y venablo" (huntsman's hat, long tunic, and short spear) Doña Sancha wears when she kills the bear also link her, as Case ("A Time for Heroines") and Matthew Stroud ("Taking Matters") have pointed out, to the *cazadora* or huntress type identified by McKendrick (*Woman and Society*, 242–261). Boyer ("*Las famosas asturianas* y la mujer heroica") has also stressed this connection by identifying Doña Sancha with the goddess Artemis from Greek mythology.

25. Luzmila Camacho Platero, "Political and Gender Transgressions in Lope de Vega's *La varona castellana*," *West Virginia University Philological Papers* 51 (2004): 5.

26. François Rigolot, *Poétique et onomastique. L'exemple de la Renaissance* [Poetics and Onomastics. The Example of the Renaissance] (Geneva: Droz, 1977), 17.

27. Fernando Copello, "Milieu naturel et jardín à l'époque de Philippe II: à propos de *l'Agricultura de jardines* de Gregorio de los Ríos" [Natural Environment and Garden in the Age of Philip II: On Gregorio de los Ríos's *Agricultura de jardines*], in *Le milieu naturel en Espagne et en Italie: savoirs et representations* [The Natural Environment in Spain and Italy: Knowledge and Representations], ed. Nathalie Peyrebonne and Pauline Renoux-Caron (Paris: Presses Sorbonne Nouvelle, 2011), 106. Copello makes this remark in relation to Gregorio de los Rios's *Agricultura de jardines* (1592), the first treatise on gardening written in early modern Spain. His views reflect those of the Italian philosopher Rosario Assunto as presented in his book *Filosofia del giardino e filosofía nel giardino: saggi di teoría e storia dell'estica* [Philosophy of the Garden and Philosophy in the Garden: Essays on Theory and the History of Aesthetics] (Roma: Bulzoni, 1981).

28. John Brinckerhoff Jackson, *The Necessity for Ruins, and Other Topics* (Amherst: University of Massachusetts Press, 1980), 20–21.

29. Sebastián de Covarrubias Horozco, *Tesoro de la lengua castellana o española* [Thesaurus of the Castilian or Spanish Language] (Madrid: Castalia, 1995), 712.

30. For the role played by the *demos* in Lopian drama, see also Cascardi, *Ideologies of History*, 17–46. For Cascardi, the Lopian comedia does more than simply recognize the power of the popular masses onstage; it provides a mechanism "for the subjection of the *vulgo* to the 'traditional' values enforced by the Absolutist State" (37).

31. The phrase "Casto me llaman" [They call me "The Chaste"], which Alfonso uses in his response to Don Nuño, seems to suggest that Alfonso's nickname was widely used by his subjects. However, as historians have noted, it was coined by the officials who chronicled his reign. The fact that Alfonso had no children out of wedlock inspired the chroniclers to choose this nickname. The king's overt and insistent reference to it

at the end of the comedia may be related to Lope's desire to highlight the originality of his play for those familiar with his sources. As Camacho Platero has indicated ("*Las famosas asturianas*," 503), Lope decided to situate the events he dramatizes in *Las famosas asturianas* during the reign of Alfonso II and not during the reign of Ramiro I (842–850), as established by his models—Lope García de Salazar's historiographical and legendary mélange *Las bienandanzas e fortunas* [Prosperous and Fortunate Events] (1471) and Pedro de La Vecilla Castellanos's epic *El león de España* [The Lion of Spain] (1586). Lope's decision to depart from his sources remains unexplained and constitutes, as David Arbesú has pointed out, "una de las particularidades más intrigantes de la obra" (one of the most intriguing features of the work) (prologue to "*Las famosas asturianas*," 215).

32. McKendrick (*Playing the King*, 53–70) discusses specifically how Lope addresses the king's education in a handful of historical dramas. The problem of masculinity as a source of cultural, social, and political anxiety in Lope's society has been meticulously examined by Cartagena Calderón in *Masculinidades en obras*, 54–113. This critic provides a detailed account of how comedia texts connect Spain's decadence as an imperial power to the feminization of its ruling elites.

33. I. A. A. Thompson, "Castile, Spain, and the Monarchy: The Political Community from *patria natural* to *patria nacional*," in *Spain, Europe, and the Atlantic: Essays in Honour of John H. Elliott*, ed. Richard L. Kagan and Geoffrey Parker (Cambridge: Cambridge University Press, 1995), 128. Historian Henry Kamen has made a similar point: "In Spain there was little consciousness of the 'nation' and daily reality was centered almost exclusively on the local community. Social ties were formed not at a national but at a regional level, and loyalties were heavily localized, fundamentally in the rural villages (*pueblos*) and at a broader level in cantons (*comarcas*) and towns." *Spain 1469–1714: A Society of Conflict* (London: Longman, 1991), 249–250. Ruth Mackay has summarized in the following terms the negative effect this situation had in terms of government: "maintaining authority over the Iberian Peninsula and much of Europe and the Americas in an equitable and efficient way was virtually impossible." *The Limits of Royal Authority: Resistance and Obedience in Seventeenth-Century Castile* (Cambridge: Cambridge University Press, 1999), 21.

CHAPTER 4 — ENDANGERED FROM WITHIN

1. For the charges of collusion with the Turks and French Protestants brought against the Moriscos, see Andrew C. Hess, "The Moriscos: An Ottoman Fifth Column in Sixteenth-Century Spain," *The American Historical Review* 74, no. 1 (1968): 1–25; Louis Cardaillac, *Moriscos y cristianos: un enfrentamiento polémico (1492–1640)* [Moriscos and Christians: A Controversial Clash (1492–1640)] (Ciudad de México, DF: Fondo de Cultura Económica, 1979), 78–84; and Benjamin Ehlers, *Between Christians and Moriscos: Juan de Ribera and Religious Reform in Valencia, 1568–1614* (Baltimore: Johns Hopkins University Press, 2006), 20–21. As François Soyer has pointed out, the fact that the majority of the Morisco population lived close to the coast in Granada and Valencia "increased anxiety about the assistance they could offer to an invasion force." "Faith, Culture, and Fear: Comparing Islamophobia in Early Modern Spain and in Twenty-First-Century Europe," *Ethnic and Racial Studies* 36, no. 3 (2013): 406.

2. On the mass hysteria caused by anti-Morisco literature, see L. P. Harvey, *Muslims in Spain 1500–1614* (Chicago: University of Chicago Press, 2005), 88–89; Trevor Dadson,

"Official Rhetoric versus Local Reality: Propaganda and the Expulsion of the Moriscos," in *Rhetoric and Reality in Early Modern Spain*, ed. Richard J. Pym (Woodbridge, UK: Tamesis, 2006), 1–25; and Antonio Feros, "Rhetorics of Expulsion."

3. Miguel de Cervantes Saavedra, *Don Quijote de la Mancha*, ed. Francisco Rico (Madrid: Real Academia Española, 2015), 2:450–451.

4. For the translation of this passage I have used *Don Quixote*, trans. Edith Grosman (New York: HarperCollins, 2003).

5. As Julián Acebrón has pointed out in the prologue to his critical edition of the play in *Comedias de Lope de Vega. Parte VII*, ed. Enrico di Pastena, vol. 2 (Lérida: Editorial Milenio-Universitat Atònoma de Barcelona, 1997), 595, the play could have been written in 1605, some eight years earlier than the date of composition provided by Morley and Bruerton in *Cronología de las comedias de Lope de Vega*. Acebrón arrives at this conclusion following information collected by Thornton Wilder in "Lope, Pinedo, Some Child-Actors, and a Lion," *Romance Philology* 7 (1953): 21–24 about the company of Baltasar de Pinedo, with whom Lope collaborated with between 1603 and 1608. Roser López Cruz, in "'Virgen bella, nuestras paces os encargo': *Las paces de los reyes y judía de Toledo* o la apuesta política por una imagen milagrosa" [Beautiful Virgin, Our Reconciliation I Entrust to You: *Las paces de los reyes y judía de Toledo* or Making a Political Bet on a Miraculous Image], *Anuario Lope de Vega* 25 (2019): 257–280), has suggested that the play was written between 1603 and 1607 and that it was probably first performed during the *Corpus Christi* celebrations that took place in the town of Illescas—where *Las paces* ends—in the spring of 1607.

6. For a detailed discussion of how King Alfonso's affair is depicted in the *Castigos e documentos* and other contemporary medieval historiographical sources, see Amaia Arizaleta, "Una historia en el margen: Alfonso VIII de Castilla y la judía de Toledo" [A Story in the Margin: Alfonso VIII of Castile and the Jewess of Toledo], *Cahiers d'études hispaniques médiévales* 28 (2005): 37–68.

7. For an analysis of the connection between *Las paces* and Ocampo's chronicle, see James A. Castañeda, "Preliminary Study," in *A Critical Edition of Lope de Vega's Las paces de los reyes y judía de Toledo*, ed. James A. Castañeda (Chapel Hill: University of North Carolina Press, 1962), 11–34.

8. The name *Raquel* is used for the first time in relation to the Jewish woman in book XIX of Lope's *Jerusalén Conquistada* [Jerusalem Conquered] (1609), an epic devoted to narrating Alfonso VIII's exploits in the Third Crusade (an event the Castilian monarch did not actually participate in). Before Lope's epic, the king's mistress is referred to as *Fermosa* in the *Tercera Crónica General* of 1390. No name is used to identify her in earlier documents.

9. As José Ramón Martín Largo has noted, during the conflict the Lara family sustained with the rival Castros clan after the death of Alfonso's father (King Sancho III), "Don Manrique Pérez de Lara, alférez mayor de Castilla, se autoproclamó regente, asumiendo el derecho a la formación del Rey Chico [King Alfonso]" (Don Manrique Pérez de Lara, highest-ranking military official in Castile, proclaimed himself regent, appropriating thus the right to educate "the Child King" [King Alfonso]). *La judía de Toledo: desde Lope de Vega hasta Franz Grillparzer* [The Jewess of Toledo: From Lope de Vega to Franz Grillparzer] (Madrid: Brand, 2000), 36–37. For an overview of this conflict and its representation in Lope's play, see Martín Largo, 36–38, and Castañeda, "Preliminary Study," 5–10.

10. Lope de Vega, *Comedia famosa de las paces de los reyes y judía de Toledo*, ed. Julián Acebrón, vol. 2 of *Comedias de Lope de Vega. Parte VII*, ed. Enrico di Pastena (Lérida: Editorial Milenio-Universitat Atònoma de Barcelona, 1997), act 1, lines 1–24. Text references are to the acts and lines of this edition.

11. Frederick A. de Armas, "Passion, Treason, and Blindness in Lope de Vega's *Las paces de los reyes*," in *Studies in the Spanish Golden Age: Cervantes and Lope de Vega*, ed. Dana B. Drake and José A. Madrigal (Miami: Ediciones Universal, 1978), 65–75.

12. Raymond McCurdy, "The Bathing Nude in Golden Age Drama," *Romance Notes* 1, no. 1 (1959): 36–39. The parallel between Alfonso and King David is part of a larger pattern of correspondences that Lope establishes in the play between the Castilian monarch and other biblical and legendary figures: Adam, Jacob, and King Rodrigo. William McCrary has called this pattern "homologous retrospection" and argued that it allows Lope to transform the simple plot of *Las paces* into "a vibrant drama of redemptive election." "Plot, Action, and Imitation: The Art of Lope's *Las paces de los reyes*," *Hipanófila* 48 (1973): 15.

13. Lope's decision to avoid dramatizing these youthful exploits in the play has garnered much criticism from scholars. Castañeda, for instance, has stated that "*Las paces de los reyes* lacks the unity of texture and continuity of inspiration without which it could never be classified as one of Lope's best works" ("Preliminary Study," 2). In a similar vein, McKendrick has referred to an abrupt "chronological lunge forward" (*Playing the King*, 46) between acts 1 and 2 of the play, an aspect that Juián Acebrón has also highlighted in the prologue to his recent edition of *Las paces*: "puede decirse que en *Las paces de los reyes y judía de Toledo* la trabazón argumental del acto primero con el resto de la comedia es muy débil" (one could say that in *Las paces de los reyes y judía de Toledo* the plot connection between act 1 and the rest of the comedia is very weak) (596). For a summary of these views, see Susan Niehoff McCrary, "Theatrical Consciousness and Redemption," in *The Golden Age Comedia: Text, Theory, and Performance*, ed. Charles Ganelin and Howard Mancing (West Lafayette, IN: Purdue University Press, 1994), 24–25.

14. See David Nirenberg, "Race and the Middle Ages: The Case of Spain and Its Jews," in *Rereading the Black Legend: The Discourses of Religious and Racial Difference in the Renaissance Empires*, ed. Maureen Quilligan, Walter Mignolo, and Margaret Rich Greer (Chicago: University of Chicago Press, 2008), 71–87.

15. Antonio Feros, "Reflexiones atlánticas: identidades étnicas y nacionales en el mundo hispánico moderno" [Atlantic Reflections: Ethnic and National Identities in the Modern Hispanic World], in *Cultura escrita y sociedad* vol. 2, ed. Verónica Sierra Blas (2006): 86.

16. Don Lope's words are repeated almost verbatim by Doña Costanza a few moments later when she reflects upon her husband's death: "¡Con qué justísima ley / merece un hombre morir / que cerca del alma pone / hombre de vil nacimiento . . . !" (How justly a man deserves to die when he allows a man of contemptible birth near his bosom . . . !) (act 1, lines 848–851).

17. For a detailed account of the origin and evolution of the story of La Cava and Don Rodrigo in Spanish historiography and literature from the Middle Ages to the modern era, see Patricia E. Grieve, *The Eve of Spain: Myths of Origins in the History of Christian, Muslim, and Jewish Conflict* (Baltimore: Johns Hopkins University Press, 2009).

18. See McCurdy, "The Bathing Nude," 36.

19. Martín Largo, *La judía de Toledo*, 17–18.

20. López Cruz ("'Virgen bella,'" 270–271) has identified a direct reference to the defeat at Alarcos in Queen Leonor's warning to the Castilian nobles regarding the advance of the Moors (see act 3, lines 1998–2017, quoted previously in this chapter). The connection between Raquel and Alarcos is already established in the *Castigos e documentos para bien vivir ordenados por el rey don Sancho* [Documents and Admonishments for Living Well Ordered by King Sancho] (1292), the earliest document containing a reference to the affair between King Alfonso and the Toledan Jewish woman, where Alfonso's military defeat is presented as divine punishment: "Por siete años que viscó mala vida con una judia de Toledo, diole Dios grand llaga e grand majamiento en la batalla de Alarcos, en que fue vencido, e fuyó e fue mal andante él e todos los de su reino, e los que mejor andanza hobieron fueron aquellos que y morieron" (Because for seven years he led a sinful life with a Jewess from Toledo, God inflicted harm and hardship on him in the battle of Alarcos, where he was defeated. He fled and suffered misfortunes with all his men. The luckiest ones were those who died there) (quoted in Martín Largo, *La judía de Toledo*, 33).

21. Catherine Swietlicki, "Lope's Dialogic Imagination: Writing Other Voices in 'Monolithic Spain,'" *Bulletin of the Comediantes* 40, no. 2 (1988): 218.

22. This sympathetic picture extends for many critics to the description of herself that Raquel makes in act 2, when she sees Alfonso enter Toledo in the company of Leonor after his victory in the Crusades: "Yo, Sibila, aunque no soy / cristiana, soy española; / que basta esta gracia sola" (I, Sibila, though I am not a Christian, I'm Spanish; and this grace is good enough) (act 1, lines 1141–1143).

23. Gustavo Faverón Patriau, "Siete años en el purgatorio: judíos y cristianos en *Las paces de los reyes y judía de Toledo* de Lope de Vega" [Seven Years in Purgatory: Jews and Christians in Lope de Vega's *Las paces de los reyes y judía de Toledo*], *Bulletin of the Comediantes* 58, no. 2, (2006): 367 (italics in the original).

24. It is worth remembering in this context that, according to a popular notion inherited from medieval political theory, the figure of the king was understood both in terms of a *body politic* (his symbolic and transcendental role as representative of the entire polity) and a *body natural* (the reality of his physical presence as a human).

25. Lope de Vega, *El cuerdo loco* [The Sane Madman], ed. José F. Montesinos (Madrid: Impresora de los Sucesores de Hernando, 1922), 178; and Karl Vossler, *Lope de Vega y su tiempo* [Lope de Vega and His Times], trans. Ramón de la Serna (Madrid: Revista de Occidente, 1933), 262 have been especially critical regarding Lope's use of divine intervention in the play. Their views have been tempered by Fernando Rodríguez Gallego, who sees *Las paces* as a play that simply incorporates elements typical of the *comedias de cuerpo o aparato* (plays that bring to the stage the lives of saints): "Este proceso de santificación de Alfonso llegará hasta *Las paces de los reyes y judía de Toledo*, que ya se plantea como una comedia de cuerpo o aparato, que normalmente suelen dramatizar la vida de un santo" (The santification of Alfonso also reaches *Las paces de los reyes y judía de Toledo*, which was written as a *comedia de cuerpo o aparato*, which usually dramatize the lives of saints). "Alfonso VIII, *La corona merecida* y la leyenda de la judía de Toledo" [Alfonso VIII, *La corona merecida* and the Legend of the Jewess of Toledo], *eHumanista* 24 (2013): 160.

26. According to López Cruz ("'Virgen bella,'" 275–276), by making Alfonso rest and receive the visit of an angel in Illescas, Lope would be contributing to this town's efforts

to have its church of La Virgen de la Caridad recognized as a prominent religious site by the Spanish monarchy. For the relation between Lope's play and the sanctuary in Illescas, see also Abraham Madroñal Durán, "Dos comedias relacionadas con Illescas: *El caballero de Illescas* y *Las paces de los reyes*" [Two comedias associated with Illescas: *El caballero de Illescas* and *Las paces de los reyes*], in *Pensamiento y literatura en los inicios de la modernidad* [Thought and Literature at the Dawn of Modernity], ed. Jaume Garau Amengual (New York: Instituto de Estudios Auriseculares, 2017), 75–93.

27. According to Pedraza, Lope's bigamy was also behind his decision to name Alfonso's mistress Raquel: "Lope fue muy aficionado al nombre de la protagonista y al mito bíblico de los amores de Jacob. Posiblemente porque veía en él un trasunto perfecto de sus circunstancias biográficas. Surge en 1598–1602, cuando, casado con Juana de Guardo, vive unos apasionados amores con Micaela de Luján. Como Jacob—pensaba el poeta—había tenido que aceptar a una Lía poco agraciada antes de gozar a la hermosa Raquel" (Lope was very fond of the name of the protagonist and of the biblical story of Jacob, Rachel, and Leah, possibly because he saw in it a perfect reflection of his biographical situation. It all began between 1598 and 1602, when he lived a passionate affair with Micaela de Luján while married to Juana de Guardo. Lope thought that, like Jacob, he had to put up with an unattractive Leah before he could enjoy the beautiful Rachel). Felipe Pedraza Jiménez, "*La judía de Toledo*: génesis y cristalización de un mito literario" [*The Jewess of Toledo*: The Origin and Shaping of a Myth], in *Marañón en Toledo (sobre "Elogio y nostalgia de Toledo")* [Marañón in Toledo (on *Praise and Nostalgia of Toledo*)], ed. José Botella Llusiá and Antonio Fernández de Molina (Cuenca: Ediciones de la Universidad de Castilla-La Mancha, 1999), 28. For a summary of Lope's simultaneous relationship with Juana de Guardo and Micaela de Luján, see Sánchez Jiménez, *Lope. El verso y la vida*, 124 and 128–131.

28. Antonio Sánchez Jiménez, in "Quevedo y Lope (poesía y teatro) en 1609: patriotismo y construcción nacional en la *España defendida* y la *Jerusalén conquistada*" [Quevedo and Lope (Poetry and Theater) in 1609: Patriotism and Nation-Building in *España defendida* and *Jerusalén conquistada*], *La Perinola* 17 (2013): 27–56, has also cited the peace treaty with England as a motivating factor for Lope's decision to write *La Jerusalén conquistada*, in which Alfonso earns the respect of King Richard I, "the Lionheart," while making war in the Holy Land. It should also be kept in mind, as Roser López Cruz has pointed out, that "para el público de la época, *Las paces de los reyes* no solo no recordaría la historia de Alfonso VIII . . . sino que habría tenido ecos más bien de asuntos de política internacional, pues esta [las paces de los reyes] era una fórmula utilizada para tratar estos temas" (Contemporary audiences would have been reminded in *Las paces de los reyes* not only of the life story of Alfonso VIII . . . they would have also heard in it echoes of international politics because the phrase [the reconciliation of the monarchs] was a formula often used to discuss that subject) ("'Virgen bella,'" 270).

29. After 1609, dissent regarding the monarchy's decision to expel the Moriscos waned significantly. As Feros has acknowledged: "What had formally been a vigorous debate, carried out for the most part within societal institutions, hardened after 1609 into a single point of view that was proclaimed in all types of printed texts written by a great variety of authors. Official discourse and 'public opinion' merged into one, and affected all the literary genres of the seventeenth century" ("Rhetorics of Expulsion," 62).

30. As Feros notes: "The printing press made possible a massive pro-Expulsion literature that covered all genres—official documents, novels, and plays—to which were

added paintings and even royal progresses" (76). To this sizable body of literature, we must add the edicts of expulsion themselves, which were printed and widely circulated throughout Spain.

31. Rafael Benítez Sánchez-Blanco, "The Religious Debate in Spain," in *The Expulsion of the Moriscos from Spain: A Mediterranean Diaspora*, ed. Mercedes García Arenal and Gerard A. Wiegers (Leiden: Brill, 2014), 102. This doctrinal concern was expressed, for instance, by the all-powerful Duke of Lerma, who, as Feros has explained, had "grave doubts about whether that action [expelling the Moriscos to Islamic territories] was desirable or convenient, arguing that the Moriscos were baptized Christians and should therefore not be treated as infidels" ("Rhetorics of Expulsion," 75).

32. On Ribera and the *memoriales* he addressed to Philip III, see Rafael Benítez Sánchez-Blanco, *Heroicas decisiones: la monarquía católica y los moriscos* [Heroic Decisions: The Catholic Monarchy and the Moriscos] (Valencia: Institució Alfons el Magnànim/Diputació de València, 2001), 363–411; and Benjamin Ehlers, *Between Christians and Moriscos*, 126–151.

33. Bleda's *Defensio* was one of the most important anti-Morisco treatises written in the years leading up to the Expulsion. Although Bleda was not granted permission to publish the original Latin version of the text in 1601, a Spanish translation was printed in Valencia in 1610.

34. Baltasar Álamos de Barrientos, *Discurso político al rey Felipe III al comienzo de su reinado* (Barcelona: Anthropos, 1990), 50.

35. On the relation between the Expulsion of the Moriscos and the impact that events in the Netherlands had on Spain during the reign of Philip III, see Benítez Sánchez-Blanco, *Heroicas decisiones*, 374–378; and Juan E. Gelabert, "1609: cuestiones de reputación" [1609: Matters of Reputation], in *Cartas de La Goleta* 2 (2008): 39–52, https://issuu.com/bibtun/docs/cartas_goleta_2.

36. Lilia Dapaz Strout, "Psicomaquia o el conflicto de Eros y Logos en *Las paces de los reyes y judía de Toledo*" [Psichomachia or the Conflict Between Eros and Logos in *Las paces de los reyes y judía de Toledo*], in *Studies in Honor of William C. McCrary*, ed. Robert Fiore (Lincoln, NE: Society of Spanish and Spanish-American Studies, 1986), 82.

37. John Beusterien, "Lope de Vega's *Auto sacramental de la circuncisión y sangría de Cristo*: A Focal Point of Antisemitism in Seventeenth-Century Spain," *Hispanic Review* 72, no. 3 (2004): 363, https://www.jstor.org/stable/3247123.

38. Other Morisco practices that were regularly attributed to Jews were, for instance, the reading of the Quran and burials in the countryside, such as the one described by Cervantes in *Don Quixote* part I, chapter 12 in relation to the character of Grisóstomo. For more details on these practices and their attribution to Jewish communities in the Iberian Peninsula, see Francisco Burgos Esteban, "Los estatutos de limpieza y sus pruebas en el siglo XVII: la figura del converso en denuncias y testimonios" [The Statutes of Purity of Blood and Their Requirements in the Seventeenth Century: The Figure of the Convert in Reports and Testimonies], in *Xudeus e conversos na historia. Actas do Congreso Internacional, Ribadavia 14–17 de outubro de 1991* [Jews and Converts in History. Proceedings of the International Symposium in Ribadavia, October 14–17, 1991], ed. Carlos Barros (Santiago de Compostela: Editorial de la Historia, 1994), 373.

39. Pedro de Valencia, *Tratado acerca de los moriscos de España*, in *Obras completas* [Complete Works], ed. Rafael González Cañal and Hipólito B. Riesco Álvarez (León: Universidad de León, 1999), 2:81–82.

40. Thomas E. Case, "Lope and the Moriscos," *Bulletin of the Comediantes* 44, no. 2 (1992): 204.

CHAPTER 5 — ATLANTIC CONQUESTS, TRANSATLANTIC ECHOES

1. Louise Mirrer, "Representing 'Other' Men: Muslims, Jews, and Masculine Ideals in Medieval Castilian Epic and Ballad," in *Medieval Masculinities: Regarding Men in the Middle Ages*, ed. Claire A. Lees (Minneapolis: University of Minnesota Press, 1994), 182.

2. Allen Carey-Webb, *Making Subject(s): Literature and the Emergence of National Identity* (New York: Garland Publishing, 1998), 50.

3. Morley and Bruerton (*Cronología de las comedias*) base their dating of *Los guanches* on the use Lope makes in this play of *Las Antigüedades de las Islas Afortunadas de la Gran Canaria, conquista de Tenerife y aparición de la santa imagen de Candelaria* [Antiquities of the Fortunate Island of Gran Canaria, Conquest of Tenerife, and Apparition of the Sacred Image of the *Candelaria* Virgin], an epic poem written by the Canarian native Antonio de Viana that was published in Seville in 1604. Viana's poem was commissioned by Juan Guerra de Ayala, head of the powerful Guerra family of Tenerife, to change the negative image of his ancestors presented by the Dominican Fray Alonso de Espinosa in *Del origen y Milagros de la Santa Imagen de Nuestra Señora de Candelaria* [On the Origin and Miracles Performed by the Holy Image of Our Lady of La Candelaria] (Seville, 1594), a work of the Marian cult that includes in its pages an ethnography and a topography of Tenerife. As scholars have argued, Lope probably met Viana in Seville through his friend and fellow poet Juan de Arguijo while Viana was finishing *Las Antigüedades*. It is quite possible, as José Miguel Martínez Torrejón notes, that *Los guanches* may have been represented in Gran Canaria in 1604 during the festivities of *Corpus Christi*: "No hay pruebas documentales de la representación de esta comedia, pero los archivos de la catedral de Gran Canaria muestran que hubo ocasión de hacerlo allí. En 1604, en el marco de las habituales representaciones teatrales en torno a la fiesta del Corpus, se solicitó permiso del obispo para representar una comedia de Lope. . . . no se menciona el título, pero la coincidencia de fechas nos hace pensar si no se trataría de *Los guanches*" (There is no documentary evidence of the representation of this play, but the archives of the cathedral of Gran Canaria show that it could have been represented there. In 1604, a request was sent to the bishop to allow the staging of one of Lope's plays as part of the customary representations for the festivity of *Corpus Christi*. . . . the request does not mention the title of the play in question, but the coincidence in the dates makes us think it could have been *Los guanches*). Prologue to *Los guanches de Tenerife*, 780.

4. The question of space and the representation of Tenerife has not been explored in depth in critical interpretations of *Los guanches*. Instead, most studies have focused on the ethnographic, anthropological, and ideological aspects of the play by exploring its connection to the small corpus of "American comedias" written by Lope. See in this respect José A. Madrigal, "El discurso primitivista en las obras de colonización de Lope de Vega" [Primitivist Discourse in Lope de Vegas's Works Dealing with Colonization], *Círculo: Revista de Cultura* 20 (1991): 147–155; Jack Weiner, "La guerra y la paz espirituales en tres comedias de Lope de Vega" [War and Spiritual Peace in Three Plays by Lope de Vega], *Revista de Estudios Hispánicos* 17 (1983): 65–79; Isabel Castells,"'Suele amor trocar con Marte las armas': la conquista erótica y militar del nuevo mundo en tres comedias de Lope de Vega" ["Love Usually Trades Weapons with Mars":

The Military and Erotic Conquest of the New World in Three plays by Lope de Vega], *Anuario Lope de Vega* 4 (1998): 87–96; and Eyda M. Merediz, *Refracted Images: The Canary Islands through a New World Lens* (Tempe: Arizona Center for Medieval and Renaissance Studies, 2004). All these critics have devoted special attention to the "techniques of othering" employed by Lope to represent both *guanches* and Amerindians in his theater. For brief allusions to the significance of geography in *Los guanches* (only in the restricted context of the Spanish conquest of the Canaries) see Sebastián La Nuez y Caballero, "Las Canarias en la obra de Lope de Vega" [The Canaries in the Work of Lope de Vega], *Anuario de Estudios Atlánticos* 10 (1964): 11–159; Carlos Brito Díaz, "Visiones del indígena canario en el teatro español del Siglo de Oro" [Representations of Native Canarians in Golden Age Spanish Theater], *Revista de Literatura* 61 (1999): 225–237; and Florencia Calvo, "La desaparición del conflicto: la comicidad como una opción ideológica en *Los guanches de Tenerife* de Lope de Vega" [Erasing Conflict: Humor as an Ideological Strategy in Lope de Vega's *Los guanches de Tenerife*], *Rilce* 17, no.1 (2001): 33–44.

5. The image of the Canaries in ancient literature has been exhaustively discussed by Antonio Cabrera Perera in *Las Islas Canarias en el mundo clásico* [The Canary Islands in the Classical World] (Santa Cruz de Tenerife: Vice-Consejería de Cultura y Deportes y Gobierno Canario, 1988), 53–78; and Marcos Martínez Hernández, *Las Islas Canarias de la Antigüedad al Renacimiento. Nuevos Aspectos* [The Canary Islands from Antiquity to the Renaissance. New Perspectives] (Santa Cruz de Tenerife: Cabildo de Tenerife y Centro de la Cultura Popular Canaria, 1996). For references to the archipelago in Greco-Roman mythology, see also Marcos Martínez Hernández, *Canarias en la mitología. Historia mítica del archipiélago* [The Canaries in Mythology. A Mythical History of the Archipelago] (Santa Cruz de Tenerife: Centro de la Cultura Popular Canaria, 1992). Jean Delumeau has also touched on the idyllic image of the islands in ancient myths in *History of Paradise: The Garden of Eden in Myth and Tradition*, trans. Matthew O'Connell (New York: Continuum, 1995). The changing picture of the Canaries that emerged from late medieval sources has been examined in detail by Theodore J. Cachey Jr. in "Petrarch, Boccaccio, and the New World Encounter," *Stanford Italian Review* 10 (1991): 45–59; Martínez Hernández, *Las Islas Canarias*; and Eyda M. Merediz, *Refracted Images*, 38–82. Felipe Fernández Armesto provides a summary of the explorations (Italian, Portuguese, and Spanish) on which these sources were based in *Before Columbus: Exploration and Colonization from the Mediterranean to the Atlantic, 1229–1492* (Philadelphia: University of Pennsylvania Press, 1987), 151–195.

6. The Castilian campaign in the Canaries began in the early 1400s with the seizure of Lanzarote, Fuerteventura, El Hierro, and La Gomera and culminated almost a century later with the conquest of Gran Canaria in 1483—where Fernández de Lugo also played a leading role—and finally of Tenerife in 1496. Fernández Armesto has offered a detailed account of the latter stage of the campaign and the ensuing colonization in *The Canary Islands after the Conquest*. For the specific case of Tenerife, see Antonio Rumeu de Armas, *La conquista de Tenerife: 1494–1496* [The Conquest of Tenerife: 1494–1496] (Santa Cruz de Tenerife: Aula de Cultura de Tenerife, 1975).

7. Gonzalo Fernández de Oviedo, *Sumario de la natural historia de las Indias*, ed. Álvaro Baraibar (Pamplona: Universidad de Navarra, 2010), 69.

8. Peter Mason, *El drago en el jardín del Edén. Las islas Canarias en la circulación transatlántica de imágenes en el mundo ibérico, siglos XVI–XVII* [The Dragon Tree in

the Garden of Eden. The Place of the Canary Islands in the Sixteenth- and Seventeenth-Century Transatlantic Traffic of Images in the Iberian World] (Madrid and Frankfurt: Iberoamericana/Vervuert, 2018), 31.

9. Gladys Robalino, introduction to *Female Amerindians in Early Modern Spanish Theater*, ed. Gladys Robalino (Lewisburg, PA: Bucknell University Press, 2014), 13.

10. Castells, "'Suele amor,'" 88.

11. In addition to Dacil, Castells has found incarnations of this type in the characters of Palca and Tacuana in *El nuevo mundo descubierto por Cristobal Colón* and in the character of Gualeva in *Arauco domado*. For a complementary discussion of these characters, see Melissa Figueroa, "Courting the Female Body: Towards a Poetics of the Conquest in Lope de Vega's *El Nuevo Mundo descubierto por Cristóbal Colón*," in *Female Amerindians*, 17–36; and María Quiroz Taub, "Love and Fury: The Evolution of Fresia in *Arauco domado* of Lope de Vega," in *Female Amerindians*, 183–214.

12. Louis Montrose, "The Work of Gender in the Discourse of Discovery," in *New World Encounters*, ed. Stephen Greenblatt (Berkeley: University of California Press, 1993), 178. Montrose has examined this process of gendering in the colonialist discourse of sixteenth-century Europe by focusing on one text, Walter Raleigh's *The Discoverie of the large, rich, and beautiful Empire of Guiana* (1596). His conclusions, however, have had far-reaching implications for postcolonial criticism, as Marianna Torgovnick's commentary on nineteenth-century European perceptions of Africa has demonstrated: "The masculine sexual metaphors of penetrating closed dark spaces no doubt help account for the West's attachment to the trope of [the] center, heart or core of Africa. [The] African landscape is to be entered, conquered; its reaches are to be reaped, enjoyed. The phallic semiology accompanies the imperialist topoi, a conjunction based on the assumption that if explorers are . . . 'manly,' then what they explore must be female." *Gone Primitive: Savage Intellects, Modern Lives* (Chicago: University of Chicago Press, 1990), 61.

13. For the impact of gender on early modern cosmography and cartography, see Caterina Albano, "Visible Bodies: Cartography and Anatomy," in *Literature, Mapping, and the Politics of Space in Early Modern Britain*, ed. Andrew Gordon and Bernhard Klein (Cambridge: Cambridge University Press, 2001), 89–106; and Benito Quintana, "*Damas indias*: America's Iconic Body and the Wars of Conquest in the Spanish Comedia," *Bulletin of the Comediantes* 62, no.1 (2010): 103–122. Quintana has included in his work reproductions of the allegorical figures of the continents found in Cesare Ripa's *Iconologia* (1593), an emblem book heavily influenced by Abraham Ortelius's *Theatrum Orbis Terrarum*, which shaped the geographical imagination of Europeans in the sixteenth and seventeenth centuries.

14. Abraham Ortelius, *Theatrum orbis terrarium* (Antwerp: Coppenium Diesth, 1570), 3, https://www.loc.gov/resource/g3200m.gct00126/?st=gallery.

15. Lope de Vega, *Los guanches de Tenerife*, ed. José Miguel Martínez Torrejón, vol. 2 of *Comedias de Lope de Vega. Parte X*, ed. Ramón Valdés and María Morrás (Lérida: Editorial Milenio-Universitat Atònoma de Barcelona, 2010), act 1, line 34. Text references are to the acts and lines of this edition.

16. José María Ruano, in *La puesta en escena de los teatros comerciales del Siglo de Oro* [Staging in Golden Age Commercial Theaters] (Madrid: Castalia, 2000), 264, has explained that this stage direction reflects the use of a *devadanera*, a wooden device shaped like an inverted pyramid that could be turned to show audiences different settings or environments on stage in a matter of seconds.

17. It would be difficult to identify a specific iconographic source for the opening of Lope's play. As Benito Quintana has noted in relation to the adoption of cosmographic and cartographic iconography in the Spanish comedia, "Renaissance painters—particularly the Florentine and Flemish Mannerists—promoted the iconic characteristics of America as a young, naked woman with warring attributes. Through books and printed engravings, the allegorical images of America became part of Europe's sixteenth- and seventeenth-century popular culture" ("*Damas indias*," 107). Despite this vagueness, Quintana has posited that the van der Straet drawing depicting Vespucci's encounter with America also inspired the playwright Luis Vélez de Guevara in act 1 of *Las palabras a los reyes y gloria de los Pizarros* [The Words Uttered to the Monarchs and the Glory of the Pizarros] (ca. 1625–1630), which describes the meeting between the conquistador Francisco Pizarro and the local female leader Tucapela.

18. Viana fleshed out the story of the relationship between Dacil and Castillo from a few lines he found in Espinosa's *Del origen*. Espinosa's text contained a note referring to a gentleman called Gonzalo Castillo, who married the daughter of King Taoro, one of Tenerife's chieftains. The name *Dacil* was later added by Viana in his poem. Neither Dacil nor Castillo are mentioned in Francisco López de Gómara's *Historia general de las Indias y conquista de México* [A General History of the Indies and the Conquest of Mexico] (1552), which devotes chapters 21–23 to the geography, ethnography, and history of the Canary Islands. Lope knew Gómara's text and may have consulted it for the composition of *Los guanches*.

19. For the impact of Lascasian thought on Espinosa's work, see also Antonio Sánchez Jiménez, "¿Leyenda negra o lascasianismo?: la polémica del Nuevo Mundo y la reescritura de la historia de *Los guanches de Tenerife*" [Black Legend or Lascasianism? New World Controversy and the Rewriting of History in *Los guanches de Tenerife*], in *La leyenda negra en el crisol de la comedia. El teatro del Siglo de Oro frente a los estereotipos antihispánicos* [The Black Legend in the Crucible of the Comedia. Golden Age Theater vis-à-vis Anti-Hispanic Stereotypes], ed. Yolanda Rodríguez Pérez and Antonio Sánchez Jiménez (Madrid and Frankfurt: Iberoamericana/Vervuert, 2016), 89–100.

20. In the encounter between Dacil and Castillo, Lope condensed the three love stories between *guanches* and Spaniards that Viana included in his epic. The presence of these stories in Viana's poem reflects, according to Mérediz (*Refracted Images*, 111), his opposition to the epic model represented by Alonso de Ercilla's *La Araucana* [The Araucaniad] (1569), in which love occupies a marginal position in relation to the heroic deeds of Araucanians and Europeans.

21. The pond and the pastoral environment where the encounter between Dacil and Castillo takes place in *Los guanches* echoes the landscape described in canto 5 of Viana's *Las Antigüedades*, which places the meeting between the conquistador and the princess in an "estanque . . . grande, / largo, espacioso y hecho de artificio" (A big, long, spacious pond, artfully made) surrounded by a "bosque y prado ameno" (a forest and a pleasant meadow). *Las Antigüedades*, 124.

22. This image of Amerindian women as friendly and eager to seduce constitutes, as Gladys Robalino has argued in relation to Fernando de Zárate's *La conquista de México* [The Conquest of Mexico] (ca. 1650–1661), an extremely "inaccurate representation of their encounter with the Spanish." "The Role of Amerindian Women in Fernando de Zárate's *La conquista de México*," in *Female Amerindians in Early Modern Spanish Theater*, ed. Gladys Robalino (Lewisburg, PA: Bucknell University Press, 2014), 39. Cit-

ing Blanca López de Mariscal's book *La figura femenina en los narradores testigos de la Conquista* [The Female Figure in Witness Accounts of the Conquest] (Ciudad de México, DF: Colegio de México, 1997), Robalino points out that "in Mesoamerica, when the Spaniards arrived, native husbands had to secure their wives in safe locations, and women would run away—often to the mountains—to hide from the Spaniards, who were known for their violence and abuses" ("The Role of Amerindian Women," 39).

23. A very similar image of America as a nude woman with a feathered headdress appears, as Quintana has noted ("*Damas indias*," 105–107), in Cesare Ripa's *Iconologia*. The emblems contained in Ripa's book circulated widely throughout Europe when Lope was writing *Los guanches*.

24. Melissa Figueroa also points out in this context the relation between conquest and sexual desire that lies behind Lope's decision to incorporate *La Deseada* [The Desired One] as one of the geographical settings in *El Nuevo Mundo descubierto por Cristóbal Colón*: "By mixing historical facts and fictional elements, Lope takes advantage of the rhetorical possibilities of the name of an island Columbus discovered in his second voyage . . . the incorporation of the island highlights the sexual character intrinsic to the colonizing process" ("Courting the Female Body," 30).

25. See also in this regard the remarks made by Manuel Alvar in *El romancero. Tradicionalidad y pervivencia* [The Medieval Ballad Collections. Tradition and Survival] (Barcelona: Planeta, 1970), 141, regarding the feminization of Muslim towns in medieval Castilian ballads, as well as in Veronika Ryjik's commentary (*Lope de Vega en la invención*, 105) on Lope's use of the image of a spear piercing the walls of Granada in his comedia *El cerco de Santa Fe* [The Siege of Santa Fe] (ca. 1596–1598).

26. According to Florencia Calvo, this scene underlines "la absoluta incomprensión de las convenciones neoplatónicas del amor por parte de los guanches" (the guanches' utter ignorance regarding Neoplatonic love conventions) ("La desaparición del conflicto," 36), a situation designed to produce laughter among the audience and thereby diffuse the inherent tensions resulting from the military and cultural clash between *guanches* and Spaniards. Fausta Antonucci, for her part, has referred to Manil's words in this scene as representing "una visión de las cosas rebajada con respecto a los ideales más elevados de los héroes o de los nobles" (a view of things below the lofty ideals embraced by heroes and nobles). *El salvaje en la comedia del Siglo de Oro. Historia de un tema de Lope a Calderón* [The Wild Man in the Golden Age Comedia: Its History from Lope to Calderón] (Pamplona: Universidad de Navarra, 1995), 38. This view, as she points out, is characteristic of the fool or *gracioso* type in the comedia.

27. Anne McClintock, "Maidens, Maps, and Mines: The Reinvention of Patriarchy in Colonial South Africa," *South Atlantic Quarterly* 87 (1988): 151.

28. The impact that the *crónicas de Indias*—in particular Francisco López de Gómara's *Historia general de las Indias y conquista de México* (1552)—had on Lope's comedias has been amply documented by scholars. See in this respect Raquel Minián de Alfie, "Lope, lector de cronistas de Indias" [Lope, Reader of the Chronicles of the Indies], *Filología* 11 (1965): 1–21; and Francisco Ruiz Ramón, *Celebración y catarsis*, 69–137, and "El héroe americano en Lope y Tirso: de la guerra de los hombres a la guerra de los dioses" [The American Hero in Lope and Tirso: From War Among Men to War Among the Gods], in *El mundo del teatro español en su Siglo de Oro: ensayos dedicados a John E. Varey* [The World of Spanish Theater in the Golden Age: Essays in Honor of John E. Varey], ed. José María Ruano de la Haza (Ottawa: Dovehouse, 1989), 229–248. Especially

relevant for the argument I present in this chapter is the intertextual relation Robert M. Shannon established in *Visions of the New World* between Gonzalo Fernández de Oviedo's *Historia general y natural de las Indias* and Lope's *El Nuevo Mundo descubierto por Cristóbal Colón*.

29. Gonzalo Fernández de Oviedo, *Historia general y natural de las Indias*, 1:280–281.

30. *Fernández de Oviedo's Chronicle of America: A New History for a New World*, ed. Kathleen Myers, trans. Nina M. Scott (Austin: University of Texas Press, 2007), 160. All subsequent translations from Fernández de Oviedo's work are from this edition.

31. José Rabasa, *Inventing America: Spanish Historiography and the Formation of Eurocentrism* (Norman: University of Oklahoma Press, 1993), 141.

32. Juan José Daneri, "Fernández de Oviedo's Pineapple and Cultural Authority in Imperial Spain," *Monographic Review/Revista Monográfica* 21 (2005): 27.

33. Rebecca Earle has also underlined the importance of fruits as symbols of the Americas in colonial writing: "With time the abundance of syrupy tropical fruits came to symbolize the grandeur and magnificence of the colonies for both residents and the newly arrived." *The Body of the Conquistador: Food, Race and the Colonial Experience in Spanish-America, 1492–1700* (New York: Cambridge University Press, 2013), 129.

34. For more details on this emblem and how it relates to the representation of Dacil in *Los guanches*, see Javier Lorenzo, "Una adelfa en tierras extrañas: emblemática y misoginia en la *Comedia famosa de los guanches de Tenerife y conquista de Canaria*" [An Oleander in Strange Lands: Emblematics and Misogyny in the *Comedia famosa de los guanches de Tenerife y conquista de Canaria*], *Anuario Lope de Vega* 23 (2017): 485–498.

35. Ken Albala, *Eating Right in the Renaissance* (Berkeley: University of California Press, 2002), 232.

36. The cause of these negative effects was attributed, as Earle has explained (*The Body of the Conquistador*, 19–53), to the transformative potential of the diet on the humoral complexion of individuals according to Galenic medical theory.

37. Fabio López-Lázaro, "Sweet Food of Knowledge: Botany, Food, and Empire in the Early Modern Spanish Kingdoms," in *At the Table: Metaphorical and Material Cultures of Food in Medieval and Early Modern Europe*, ed. Timothy J. Tomasik and Juliann M. Vitullo (Leiden: Brepols, 2007), 3–5. The decision to limit the importation of New World ingredients had limited success, for, as Earle has pointed out (*The Body of the Conquistador*, 118–155), products like chilies, chocolate, and tomatoes were soon exported from the colonies and, in some cases, began to be cultivated in Europe.

38. Francisco de Medina, prologue, *Annotaciones a la poesía de Garcilaso* [Commentaries to the Poetry of Garcilaso], by Fernando de Herrera, ed. Inoria Pepe Sarno and José María Reyes Cano (Madrid: Cátedra, 2001), 189.

39. This tendency to Europeanize exotic food products is a point stressed by both Earle (*The Body of the Conquistador*, 156–186) and López-Lázaro ("Sweet Food of Knowledge"). They have attributed this phenomenon to the fear of "becoming Indian" if local crops and culinary habits were allowed to take root among the Spanish colonists.

40. Rebecca Weaver-Hightower, *Empire Islands: Castaways, Cannibals, and Fantasies of Conquest* (Minneapolis: University of Minnesota Press, 2007). Weaver-Hightower's study is mainly focused on French and Anglo-American castaway narratives of the nineteenth century. Despite the obvious chronological and cultural gap between these

works and Lope's comedias, her conclusions are quite valuable for a critical reading of *Los guanches.*

41. La Nuez y Caballero ("Las Canarias") and Merediz (*Refracted Images*) have also referred to the early disappearance of the language barrier in the play. As the latter has noted, by doing so, Lope "ignores Viana's claims of the lack of interpreters which prevented communication between Castillo and Dacil" (142).

42. José Miguel Martínez Torrejón has also seen a direct echo of Guevara's *Marco Aurelio* [Marcus Aurelius] (1528) in the speech against imperial ambition King Bencomo gives at the start of the play (act 1, lines 232–251), which, in his view, "se hace eco de su más célebre expresión, el cuento del villano del Danubio inserto en el *Marco Aurelio* de Fr. Antonio de Guevara" (echoes its most famous manifestation, the tale told by a villager from the Danube in Fray Antonio de Guevara's *Marco Aurelio*). Prologue to *Los guanches de Tenerife*, 778.

43. See Hernando de Acuña, "Al Rey nuestro señor," in *Varias poesías* [Collected Poems], ed. Luis F. Díaz Larios (Madrid: Cátedra, 1982), 328.

44. On the origin and history of the cult of the Virgin of La Candelaria in the Canaries, see Merediz, "Traveling Icons," 118–126.

45. This final showdown resulted in a Spanish victory at the second battle of Acentejo (December 1494), which effectively concluded the conquest of Tenerife. Prior to this victory, in May of 1494, the Spanish suffered a crushing defeat at the same spot that left many stranded on the island. Lope makes Castillo one of these marooned Spaniards in *Los guanches*, which explains why he appears dressed in barbarian attire in act 3.

CONCLUSION

1. David Woodward, "Maps and the Rationalization of Geographic Space," in *Circa 1492: Art in the Age of Exploration*, ed. J. A. Levinson (Washington, DC: National Gallery of Art, 1991), 87.

2. Lope de Vega, preface, *La campana de Aragón*, 328.

3. Stephen Gilman, "Lope, dramaturgo de la historia" [Lope, Dramatist of History], in *Lope de Vega y los orígenes del teatro español* [Lope de Vega and the Origin of Spanish Theater], ed. Manuel Criado de Val (Madrid: EDI-6, 1981), 19–26.

4. Luis Cabrera de Córdoba, *Relaciones de las cosas sucedidas en la corte de España desde 1599 hasta 1614* [Relation of the Things That Happened in the Court of Spain from 1599 to 1614], ed. Ricardo García Cárcel (Valladolid: Junta de Castilla y León, 1997), 59.

Bibliography

Acebrón, Julián. Prologue to *Comedia famosa de las paces de los reyes y judía de Toledo*, by Lope de Vega, 595–604. Vol. 2 of *Comedias de Lope de Vega. Parte VII*, edited by Enrico di Pastena. Lérida: Editorial Milenio-Universitat Atònoma de Barcelona, 1997.

Acuña, Hernando de. "Al Rey nuestro señor." In *Varias poesías*, edited by Luis F. Díaz Larios, 328. Madrid: Cátedra, 1982.

Adams, Kenneth, Ciaran Cosgrove, and James Whiston, eds. *Spanish Theatre: Studies in Honour of Victor F. Dixon*. Woodbridge, UK: Tamesis, 2001.

Álamos de Barrientos, Baltasar. *Discurso político al rey Felipe III al comienzo de su reinado*. Barcelona: Anthropos, 1990.

Albala, Ken. *Eating Right in the Renaissance*. Berkeley: University of California Press, 2002.

Albano, Caterina. "Visible Bodies: Cartography and Anatomy." In *Literature, Mapping, and the Politics of Space in Early Modern Britain*, edited by Andrew Gordon and Bernhard Klein, 89–106. Cambridge: Cambridge University Press, 2001.

Allan, Madera. "Shouting Distance: Local History and a Global Empire in Lope de Vega's *Famosa comedia del nuevo mundo descubierto por Cristóbal Colón*." In *Imagining Early Modern Histories*, edited by Allison Kavey and Elizabeth Ketner, 13–26. Farnham, UK: Ashgate, 2016.

Allen, John Jay, and José María Ruano de la Haza. *Los teatros comerciales del siglo XVII y la escenificación de la comedia*. Madrid: Castalia, 1994.

Allen, Paul C. *Philip III and the Pax Hispanica, 1598–1621: The Failure of Grand Strategy*. New Haven: Yale University Press, 2000.

Alonso Acero, Beatriz. *España y el Norte de África en los siglos XVI y XVII*. Madrid: Síntesis, 2017.

———. *Orán-Mazalquivir, 1589–1639: una sociedad española en la frontera de Berbería*. Madrid: Consejo Superior de Investigaciones Científicas, 2000.

Alvar, Manuel. *El romancero. Tradicionalidad y pervivencia*. Barcelona: Planeta, 1970.

Amezcua, José. "El espacio simbólico: el caso del teatro español del Siglo de Oro." *Signos* 1 (1987): 291–301.

———. *Espectáculo, texto y fiesta. Juan Ruiz de Alarcón y el teatro de su tiempo*. Iztapalapa, Mexico: Universidad Autónoma Metropolitana Iztapalapa, 1990.

———. "Hacia el centro: espacio e ideología en la *Comedia nueva*." In *Espectáculo, texto y fiesta. Juan Ruiz de Alarcón y el teatro de su tiempo*, edited by José Amezcua and Serafín González, 159–172. Iztapalapa, México: Universidad Autónoma Metropolitana, 1990.

Anderson, Benedict. *Imagined Communities: Reflections on the Origin and Spread of Nationalism*. London: Verso, 2006.

Antonucci, Fausta. *El salvaje en la comedia del Siglo de Oro. Historia de un tema de Lope a Calderón*. Pamplona: Universidad de Navarra, 1995.

———. "La tradición manuscrita e impresa de *El mejor alcalde, el rey*, desde finales del siglo XVII hasta finales del siglo XVIII." *Anuario Lope de Vega* 27 (2022): 262–298. https://doi.org/10.5565/rev/anuariolopedevega.446.

Arbesú, David. "*Las famosas asturianas* y los tratados de nobleza: otra comedia histórico-genealógica de Lope de Vega." *Hispanófila* 183 (June 2018): 215–229. https://doi.org/10.1353/hsf.2018.0027.

———. Prologue to *Las famosas asturianas*, by Lope de Vega, 157–173. Vol. 2 of *Comedias de Lope de Vega. Parte XVIII*, edited by Adrián J. Sáez and Antonio Sánchez Jiménez. Madrid: Gredos, 2019.

Arellano, Ignacio. "Valores visuales de la palabra en el espacio escénico del Siglo de Oro." *Revista Canadiense de Estudios Hispánicos* 19, no. 3 (Spring 1995): 411–443. https://www.jstor.org/stable/27763210.

Argensola, Lupercio Leonardo. "La Alejandra." In *Tragedias*, edited by Luigi Giuliani, 3–156. Zaragoza: Prensas Universitarias de Zaragoza, 2009.

Arizaleta, Amaia. "Una historia en el margen: Alfonso VIII de Castilla y la judía de Toledo." *Cahiers d'études hispaniques médiévales* 28 (2005): 37–68. https://www.persee.fr/doc/cehm_0396-9045_2005_num_28_1_1694.

Armas, Frederick A. de. "Passion, Treason, and Blindness in Lope de Vega's *Las paces de los reyes*." In *Studies in the Spanish Golden Age: Cervantes and Lope de Vega*, edited by Dana B. Drake and José A. Madrigal, 65–75. Miami: Ediciones Universal, 1978.

Artigas, María del Carmen. "Erotismo en *El mejor alcalde, el rey*." *Bulletin of Hispanic Studies* 71, no. 2 (1994): 185–196. https://doi.org/10.1080/1475382942000371185.

———. "*Las paces de los reyes y la judía de Toledo* de Lope de Vega: una aproximación al lenguaje equívoco." *Explicación de Textos Literarios* 27, no. 1 (1998–1999): 1–13.

Assunto, Rosario. *Filosofia del giardino e filosofía nel giardino: saggi di teoría e storia dell'estica*. Roma: Bulzoni, 1981.

Asunción Flórez Asensio, María. "'Cantaron desta suerte . . .': funciones de la música en el auto *Bodas entre el alma y el amor divino* de Lope de Vega, trasposición a lo divino de las Bodas Reales de 1599." *Anuario Lope de Vega* 18 (2012): 233–255.

Ayala Martínez, Carlos. "The Episcopate and Reconquest in the Times of Alfonso VII of Castile and León." In *Between Sword and Prayer: Warfare and Medieval Clergy in Cultural Perspective*, edited by Radoslaw Kotecki, Jacek Maciejewski, and John S. Ottet, 207–232. Leiden: Brill, 2018.

Badía, Mindy, and Bonnie L. Gasior, eds. *Crosscurrents: Transatlantic Perspectives on Early Modern Spanish Drama*. Lewisburg, PA: Bucknell University Press, 2006.

Baron, Hans. *In Search of Florentine Civic Humanism: Essays in the Transition from Medieval to Modern Thought*. Vol. 1. Princeton: Princeton University Press, 1988.

Barreiro Mallón, Baudilio. "La Audiencia de Galicia en la época de Felipe II." In *El reino de Galicia en la monarquía de Felipe II*, edited by Antonio Eiras Roel, 191–213. Santiago de Compostela: Xunta de Galicia, 1998.

Barros, Carlos, ed. *Xudeus e conversos na historia. Actas do Congreso Internacional, Ribadavia 14–17 de outubro de 1991*. Santiago de Compostela: Editorial de la Historia, 1994.

Bass, Laura R., and Margaret R. Greer, eds. *Approaches to Teaching Early Modern Spanish Drama*. New York: Modern Language Association of America, 2006.

Beaumont, Alexander. "Literary Studies after the Spatial Turn." *Journal of Urban Cultural Studies* 3, no. 3 (2016): 395–405. https://doi.org/10.1386/jucs.3.3.395_1.

Benítez Sánchez-Blanco, Rafael. *Heroicas decisiones: la monarquía católica y los moriscos*. Valencia: Institució Alfons el Magnànim/Diputació de València, 2001.

———. "The Religious Debate in Spain." In *The Expulsion of the Moriscos from Spain: A Mediterranean Diaspora*, edited by Mercedes García Arenal and Gerard A. Wiegers, 102–131. Leiden: Brill, 2014.

Besga Marroquín, Armando. *Orígenes Hispano-godos del Reino de Asturias*. Oviedo: Real Instituto de Estudios Asturianos, 2000.

Beusterien, John. "Lope de Vega's *Auto sacramental de la circuncisión y sangría de Cristo*: A Focal Point of Antisemitism in Seventeenth-Century Spain." *Hispanic Review* 72, no. 3 (2004): 357–374. https://www.jstor.org/stable/3247123.

Bhaduri, Saugata. "Polycolonial Angst: Representations of Spain in Early Modern English Drama." In *Theater Cultures within Globalising Empires: Looking at Early Modern England and Spain*, edited by Joachim Küpper and Leonie Pawlita, 150–159. Berlin: De Gruyter, 2018.

Biedma Torrecillas, Aurora. "Influencia del vestuario en el teatro del Siglo de Oro." In *Moda y sociedad. Estudios sobre educación, lenguaje e historia del vestido*, edited by Emilio J. García Wiedemann and María Isabel Montoya Ramírez, 125–134. Granada: Universidad de Granada, 1998.

Bingham Kirby, Carol. "Observaciones preliminares sobre el teatro histórico de Lope de Vega." In *Lope de Vega y los orígenes del teatro español. Actas del I Congreso Internacional sobre Lope de Vega*, edited by Manuel Criado de Val, 329–337. Madrid: Edi-6, 1981.

Binotti, Lucia. "*Restauratio imperii, restitutio linguae*: The Sixteenth-Century Spanish Historiographical Tradition and the Linguistic Definition of the Middle Ages." In *Recuerde el alma dormida: Medieval and Early Modern Spanish Essays in Honor of Frank Dominguez*, edited by John K. Moore Jr. and Adriano Duque, 39–77. Newark, DE: Juan de la Cuesta, 2009.

Botella Llusiá, José, and Antonio Fernández de Molina, eds. *Marañón en Toledo (sobre "Elogio y nostalgia de Toledo")*. Cuenca: Ediciones de la Universidad de Castilla-La Mancha, 1999.

Boyer, Harriet P. "*Las famosas asturianas* y la mujer heroica." In *Lope de Vega y los orígenes del teatro español*, edited by Manuel Criado de Val, 479–484. Madrid: EDI-6, 1981.

Braudel, Fernand. *The Mediterranean and the Mediterranean World in the Age of Philip II*. Translated by Siân Reynolds. Vol. 1. New York: Harper & Row, 1972.

Braun, Harald E. *Juan de Mariana and Early Modern Spanish Political Thought*. Aldershot, UK: Ashgate, 2007.

Brito Díaz, Carlos. "Visiones del indígena canario en el teatro español del Siglo de Oro." *Revista de Literatura* 6 (1999): 225–237.

Brownlee, Marina S., and Hans S. Gumbrecht, eds. *Cultural Authority in Golden Age Spain*. Baltimore: Johns Hopkins University Press, 1995.

Bunes Ibarra, Miguel Ángel de. "The Expulsion of the Moriscos in the Context of Philp III's Mediterranean Policy." In *The Expulsion of the Moriscos from Spain: A Mediterranean Diaspora*, edited by Mercedes García Arenal and Gerard A. Wiegers, 37–59. Leiden: Brill, 2014.

Burgos Esteban, Francisco. "Los estatutos de limpieza y sus pruebas en el siglo XVII: la figura del converso en denuncias y testimonios." In *Xudeus e conversos na historia. Actas do Congreso Internacional, Ribadavia 14–17 de outubro de 1991*, edited by Carlos Barros, 359–381. Santiago de Compostela: Editorial de la Historia, 1994.

Burningham, Bruce. "Beleaguered Hegemony and Triangular Desire in Lope de Vega's *Las famosas asturianas* and John Ford's *Stagecoach*." *Bulletin of the Comediantes* 56, no. 1 (2004): 115–142. https://doi.org/10.1353/boc.2004.0024.

Cabal, Constantino. *Alfonso II, El Casto*. Madrid: Ediciones GEA, 1991.

Caballero Fernández-Rufete, Carmelo. "La música en el teatro clásico." In *Historia del teatro español*, edited by Javier García Calvo, 677–716. Vol. 1. Madrid: Gredos, 2003.

Cabrera de Córdoba, Luis. *Relaciones de las cosas sucedidas en la corte de España desde 1599 hasta 1614*. Edited by Ricardo García Cárcel. Valladolid: Junta de Castilla y León, 1997.

Cabrera Perera, Antonio. *Las Islas Canarias en el mundo clásico*. Santa Cruz de Tenerife: Vice-Consejería de Cultura y Deportes y Gobierno Canario, 1988.

Cachey, Theodore J., Jr. "Petrarch, Boccaccio, and the New World Encounter." *Stanford Italian Review* 10 (1991): 45–59.

Calvo, Florencia. "La desaparición del conflicto: la comicidad como una opción ideológica en *Los guanches de Tenerife* de Lope de Vega." *Rilce* 17, no.1 (2001): 33–44.

Camacho Platero, Luzmila. "*Las famosas asturianas*: celebración de la castidad y la mujer varonil." In *Cuatro triunfos áureos y otros dramaturgos del Siglo de Oro*, edited by Serafín González García and Lillian von der Walde Moheno, 497–510. Ciudad de México, DF: Colegio de México, 2010.

———. "Political and Gender Transgressions in Lope de Vega's *La varona castellana*." *West Virginia University Philological Papers* 51 (2004): 1–11.

Campbell, Brian. *Rivers and the Power of Ancient Rome*. Chapel Hill: University of North Carolina Press, 2012.

Canavaggio, Jean. *Cervantes dramaturge. Un théâtre à naître*. Paris: Presses Universitaires de France, 1977.

Cañadas, Iván. "Nation, Empire, and Local Community in Lope de Vega's Peasant Drama and *El nuevo mundo descubierto por Cristóbal Colón*." *Journal of Iberian and Latin American Studies* 8, no. 2 (2002): 81–92.

Cardaillac, Louis. *Moriscos y cristianos: un enfrentamiento polémico (1492–1640)*. Ciudad de México, DF: Fondo de Cultura Económica, 1979.

Carey-Webb, Allen. *Making Subject(s): Literature and the Emergence of National Identity*. New York: Garland Publishing, 1998.

———. "Other-Fashioning: The Discourse of Empire and Nation in Lope de Vega's *El nuevo mundo descubierto por Cristóbal Colón*." In *Amerindian Images and the Legacy of Columbus*, edited by René Jara and Nicholas Spadaccini, 425–451. Minneapolis: University of Minnesota Press, 1992.

Carranza, Paul. "Garcilaso's Third Eclogue, Verses 65–68: The Tagus River, Exile, and Caesar's Campaign in Gaul." *Revista Canadiense de Estudios Hispánicos* 41, no. 3 (2017): 499–524. https://www.jstor.org/stable/26393651.

Carreño, Antonio. "La fuerza de las historias representadas: Lope de Vega y las alegorías del poder." In *El teatro del Siglo de Oro ante los espacios de la crítica: encuentros y revisiones*, edited by Enrique García Santo-Tomás, 205–236. Madrid and Frankfurt: Iberoamericana/Vervuert, 2002.

Carrión, María M. "The Balcony of the *Chapín*, or the Vain Architecture of Shoes in Early Modern Spain." *Journal of Spanish Cultural Studies* 14, no. 2 (2013): 143–158. https://doi.org/10.1080/14636204.2013.868242.

Cartagena Calderón, José R. "Lope and the Matter of America: Approaching the *Comedia* from a Trans-Atlantic Perspective." In *Approaches to Teaching Early Modern Spanish Drama*, edited by Margaret R. Greer and Laura R. Bass, 152–158. New York: Modern Language Association of America, 2006.

———. *Masculinidades en obras: el drama de la hombría en la España imperial.* Newark, DE: Juan de la Cuesta, 2008.

Carter, Robin. "History and Poetry: A Re-Examination of Lope de Vega's *El mejor alcalde, el rey.*" *Forum for Modern Language Studies* 16 (1980): 193–233.

Cascardi, Anthony. *Ideologies of History in the Spanish Golden Age*. University Park: Penn State University Press, 1997.

Case, Thomas E. "El indio y el moro en las comedias de Lope de Vega." In *Looking at the Comedia in the Year of the Quincentennial: Proceedings of the 1992 Symposium on Golden Age Drama at the University of Texas*, edited by Barbara Mújica and Sharon D. Voros, 13–21. Lanham, MD: University Press of America, 1992.

———. "Lope and the Moriscos." *Bulletin of the Comediantes* 44, no. 2 (1992): 195–216.

———. "A Time for Heroines in Lope." In *The Perception of Women in Spanish Theater of the Golden Age*, edited by Anita K. Stoll and Dawn L. Smith, 202–219. Cranbury, NJ: Associated University Presses, 1991.

Castañeda, James A. "Preliminary Study." In *A Critical Edition of Lope de Vega's Las paces de los reyes y judía de Toledo*, edited by James A. Castañeda, 5–124. Chapel Hill: University of North Carolina Press, 1962.

Castells, Isabel. "'Suele amor trocar con Marte las armas': la conquista erótica y militar del nuevo mundo en tres comedias de Lope de Vega." *Anuario Lope de Vega* 4 (1998): 87–96.

Castillo, David. "Monumental Landscapes in the Society of the Spectacle: From *Fuenteovejuna* to New York." In *Spectacle and Topophilia: Reading Early Modern and Postmodern Hispanic Cultures*, edited by David Castillo and Bradley Nelson, 3 18. Nashville: Vanderbilt University Press, 2011.

Castillo, David, and Bradley Nelson. Introduction. In *Spectacle and Topophilia: Reading Early Modern and Postmodern Hispanic Cultures*, edited by David Castillo and Bradley Nelson, ix–xxiv. Nashville: Vanderbilt University Press, 2011.

Castillo, David, and Bradley Nelson, eds. *Spectacle and Topophilia: Reading Early Modern and Postmodern Hispanic Cultures.* Nashville: Vanderbilt University Press, 2011.

Castillo, Moisés. *Indios en escena: la representación del amerindio en el teatro del Siglo de Oro.* West Lafayette, IN: Purdue University Press, 2009.

Castillo, Susan. "Performing Encounters: Lope's *El nuevo mundo descubierto por Cristóbal Colón.*" *Bulletin of the Comediantes* 58, no. 1 (2006): 57–72. https://doi.org/10.1353/boc.2006.0003.

Catalán, Diego. "España en su historiografía: de objeto a sujeto de la historia." Introduction to *Los españoles en su historia*, by Ramón Menéndez Pidal, 9–67. Madrid: Espasa-Calpe, 1982.

Cazal, Françoise, Christophe González, and Marc Vitse, eds. *Homenaje a Frédéric Serralta. El espacio y sus representaciones en el teatro español del Siglo de Oro.* Madrid and Frankfurt: Iberoamericana/Vervuert, 2002.

Cervantes Saavedra, Miguel de. *Don Quijote de la Mancha.* Edited by Francisco Rico. 2 vols. Madrid: Real Academia Española, 2015.

———. *Don Quixote.* Translated by Edith Grosman. New York: HarperCollins, 2003.

———. *El rufián dichoso.* Edited by Valentín Núñez Rivera. In *Miguel de Cervantes. Comedias y tragedias*, edited by Luis Gómez Canseco, 364–467. Madrid: Real Academia Española, 2015.

Childers, William. "'Ese tan borrado escrito': The Deconstruction of Lope's Religious Theater in *El retablo de las maravillas* and *El rufián dichoso*." *Bulletin of the Comediantes* 56, no. 2 (2004): 241–268. https://doi.org/10.1353/boc.2004.0000.

Clavería, Carlos. "Notas generales sobre los godos y su proyección histórica." *Cuadernos Hispanoamericanos* 280–282 (1973): 541–556.

———. "Reflejos del goticismo español en la fraseología del Siglo de Oro." In *Studia Philologica: Homenaje a Dámaso Alonso*, 357–372. Vol. 1. Madrid: Gredos, 1960.

Coates, Geraldine. "The 1541 *Crónica general* and the Historical Theater of Juan de la Cueva and Lope de Vega: An Epic Debt." *Bulletin of the Comediantes* 60, no. 1 (2008): 1–29. https://doi.org/10.1353/boc.2008.0015.

———. "Lope de Vega, the Chronicle-Legend Plays and Collective Memory." In *A Companion to Lope de Vega*, edited by Alexander Samson and Jonathan Thacker, 131–146. Woodbridge, UK: Tamesis, 2008.

Cochrane, Eric. *Historians and Historiography in the Italian Renaissance.* Chicago: University of Chicago Press, 1981.

Cohen, Walter. *Drama of a Nation: Public Theater in Renaissance England and Spain.* Ithaca: Cornell University Press, 1985.

Copello, Fernando. "Milieu naturel et jardín à l'époque de Philippe II: à propos de *l'Agricultura de jardines* de Gregorio de los Ríos." In *Le milieu naturel en Espagne et en Italie. savoirs et representations*, edited by Nathalie Peyrebonne and Pauline Renoux-Caron, 105–120. Paris: Presses Sorbonne Nouvelle, 2011.

Cosgrove, Denis. "Spectacle and Society: Landscape and Theater in Premodern and Postmodern Cities." In *Understanding Ordinary Landscapes*, edited by Paul Groth and Todd W. Bressi, 99–110. New Haven: Yale University Press, 1997.

Covarrubias Horozco, Sebastián de. *Tesoro de la lengua castellana o española.* Madrid: Castalia, 1995.

Criado de Val, Manuel, ed. *Lope de Vega y los orígenes del teatro español. Actas del I Congreso Internacional sobre Lope de Vega.* Madrid: Edi-6, 1981.

Cuart Moner, Baltasar. "La larga marcha hacia las historias de España en el siglo XVI." In *La construcción de las historias de España*, edited by Ricardo García Cárcel, 45–126. Madrid: Marcial Pons, 2004.

Dadson, Trevor. "Official Rhetoric versus Local Reality: Propaganda and the Expulsion of the Moriscos." In *Rhetoric and Reality in Early Modern Spain*, edited by Richard J. Pym, 1–25. Woodbridge, UK: Tamesis, 2006.

Dandelet, Thomas. *The Renaissance of Empire in Early Modern Europe.* New York: Cambridge University Press, 2014.

Daneri, Juan José. "Fernández de Oviedo's Pineapple and Cultural Authority in Imperial Spain." *Monographic Review/Revista Monográfica* 21 (2005): 26–39.

Dapaz Strout, Lilia. "Psicomaquia o el conflicto de Eros y Logos en *Las paces de los reyes y judía de Toledo.*" In *Studies in Honor of William C. McCrary*, edited by Robert Fiore, 77–90. Lincoln, NE: Society of Spanish and Spanish-American Studies, 1986.

Darst, David. "The Unity of *Las paces de Toledo y judía de Toledo.*" *Symposium* 25 (1975): 225–235.

Dawson, David. *Christian Figural Reading and the Fashioning of Identity.* Berkeley: University of California Press, 2004.

Delgado, María M., and David T. Gies, eds. *A History of Theater in Spain.* Cambridge: Cambridge University Press, 2012.

Delumeau, Jean. *History of Paradise: The Garden of Eden in Myth and Tradition.* Translated by Matthew O'Connell. New York: Continuum, 1995.

Deyermond, Alan S. "The Death and Rebirth of Visigothic Spain in the *Estoria de España.*" *Revista Canadiense de Estudios Hispánicos* 9, no. 3 (1985): 345–367.

Dixon, Victor. "Lope de Vega and America: *The New World* and *Arauco Tamed.*" *Renaissance Studies* 6, no. 3/4 (1992): 249–269.

Domínguez Matito, Francisco, and María Luisa Lobato López, eds. *Memoria de la palabra. Actas del VI Congreso de la Asociación Internacional Siglo de Oro.* Madrid: Iberoamericana-Vervuert, 2004.

Drake, Dana B., and José A. Madrigal, eds. *Studies in the Spanish Golden Age: Cervantes and Lope de Vega.* Miami: Ediciones Universal, 1978.

Dubert, Isidro. "Galicia en la incorporación de Portugal, 1579–1581." In *El reino de Galicia en la monarquía de Felipe II*, edited by Antonio Eiras Roel, 139–168. Santiago de Compostela: Xunta de Galicia, 1998.

Dünne, Jörg. "'Ya la comedia es un mapa.' Cervantes y la teatralización del espacio geográfico." *Olivar* 13, no. 17 (2012): 33–54.

Dustagheer, Sarah. "Shakespeare and the Spatial Turn." *Literature Compass* 10, no. 7 (2013): 570–581.

Earle, Rebecca. *The Body of the Conquistador: Food, Race and the Colonial Experience in Spanish-America, 1492–1700.* Cambridge: Cambridge University Press, 2013.

Ehlers, Benjamin. *Between Christians and Moriscos: Juan de Ribera and Religious Reform in Valencia, 1568–1614.* Baltimore: Johns Hopkins University Press, 2006.

Eiras Roel, Antonio, ed. *El reino de Galicia en la monarquía de Felipe II.* Santiago de Compostela: Xunta de Galicia, 1998.

Eiroa, Sofía. "Galicia y los gallegos, tópicos y contrastes en Tirso de Molina: *Mari Hernández, la Gallega.*" *Hesperia: Anuario de Filología Hispánica* 5 (2002): 51–67.

Elam, Keir. *The Semiotics of Theater and Drama.* London: Methuen, 1980.

Elliott, J. H. *Imperial Spain, 1469–1716.* 3rd ed. London: Penguin, 1990.

Escudero Baztán, Juan Manuel, and Victoriano Roncero López, eds. *La violencia en el mundo hispánico en el Siglo de Oro.* Madrid: Visor, 2010.

Faverón Patriau, Gustavo. "Siete años en el purgatorio: judíos y cristianos en *Las paces de los reyes y judía de Toledo* de Lope de Vega." *Bulletin of the Comediantes* 58, no. 2 (2006): 359–382.

Fernández Albaladejo, Pablo, ed. *Monarquía, imperio y pueblos en la España moderna. Actas de la IV reunión científica de la Asociación Española de Historia Moderna.* Alicante: Caja de Ahorros del Mediterráneo/Universidad de Alicante, 1997.

Fernández Armesto, Felipe. *Before Columbus: Exploration and Colonization from the Mediterranean to the Atlantic, 1229–1492.* Philadelphia: University of Pennsylvania Press, 1987.

———. *The Canary Islands after the Conquest: The Making of a Colonial Society in the Early Sixteenth Century*. Oxford: Clarendon Press, 1982.

Fernández Catón, José María. *El reino de León en la alta Edad Media*. 3 vols. León: Centro de Estudios e Investigación San Isidoro, 1995.

Fernández Cava, Salvador. *Constantino de la Fuente (1505–1559). El camino de la verdad*. Ciudad Real: Almud, 2007.

Fernández Cortizo, Camilo. "El señorío rural gallego en tiempos de Felipe II." In *El reino de Galicia en la monarquía de Felipe II*, edited by Antonio Eiras Roel, 379–408. Santiago de Compostela: Xunta de Galicia, 1998.

Fernández de Oviedo, Gonzalo. *Fernández de Oviedo's Chronicle of America: A New History for a New World*. Edited by Kathleen Myers. Translated by Nina M. Scott. Austin: University of Texas Press, 2007.

———. *Historia general y natural de las Indias, islas y tierra-firme del mar océano*. Edited by José Amador de los Ríos. Vol. 1. Madrid: Real Academia de la Historia, 1851.

———. *Sumario de la natural historia de las Indias*. Edited by Álvaro Baraibar. Pamplona: Universidad de Navarra, 2010.

Feros, Antonio. "Reflexiones atlánticas: identidades étnicas y nacionales en el mundo hispánico moderno." In Vol. 2 of *Cultura escrita y sociedad*, ed. Verónica Sierra Blas (2006): 85–115.

———. "Rhetorics of the Expulsion." In *The Expulsion of the Moriscos from Spain: A Mediterranean Diaspora*, edited by Mercedes García Arenal and Gerard A. Wiegers, 60–101. Leiden: Brill, 2014.

Figueroa, Melissa. "Courting the Female Body: Towards a Poetics of the Conquest in Lope de Vega's *El Nuevo Mundo descubierto por Cristóbal Colón*." In *Female Amerindians in Early Modern Spanish Theater*, edited by Gladys Robalino, 17–36. Lewisburg, PA: Bucknell University Press, 2014.

Fiore, Robert, ed. *Studies in Honor of William C. McCrary*. Lincoln, NE: Society of Spanish and Spanish-American Studies, 1986.

Flórez Asensio, Asunción. "'Cantaron desta suerte . . .': funciones de la música en el auto *Bodas entre el alma y el amor divino* de Lope de Vega, trasposición a lo divino de las Bodas Reales de 1599." *Anuario Lope de Vega* 18 (2012): 233–255.

Francomano, Emily. "The Legend of the *Tributo de las cien doncellas*: Women as Warweavers and the Coin of Salvation." *Revista Canadiense de Estudios Hispánicos* 32, no. 1 (2007): 9–25.

Fuchs, Barbara. "Imperium Studies: Theorizing Early Modern Expansion." In *Postcolonial Moves: Medieval through Modern*, edited by Patricia Clare Ingham and Michelle R. Warren, 70–90. New York: Palgrave Macmillan, 2003.

———. *The Poetics of Piracy: Emulating Spain in English Literature*. Philadelphia: University of Pennsylvania Press, 2013.

Fuchs, Barbara, and Yuen-Gen Liang. "A Forgotten Empire: The Spanish-North African Borderlands." *Journal of Spanish Cultural Studies* 12, no. 3 (2012): 261–273.

Fuente Merás, Manuel de la. "La 'España imperial' y los distintos modos de pensar su identidad." *El Catoblepas* 38 (2005): 12–49.

Ganelin, Charles, and Howard Mancing, eds. *The Golden Age Comedia: Text, Theory, and Performance*. West Lafayette, IN: Purdue University Press, 1994.

Garau Amengual, Jaume, ed. *Pensamiento y literatura en los inicios de la modernidad*. New York: Instituto de Estudios Auriseculares, 2017.

García Arenal, Mercedes, and Miguel Ángel de Bunes Ibarra. *Los españoles y el norte de África: siglos XVI-XVIII*. Madrid: Mapfre, 1992.

García Arenal, Mercedes, and Gerard A. Wiegers, eds. *The Expulsion of the Moriscos from Spain: A Mediterranean Diaspora*. Leiden: Brill, 2014.

García Calvo, Javier, ed. *Historia del teatro español*. Madrid: Gredos, 2003.

García Cárcel, Ricardo, ed. *La construcción de las historias de España*. Madrid: Marcial Pons, 2004.

García Santo-Tomás, Enrique, ed. *El teatro del Siglo de Oro ante los espacios de la crítica: encuentros y revisiones*. Madrid and Frankfurt: Iberoamericana/Vervuert, 2002.

García Wiedemann, Emilio J., and María Isabel Montoya Ramírez, eds. *Moda y sociedad. Estudios sobre educación, lenguaje e historia del vestido*. Granada: Universidad de Granada, 1998.

Gasta, Chad M. *Imperial Stagings: Empire and Ideology in Transatlantic Theater of Early Modern Spain and the New World*. Chapel Hill: University of North Carolina Press, 2012.

Gelabert, Juan E. "1609: cuestiones de reputación." *Cartas de La Goleta* 2 (2008): 39–52. https://issuu.com/bibtun/docs/cartas_goleta_2.

Gerli, Michael. "*El retablo de las maravillas*: Cervantes' 'Arte nuevo de deshacer comedias.'" *Hispanic Review* 57, no. 4 (1989): 477–492.

Giesen, Christine. "Audacia y precaución: Constantino Ponce de la Fuente, defensor del protestantismo." *Res Publica. Revista de Historia de las Ideas Políticas* 20, no. 2 (2017): 227–241.

Gillies, John. *Shakespeare and the Geography of Difference*. Cambridge: Cambridge University Press, 1994.

Gilman, Stephen. "Lope, dramaturgo de la historia." In *Lope de Vega y los orígenes del teatro español*, edited by Manuel Criado de Val, 19–26. Madrid: EDI-6, 1981.

Giuliani, Luigi. "Consideraciones preliminares sobre la tragedia de los años de 1580." In *Lupercio Leonardo de Argensola. Tragedias*, edited by Luigi Giuliani, ix–xxi. Zaragoza: Prensas Universitarias de Zaragoza, 2009.

Goldmark, Matthew. "Settling Down: Itinerant Empire and the Ends of Conquest in *El burlador de Sevilla*." *Bulletin of Hispanic Studies* 96, no. 8 (2019): 799–814.

González, Aurelio. "Espacio y dramaturgia cervantina." In *Memoria de la palabra. Actas del VI Congreso de la Asociación Internacional Siglo de Oro*, edited by Francisco Domínguez Matito and María Luisa Lobato López, 897–904. Madrid and Frankfurt: Iberoamericana-Vervuert, 2004.

González García, Serafín, and Lillian von der Walde Moheno, eds. *Cuatro triunfos áureos y otros dramaturgos del Siglo de Oro*. Ciudad de México, DF: Colegio de México, 2010.

Gordon, Andrew, and Bernhard Klein, eds. *Literature, Mapping, and the Politics of Space in Early Modern Britain*. New York: Cambridge University Press, 2001.

Greenblatt, Stephen, ed. *New World Encounters*. Berkeley: University of California Press, 1993.

Greer, Margaret R. "Espacios teatrales: su significación dramática y social." In *Espacios de representación y espacios representados en el teatro áureo español*, edited by Francisco Sáez Raposo, 297–320. Barcelona: Bellaterra, 2011

Grieve, Patricia E. *The Eve of Spain: Myths of Origins in the History of Christian, Muslim, and Jewish Conflict*. Baltimore: Johns Hopkins University Press, 2009.

Griffin, Eric J. *English Renaissance Drama and the Specter of Spain: Ethnopoetics and Empire*. Philadelphia: University of Pennsylvania Press, 2009.

Griswold Morley, S., and Courtney Bruerton. *Cronología de las comedias de Lope de Vega*. Madrid: Gredos, 1968.

Hampton, Timothy. *Writing From History: The Rhetoric of Exemplarity in Renaissance Literature*. Ithaca: Cornell University Press, 1990.

Harvey, L. P. *Muslims in Spain 1500–1614*. Chicago: University of Chicago Press, 2005.

Hausser, Christian, and Horst Pietschmann. "Empire. The Concept and Its Problems in the Historiography on the Iberian Empires in the Early Modern Age." *Culture and History Digital Journal* 3, no. 1 (2014): 1–10. http://dx.doi.org/10.3989/chdj.2014.002.

Heras Santos, José Luis de las. *La justicia penal de los Austrias en la corona de Castilla*. Salamanca: Ediciones Universidad de Salamanca, 1991.

Hermenegildo, Alfredo. Introduction to *La gran Semíramis*, by Cristóbal de Virués, 11–87. *La gran Semíramis. Elisa Dido*. Edited by Alfredo Hermengildo. Madrid: Castalia, 2003.

Herrera, Fernando de. *Anotaciones a la poesía de Garcilaso*. Edited by Inoria Pepe and José María Reyes. Madrid: Cátedra, 2001.

Herrero Sánchez, Manuel. "Spanish Theories of Empire: A Catholic and Polycentric Monarchy." In *A Companion to Early Modern Spanish Imperial Political and Social Thought*, edited by Jörg Tellkamp, 17–52. Leiden: Brill, 2020.

Hess, Andrew C. "The Moriscos: An Ottoman Fifth Column in Sixteenth-Century Spain." *The American Historical Review* 74, no. 1 (1968): 1–25.

Hillgarth, J. N. *The Visigoths in History and Legend*. Toronto: Pontifical Institute of Mediaeval Studies, 2009.

Howard, Jean E. *Theater of a City: The Places of London Comedy, 1598–1642*. Philadelphia: University of Pennsylvania Press, 2009.

Huerta Calvo, Javier. "Espacios poéticos en el primer teatro clásico." In *Espacios de representación y espacios representados en el teatro áureo español*, edited by Francisco Sáez Raposo, 15–40. Barcelona: Bellaterra, 2011.

Irigoyen García, Javier. *Moors Dressed as Moors: Clothing, Social Distinction, and Ethnicity in Early Modern Iberia*. Toronto: University of Toronto Press, 2017.

Issacharoff, Michael. *Discourse as Performance*. Stanford: Stanford University Press, 1989.

Izquierdo Domingo, Amparo. "La importancia de la música y el baile en los autos lopianos." In *Fiesta y teatro en el Siglo de Oro: ámbito hispánico*, edited by Miguel Zugasti and Joseba Andoni Cuñado, 205–213. Toulouse: Presses Universitaires du Midi, 2019.

Jackson, John Brinkerhoff. *The Necessity for Ruins, and Other Topics*. Amherst: University of Massachusetts Press, 1980.

Kagan, Richard. *Clio and the Crown: The Politics of History in Medieval and Early Modern Spain*. Baltimore: Johns Hopkins University Press, 2009.

Kagan, Richard, and Geoffrey Parker, eds. *Spain, Europe, and the Atlantic: Essays in Honour of John H. Elliott*. Cambridge: Cambridge University Press, 1995.

Kamen, Henry. *Spain 1469–1714: A Society of Conflict*. 2nd ed. London: Longman, 1991.

Kantorowicz, Ernst. *The King's Two Bodies: A Study in Medieval Political Theory*. Princeton: Princeton University Press, 1997.

Kavey, Allison, and Elizabeth Ketner, eds. *Imagining Early Modern Histories*. Farnham, UK: Ashgate, 2016.

Kotecki, Radoslaw, Jacek Maciejewski, and John S. Ottet, eds. *Between Sword and Prayer: Warfare and Medieval Clergy in Cultural Perspective*. Leiden: Brill, 2018.

Küpper, Joachim, and Leonie Pawlita, eds. *Theater Cultures within Globalising Empires: Looking at Early Modern England and Spain*. Berlin: De Gruyter, 2018.

Larson, Donald R. "Rape, Redress, and Reintegration: Ritualized Social Drama in *El mejor alcalde, el rey*." In *La violencia en el mundo hispánico en el Siglo de Oro*, edited by Juan Manuel Escudero Baztán and Victoriano Roncero López, 125–136. Madrid: Visor, 2010.

Lasso de la Vega, Gabriel. *Tragedia de la honra de Dido restaurada*. Edited by Alfredo Hermenegildo. Kassel: Edition Reichenberger, 1986.

Lázaro Carreter, Fernando. *Lope de Vega: introducción a su vida y obra*. Madrid: Anaya, 1966.

Lees, Claire A., ed. *Medieval Masculinities: Regarding Men in the Middle Ages*. Minneapolis: University of Minnesota Press, 1994.

Lefebvre, Henri. *The Production of Space*. Translated by Donald Nicholson-Smith. London: Blackwell, 1991.

Lindenberger, Herbert. *Historical Drama. The Relation of Literature and Reality*. Chicago: University of Chicago Press, 1975.

Linehan, Peter. *History and the Historians of Medieval Spain*. Oxford: Clarendon Press, 1993.

López Cruz, Roser. "'Virgen bella, nuestras paces os encargo': *Las paces de los reyes y judía de Toledo* o la apuesta política por una imagen milagrosa." *Anuario Lope de Vega* 25 (2019): 257–280.

López de Mariscal, Blanca. *La figura femenina en los narradores testigos de la Conquista*. Ciudad de México, DF: Colegio de México, 1997.

López-Lázaro, Fabio. "Sweet Food of Knowledge: Botany, Food, and Empire in the Early Modern Spanish Kingdoms." In *At the Table: Metaphorical and Material Cultures of Food in Medieval and Early Modern Europe*, edited by Timothy J. Tomasik and Juliann M. Vitullo, 3–28. Leiden: Brepols, 2007.

Lorenzo, Javier. "Una adelfa en tierras extrañas: emblemática y misoginia en la Comedia famosa de *Los guanches de Tenerife y conquista de Canaria*." *Anuario Lope de Vega* 23 (2017): 485–498.

Lupher, David A. *Romans in a New World: Classical Models in Sixteenth-Century Spanish America*. Ann Arbor: University of Michigan Press, 2009.

Mackay, Ruth. *The Limits of Royal Authority: Resistance and Obedience in Seventeenth-Century Castile*. Cambridge: Cambridge University Press, 1999.

Madrigal, José A. "El discurso primitivista en las obras de colonización de Lope de Vega." *Círculo: Revista de Cultura* 20 (1991): 147–155.

Madroñal Durán, Abraham. "Dos comedias relacionadas con Illescas: *El caballero de Illescas* y *Las paces de los reyes*." In *Pensamiento y literatura en los inicios de la modernidad*, edited by Jaume Garau Amengual, 75–93. New York: Instituto de Estudios Auriseculares, 2017.

Maestro, Jesús. *La escena imaginaria. Poética del teatro de Miguel de Cervantes*. Madrid and Frankfurt: Iberoamericana/Vervuert, 2000.

Mantecón Movellán, Tomás, and Susana Truchuelo García. "La(s) frontera(s) exteriores e interiores de la Monarquía Hispánica: perspectivas historiográficas." *Historia Crítica* 59 (2016): 19–39.

Manzanares de Cirre, Manuela. "Las cien doncellas: trayectoria de una leyenda." *PMLA* 81, no. 3 (1966): 179–184.

Maravall, José Antonio. *El concepto de España en la Edad Media*. Madrid: Instituto de Estudios Políticos, 1964.

———. *Los factores de la idea de progreso en el renacimiento español*. Madrid: Real Academia de la Historia, 1963.

Mariana, Juan de. *La dignidad real y la educación del rey (De rege et regis institutione)*. Edited by L. Sánchez-Agesta. Madrid: Centro de Estudios Constitucionales, 1981.

———. *Historia de España*. Vol. 1. Madrid: Real Academia Española, 1950.

Marino, John A. *Becoming Neapolitan: Citizen Culture in Baroque Naples*. Baltimore: Johns Hopkins University Press, 2011.

Martín Largo, José Ramón. *La judía de Toledo: desde Lope de Vega hasta Franz Grillparzer*. Madrid: Brand, 2000.

Martín Moreno, Antonio. "Música, pasión y razón: la teoría de los afectos en el teatro y la música del Siglo de Oro." *Edad de Oro* 22 (2003): 321–360.

Martínez Hernández, Marcos. *Canarias en la mitología. Historia mítica del archipiélago*. Santa Cruz de Tenerife: Centro de la Cultura Popular Canaria, 1992.

———. *Las Islas Canarias de la Antigüedad al Renacimiento. Nuevos Aspectos*. Santa Cruz de Tenerife: Cabildo de Tenerife y Centro de la Cultura Popular Canaria, 1996.

Martínez Millán, José, ed. *Carlos V y la quiebra del humanismo político en Europa (1530–1558)*. Madrid: Sociedad Estatal para la Conmemoración de los Centenarios de Felipe II y Carlos V, 2001.

Martínez Torrejón, José Miguel. Prologue to *Los guanches de Tenerife*, by Lope de Vega, 771–788. Vol. 2 of *Comedias de Lope de Vega. Parte X*, edited by Ramón Valdés and María Morrás. Lérida: Editorial Milenio, 2010.

Mason, Peter. *El drago en el jardín del Edén. Las islas Canarias en la circulación transatlántica de imágenes en el mundo ibérico, siglos XVI–XVII*. Madrid and Frankfurt: Iberoamericana/Vervuert, 2018.

McClintock, Anne. "Maidens, Maps, and Mines: The Reinvention of Patriarchy in Colonial South Africa." *South Atlantic Quarterly* 87 (1988): 147–192.

McCrary, William. "Plot, Action, and Imitation: The Art of Lope's *Las paces de los reyes*." *Hipanófila* 48 (1973): 1–17.

McCurdy, Raymond. "The Bathing Nude in Golden Age Drama." *Romance Notes* 1, no. 1 (1959): 36–39.

McGrady, Donald. "Lope de Vega's *El mejor alcalde, el rey*: Its Italian *Novella* Sources and Its Influence Upon Manzoni's *I promessi sposi*." *Modern Language Review* 80, no. 3 (1985): 604–618.

McKendrick, Melveena. *Playing the King: Lope de Vega and the Limits of Conformity*. Woodbridge, UK: Tamesis, 2000.

———. *Woman and Society in the Spanish Drama of the Golden Age: A Study of the mujer varonil*. Cambridge: Cambridge University Press, 1974.

Meadows, Harrison. "Disruptive Marginality: The Representation of Wildness in Lope de Vega's Baroque Dramatic Art." *Romance Quarterly* 65, no. 4 (2018): 180–191.

Medina, Francisco de. Prologue to *Anotaciones a la poesía de Garcilaso*, by Fernando de Herrera, 187–203. Edited by Inoria Pepe Sarno and José María Reyes Cano. Madrid: Cátedra, 2001.

Menéndez Pelayo, Marcelino. *Estudios literarios sobre el teatro de Lope de Vega*. Vol. 5. Madrid: Librería General de Victoriano Suárez, 1925.

———. "Observaciones preliminares (I)." In *Obras de Lope de Vega publicadas por la Real Academia Española*, ix–xxi. Vol. 1. Madrid: Sucesores de Ribadeneyra, 1892.

Merediz, Eyda M. "Estudio crítico." In *Comedia la famosa de los guanches de Tenerife y conquista de Gran Canaria*, edited by Eyda M. Merediz, 9–33. Newark, DE: Juan de la Cuesta, 2003.

———. *Refracted Images: The Canary Islands through a New World Lens*. Tempe: Arizona Center for Medieval and Renaissance Studies, 2004.

———. "Traveling Icons: The Virgin of Candelaria's Transatlantic Journeys." *Arizona Journal of Hispanic Cultural Studies* 5 (2001): 115–132.

Mexía, Pedro de. *Historia del Emperador Carlos V.* Edited by Juan de Mata Carriazo. Madrid: Espasa Calpe, 1945.

Minián de Alfie, Raquel. "Lope, lector de cronistas de Indias." *Filología* 11 (1965): 1–21.

Mirrer, Louise. "Representing 'Other' Men: Muslims, Jews, and Masculine Ideals in Medieval Castilian Epic and Ballad." In *Medieval Masculinities: Regarding Men in the Middle Ages*, edited by Claire A. Lees, 169–186. Minneapolis: University of Minnesota Press, 1994.

———. *Women, Jews, and Muslims in the Texts of Reconquest Castile*. Ann Arbor: University of Michigan Press, 1996.

Montero, Santiago. *El emperador y los ríos. Religión, ingeniería y política en el Imperio Romano*. Madrid: UNED, 2012.

Montrose, Louis. "The Work of Gender in the Discourse of Discovery." In *New World Encounters*, edited by Stephen Greenblatt, 177–218. Berkeley: University of California Press, 1993.

Moore, John K., and Adriano Duque, eds. *Recuerde el alma dormida: Medieval and Early Modern Spanish Essays in Honor of Frank Dominguez*. Newark, DE: Juan de la Cuesta, 2009.

Morales, Ambrosio de. *Corónica general de España*. Vol. 7. Madrid: Oficina de Don Benito Cano, 1791.

Mújica, Bárbara, and Sharon D. Voros, eds. *Looking at the Comedia in the Year of the Quincentennial*. Lanham, MD: University Press of America, 1993.

Niehoff McCrary, Susan. "Theatrical Consciousness and Redemption." In *The Golden Age Comedia: Text, Theory, and Performance*, edited by Charles Ganelin and Howard Mancin, 24–36. West Lafayette, IN: Purdue University Press, 1994.

Nieto, José. "Herejía en la capilla imperial: Constantino Ponce de la Fuente y la imagen del diablo." In *Carlos V y la quiebra del humanismo político en Europa (1530–1558)*, edited by José Martínez Millán, 213–226. Vol. 4. Madrid: Sociedad Estatal para la Conmemoración de los Centenarios de Felipe II y Carlos V, 2001.

Nirenberg, David. "Race and the Middle Ages: The Case of Spain and Its Jews." In *Rereading the Black Legend: The Discourses of Religious and Racial Difference in the Renaissance Empires*, edited by Maureen Quilligan, Walter Mignolo, and Margaret Rich Greer, 71–87. Chicago: University of Chicago Press, 2008.

Nuez y Caballero, Sebastián la. "Las Canarias en la obra de Lope de Vega." *Anuario de Estudios Atlánticos* 10 (1964): 11–159.

Ocampo, Florián de. *Las quatro partes enteras de la Crónica de España que mandó componer el serenissimo rey don Alonso llamado el Sabio: vista y emendada mucha parte de su impresión por el maestro Florián Docampo*. Zamora: Agustín de Paz y Juan Picardo, 1541.

Oleza, Joan. "Los dramas históricos de hechos particulares, de Lope de Vega: una exigencia de sujetos." *Revista sobre teatro áureo* 7 (2013): 105–140.

———. "Del primer Lope al *Arte Nuevo*." In *Lope de Vega. Peribáñez y el comendador de Ocaña*, edited by Donald McGrady, ix–lv. Barcelona: Crítica, 1997.

———. "Variaciones del drama historial en Lope de Vega." *Anuario Lope de Vega* 19 (2013): 1–38.

Ortelius, Abraham. *Theatrum Orbis Terrarum*. Antwerp: Coppenium Diesth, 1570. https://www.loc.gov/resource/g3200m.gct00126/?st=gallery.

Padrón, Ricardo. *The Spacious Word: Cartography, Literature, and Empire in Early Modern Spain*. Chicago: University of Chicago Press, 2004.

Pagden, Anthony. *Lords of All the World: Ideologies of Empire in Spain, Britain, and France, c. 1500–1800*. New Haven: Yale University Press, 1995.

Pardo de Neyra, Xulio. "El juego literario de la colonización en *El mejor alcalde, el rey*." *Anuario de Estudios Filológicos* 27 (2004): 237–258.

Parker, Geoffrey. *The Army of Flanders and the Spanish Road, 1567–1659*. 2nd ed. Cambridge: Cambridge University Press, 2004.

Paterson, Alan K. G. "Stages of History and History on Stage: On Lope de Vega and Historical Drama." In *Spanish Theatre: Studies in Honour of Victor F. Dixon*, edited by Kenneth Adams, Ciaran Cosgrove, and James Whiston, 147–156. Woodbridge, UK: Tamesis, 2001.

Pavis, Patrice. *Dictionary of the Theater: Terms, Concepts, and Analysis*. Toronto: University of Toronto Press, 1998.

———. *Languages of the Stage: Essays in the Semiology of the Theater*. New York: Performing Arts Journal Publications, 1982.

Pedraza Jiménez, Felipe. "*La judía de Toledo*: génesis y cristalización de un mito literario." In *Marañón en Toledo (sobre "Elogio y nostalgia de Toledo")*, edited by José Botella Llusiá and Antonio Fernández de Molina, 19–37. Cuenca: Ediciones de la Universidad de Castilla-La Mancha, 1999.

Peyrebonne, Nathalie, and Pauline Renoux-Caron, eds. *Le milieu naturel en Espagne et en Italie: savoirs et représentations*. Paris: Presses Sorbonne Nouvelle, 2011.

Porter, James I. "Disfigurations: Erich Auerbach's Theory of *Figura*." *Critical Inquiry* 44, no. 1 (2017): 80–113.

Pym, Richard J., ed. *Rhetoric and Reality in Early Modern Spain*. Woodbridge, UK: Tamesis, 2006.

Quilligan, Maureen, Walter Mignolo, and Margaret Rich Greer, eds. *Rereading the Black Legend: The Discourses of Religious and Racial Difference in the Renaissance Empires*. Chicago: University of Chicago Press, 2008.

Quintana, Benito. "*Damas indias*: America's Iconic Body and the Wars of Conquest in the Spanish Comedia." *Bulletin of the Comediantes* 62, no.1 (2010): 103–122.

Quiroz Taub, María. "Love and Fury: The Evolution of Fresia in *Arauco domado* of Lope de Vega." In *Female Amerindians in Early Modern Spanish Theater*, edited by Gladys Robalino, 183–214. Lewisburg, PA: Bucknell University Press, 2014.

Rabasa, José. *Inventing America: Spanish Historiography and the Formation of Eurocentrism*. Norman: University of Oklahoma Press, 1993.

Ramos, Rafael. "De Heródoto a Lope: Nota a *El mejor alcalde, el rey*." *Anuario Lope de Vega* 1 (1995): 235–240.

Regueiro, José M. *Espacios dramáticos en el teatro español medieval, renacentista y barroco*. Kassel, Germany: Edition Reichenberger, 1996.

Reilly, Bernard F. *The Kingdom of León-Castilla under King Alfonso VII, 1126–1157*. Philadelphia: University of Pennsylvania Press, 1998.

Resina, Joan Ramón. "The Role of Discontinuity in the Formation of National Culture." In *Cultural Authority in Golden Age Spain*, edited by Marina S. Brownlee and Hans S. Gumbrecht, 284–303. Baltimore: Johns Hopkins University Press, 1995.

Reyes Peña, Mercedes de los, ed. *El vestuario en el teatro español del Siglo de Oro (Cuadernos del Teatro Clásico 13–14)*. Madrid: Compañía Nacional de Teatro Clásico, 2000.

Rigolot, François. *Poétique et onomastique. L'exemple de la Renaissance*. Geneva: Droz, 1977.

Ríos Saloma, Martín. "De la Restauración a la Reconquista: la construcción de un mito nacional (Una revisión historiográfica. Siglos XVI–XIX)." *La España Medieval* 28 (2005): 379–414.

Roas, David. "Lope y la manipulación de la historia: realidad, leyenda e invención en la *Comedia de Bamba*." *Anuario Lope de Vega* 1 (1995): 189–208.

Robalino, Gladys, ed. *Female Amerindians in Early Modern Spanish Theater*. Lewisburg, PA: Bucknell University Press, 2014.

Robalino, Gladys. Introduction. *Female Amerindians in Early Modern Spanish Theater*, edited by Gladys Robalino, 10–16. Lewisburg, PA: Bucknell University Press, 2014.

———. "The Role of Amerindian Women in Fernando de Zárate's *La conquista de México*." In *Female Amerindians in Early Modern Spanish Theater*, edited by Gladys Robalino, 37–45. Lewisburg, PA: Bucknell University Press, 2014.

Rodríguez Gallego, Fernando. "Alfonso VIII, *La corona merecida* y la leyenda de la judía de Toledo." *eHumanista* 24 (2013): 147–164.

Rodríguez Garrido, José A. "El ingenio en la mujer: *La traición en la amistad* de María de Zayas entre Lope de Vega y Huarte de San Juan." *Bulletin of the Comediantes* 49, no. 2 (1997): 357–373.

Rodríguez Pérez, Yolanda, and Antonio Sánchez Jiménez, eds. *La leyenda negra en el crisol de la comedia. El teatro del Siglo de Oro frente a los estereotipos antihispánicos*. Madrid and Frankfurt: Iberoamericana/Vervuert, 2016.

Ruano de la Haza, José María. "Lope de Vega and the Theater in Madrid." In *A Companion to Lope de Vega*, edited by Alexander Samson and Jonathan Parker, 29–50. Woodbridge, UK: Tamesis, 2008.

Ruano de la Haza, José María, ed. *El mundo del teatro español en su Siglo de Oro: ensayos dedicados a John E. Varey*. Ottawa: Dovehouse, 1989.

———. *La puesta en escena de los teatros comerciales del Siglo de Oro*. Madrid: Castalia, 2000.

———. "The World as a Stage: Politics, Imperialism, and Spain's Seventeenth-Century Theater." In *A History of Theater in Spain*, edited by María M. Delgado and David T. Gies, 57–78. Cambridge: Cambridge University Press, 2012.

Rubiera Fernández, Javier. *La construcción del espacio en la comedia española del Siglo de Oro*. Madrid: Arco Libros, 2005.

Ruiz de la Peña Solar, Juan Ignacio. *El reino de León en la alta Edad Media. La monarquía astur-leonesa. De Pelayo a Alfonso VI (718–1109)*. Edited by José María Fernández Catón, 11–127. Vol. 3. León: Centro de Estudios e Investigación San Isidoro, 1995.

Ruiz, Francisco Ramón. *Calderón, nuestro contemporáneo*. Madrid: Castalia, 2000.

———. *Celebración y catarsis (leer el teatro español)*. Murcia: Universidad de Murcia, 1988.

———. "El héroe americano en Lope y Tirso: de la guerra de los hombres a la guerra de los dioses." In *El mundo del teatro español en su Siglo de Oro: ensayos dedicados a John E. Varey*, edited by José María Ruano de la Haza, 229–248. Ottawa: Dovehouse, 1989.

Ruiz, Francisco Ramón, ed. *América en el teatro clásico español: estudio y textos*. Pamplona: Universidad de Navarra, 1993.

Rumeu de Armas, Antonio. *La conquista de Tenerife: 1494–1496*. Santa Cruz de Tenerife: Aula de Cultura de Tenerife, 1975.

Ryjik, Veronika. *Lope de Vega en la invención de España. El drama histórico y la formación de la conciencia nacional*. Woodbridge, UK: Tamesis, 2011.

Saavedra Vázquez, María del Carmen. "El corsarismo inglés en Galicia: los ataques a Vigo y Coruña y la militarización del reino." In *El reino de Galicia en la monarquía de Felipe II*, edited by Antonio Eiras Roel, 115–137. Santiago de Compostela: Xunta de Galicia, 1998.

———. "Galicia en la política atlántica de Felipe II: la Gran Armada y sus efectos." In *El reino de Galicia en la monarquía de Felipe II*, edited by Antonio Eiras Roel, 89–113. Santiago de Compostela: Xunta de Galicia, 1998.

———. "Política imperial y élites locales: la evolución del concejo coruñés en los siglos XVI y XVII." In *Monarquía, imperio y pueblos en la España moderna. Actas de la IV reunión científica de la Asociación Española de Historia Moderna*, edited by Pablo Fernández Albaladejo, 279–287. Alicante: Caja de Ahorros del Mediterráneo and Universidad de Alicante, 1997.

Sáez, Adrián J. *Godos de papel. Identidad nacional y reescritura en el siglo de oro*. Madrid: Cátedra, 2019.

Sáez Raposo, Francisco, ed. *Monstruos de apariencias llenos. Espacios de representación y espacios representados en el teatro áureo español*. Barcelona: Bellaterra, 2011.

Said, Edward. "Representing the Colonized: Anthropology's Interlocutors." *Critical Inquiry* 15 (1989): 205–225.

Salomon, Noël. *Recherches sur le thème paysan dans la "Comedia" au temps de Lope de Vega*. Bordeaux: Institut d'Études Ibériques et Ibéro-Américaines, 1965.

Sánchez Albornoz, Claudio. *España, un enigma histórico*. Vol. 1. Buenos Aires: Editorial Sudamericana, 1962.

Sánchez Jiménez, Antonio. "¿Leyenda negra o lascasianismo?: la polémica del Nuevo Mundo y la reescritura de la historia de *Los guanches de Tenerife*." In *La leyenda negra en el crisol de la comedia. El teatro del Siglo de Oro frente a los estereotipos antihispánicos*, edited by Yolanda Rodríguez Pérez and Antonio Sánchez Jiménez, 89–100. Madrid and Frankfurt: Iberoamericana/Vervuert, 2016.

———. *Lope. El verso y la vida*. Madrid: Cátedra, 2018.

———. "Quevedo y Lope (poesía y teatro) en 1609: patriotismo y construcción nacional en la *España defendida* y la *Jerusalén conquistada*." *La Perinola* 17 (2013): 27–56.

Sandoval Sánchez, Alberto. "Moros por indios: ensayando una lectura ex-céntrica del discurso colonial en *La Manguilla de Melilla* de Juan Ruiz de Alarcón." *Revista Iberoamericana* 67, no. 172–173 (1995): 535–553.

Shannon, Robert. "The Staging of America in Golden Age Theater: Scenery, Costumes, Special Effects." In *Looking at the Comedia in the Year of the Quincentennial*, edited by Bárbara Mújica and Sharon D. Voros, 53–66. Lanham, MD: University Press of America, 1993.

———. *Visions of the New World in the Drama of Lope de Vega*. New York: Peter Lang, 1989.

Shergold, N. D. *A History of the Spanish Stage from Medieval Times until the End of the Seventeenth Century*. Oxford: Clarendon Press, 1967.

Simerka, Barbara. *Discourses of Empire: Counter-Epic Literature in Early Modern Spain*. University Park: Pennsylvania State University Press, 2003.

Skwirblies, Lisa. "Theaters of Colonialism: Theatricality, Coloniality, and Performance in the German Empire, 1894–1914." PhD diss., University of Warwick, 2017. http://wrap.warwick.ac.uk/106458/.

Solórzano y Pereira, Juan de. *Política indiana*. Madrid: Diego Díaz de la Carrera, 1648. http://bdh-rd.bne.es/viewer.vm?id=0000134097&page=1.

Soto, Hernando de. *Emblemas moralizadas*. Edited by Carmen Bravo Villasante. Madrid: Fundación Universitaria Española, 1983.

Soyer, François. "Faith, Culture, and Fear: Comparing Islamophobia in Early Modern Spain and in Twenty-First-Century Europe." *Ethnic and Racial Studies* 36, no. 3 (2013): 399–416.

Spadaccini, Nicholas, and Jenaro Talens. *Through the Shattering Glass: Cervantes and the Self-Made World*. Minneapolis: University of Minnesota Press, 1993.

Stoll, Anita K., and Dawn L. Smith, eds. *The Perception of Women in Spanish Theater of the Golden Age*. Cranbury, NJ: Associated University Presses, 1991.

Stroud, Matthew D. "Taking Matters into Their Own Hands: Heroic Women of the Early Reconquest in the Spanish *Comedia*." *Bulletin of the Comediantes* 66, no. 2 (2014): 55–66.

Swietlicki, Catherine. "Lope's Dialogic Imagination: Writing Other Voices in 'Monolithic Spain.'" *Bulletin of the Comediantes* 40, no. 2 (1988): 205–226.

Tally, Robert T., Jr. *Spatiality*. New York: Routledge, 2012.

Tanner, Marie. *The Last Descendant of Aeneas: The Hapsburgs and the Mythic Image of the Emperor*. New Haven: Yale University Press, 1993.

Tate, Robert. *Ensayos sobre la historiografía peninsular del siglo XV*. Translated by Jesús Díaz. Madrid: Gredos, 1970.

Teijeiro Fuentes, Miguel Ángel. "Galicia y los gallegos en la literatura española del Siglo de Oro." *Scriptura* 11, no. 1 (1996): 203–246.

Tellkamp, Jörg, ed. *A Companion to Early Modern Spanish Imperial Political and Social Thought*. Leiden: Brill, 2020.

Thompson, I.A.A. "Castile, Spain, and the Monarchy: The Political Community from *patria natural* to *patria nacional*." In *Spain, Europe, and the Atlantic: Essays in Honour of John H. Elliott*, edited by Richard L. Kagan and Geoffrey Parker, 125–159. Cambridge: Cambridge University Press, 1995.

Tomasik, Timothy J., and Juliann M. Vitullo, eds. *At the Table: Metaphorical and Material Cultures of Food in Medieval and Early Modern Europe*. Leiden: Brepols, 2007.

Torgorvnick, Marianna. *Gone Primitive: Savage Intellects, Modern Lives*. Chicago: University of Chicago Press, 1990.

Torre y del Cerro, Antonio de la, ed. *Testamentaría de Isabel la Católica*. Barcelona: Vda. Fidel Rodriguez Ferrán, 1974.

Usandizaga, Guillem. *La representación de la historia contemporánea en el teatro de Lope de Vega*. Madrid and Frankfurt: Iberoamericana/Vervuert, 2014.

Valencia, Pedro de. *Tratado acerca de los moriscos de España*. Vol. 4 of *Obras completas*, edited by Rafael González Cañal and Hipólito B. Riesco Álvarez, 15–139. León: Universidad de León, 1999.

Varey, John E. *Cosmovisión y escenografía. El teatro español en el Siglo de Oro*. Madrid: Castalia, 1987.

Vega, Garcilaso de la. *Obra poética y textos en prosa*. Edited by Bienvenido Morros. Barcelona: Crítica, 1995.

Vega, Lope de. *Arauco domado por el excelentísimo señor don García Hurtado de Mendoza*. In *América en el teatro clásico español: estudio y textos*, edited by Francisco Ruiz Ramón, 75–140. Pamplona: Universidad de Navarra, 1993.

———. *Arte nuevo de hacer comedias. Edición crítica. Fuentes y ecos latinos*. Edited by Felipe Pedraza Jiménez and Pedro Conde Parrado. Cuenca: Ediciones de la Universidad de Castilla-La Mancha, 2016.

———. *La campana de Aragón*. Edited by Diego Símini. Vol. 2 of *Comedias de Lope de Vega. Parte XVIII*, edited by Adrián J. Sáez and Antonio Sánchez Jiménez, 303–466. Madrid: Gredos, 2019.

———. *Comedia famosa de las paces de los reyes y judía de Toledo*. Edited by Julián Acebrón. Vol 2. of *Comedias de Lope de Vega. Parte VII*, edited by Enrico di Pastena, 593–703. Lérida: Editorial Milenio-Universitat Atònoma de Barcelona, 1997.

———. *El cuerdo loco*. Edited by José F. Montesinos. Madrid: Impresora de los Sucesores de Hernando, 1922.

———. *Epistolario de Lope de Vega Carpio*. Edited by Agustín González Amezúa. Madrid: Artes Gráficas Aldus, 1941.

———. *Los españoles en Flandes*. Edited by Antonio Cortijo-Ocaña. Vol. 2 of *Comedias de Lope de Vega. Parte XIII*, edited by Natalia Fernández Rodríguez, 909–1108. Madrid: Gredos, 2014.

———. *Las famosas asturianas*. Edited by David Arbesú. Vol. 2 of *Comedias de Lope de Vega. Parte XVIII*, edited by Adrián J. Sáez and Antonio Sánchez Jiménez, 157–302. Madrid: Gredos, 2019.

———. *Los guanches de Tenerife*. Edited by José Miguel Martínez Torrejón. Vol. 2 of *Comedias de Lope de Vega. Parte X*, edited by Ramón Valdés and María Morrás, 769–889. Lérida: Editorial Milenio-Universitat Atònoma de Barcelona, 2010.

———. *El mejor alcalde, el rey*. Edited by Frank P. Casa and Berislav Primorac. Madrid: Cátedra, 1993.

———. *El mejor alcalde, el rey*. Edited by Teresa Ferrer Valls. Alicante: Biblioteca Virtual Miguel de Cervantes, 2002.

———. *El nuevo mundo descubierto por Cristóbal Colón*. Edited by Luigi Giuliani. Vol. 1 of *Comedias de Lope de Vega. Parte IV*, edited by Luigi Giuiani and Ramón Valdés, 175–287. Lérida: Editorial Milenio, 1997.

———. *El premio de la hermosura*. Edited by Florence D'Artois and Héctor Ruiz. Vol. 1 of *Comedias de Lope de Vega. Parte XVI*, edited by Florence D'Artois and Luigi Giuliani, 55–210. Madrid: Gredos, 2017.

———. *El primer rey de Castilla*. Edited by Adrián J. Sáez. Vol. 1 of *Comedias de Lope de Vega. Parte XVII*, edited by Daniele Crivellari and Eugenio Maggi, 825–975. Madrid: Gredos, 2018.

———. *Los ramilletes de Madrid*. Edited by Elizabeth Wright. Vol. 1 of *Comedias de Lope de Vega. Parte XI*, edited by Laura Fernández and Gonzalo Pontón, 467–610. Madrid: Gredos, 2012.

———. *La varona castellana*. Edited by Gonzalo Pontón and Guillermo Serés. Vol. 3 of *Comedias de Lope de Vega. Parte IX*, edited by Marco Presotto, 1115–1292. Lérida: Editorial Milenio, 2007.

———. *El villano en su rincón*. Edited by Guillermo Serés. Vol. 1 of *Comedias de Lope de Vega. Parte VII*, edited by Enrico di Pastena, 67–199. Lérida: Editorial Milenio, 2008.

Viana, Antonio de. *Las Antigüedades de las Islas Afortunadas de la Gran Canaria, conquista de Tenerife y aparición de la Santa Imagen de la Candelaria en verso suelto y octava rima*. La Laguna, Tenerife: Tipografía de La Laguna, 1905.

Virgil. *Eclogues. Georgics. Aeneid: Books 1–6*. Translated by Rushton Fairclough. Cambridge, MA: Harvard University Press, 1999.

Virués, Cristóbal de. *Elisa Dido*. In *La gran Semíramis. Elisa Dido*. Edited by Alfredo Hermenegildo, 179–243. Madrid: Castalia, 2003.

Vitse, Marc. "Sobre los espacios en *La dama duende*: el cuarto de don Manuel." *Notas y Estudios Filológicos* 2 (1985): 7–32.

Vossler, Karl. *Lope de Vega y su tiempo*. Translated by Ramón de la Serna. Madrid: Revista de Occidente, 1933.

Weaver-Hightower, Rebecca. *Empire Islands: Castaways, Cannibals, and Fantasies of Conquest*. Minneapolis: University of Minnesota Press, 2007.

Weiner, Jack. "La guerra y la paz espirituales en tres comedias de Lope de Vega." *Revista de Estudios Hispánicos* 17 (1983): 65–79.

Wilder, Thornton. "Lope, Pinedo, Some Child-Actors, and a Lion." *Romance Philology* 7 (1953): 21–24.

Woodward, David. "Maps and the Rationalization of Geographic Space." In *Circa 1492: Art in the Age of Exploration*, edited by J. A. Levinson, 83–87. Washington, DC: National Gallery of Art, 1991.

Wulff, Fernando. *Las esencias patrias. Historiografía e historia antigua en la construcción de la identidad española (siglos XVI–XX)*. Barcelona: Crítica, 2003.

Zabaleta, Juan de. *Errores celebrados*. Edited by David Hershberg. Madrid: Espasa-Calpe, 1972.

Zugasti, Miguel, and Joseba Andoni Cuñado, eds. *Fiesta y teatro en el Siglo de Oro: ámbito hispánico*. Toulouse: Presses Universitaires du Midi, 2019.

Index

Note: Page numbers in *italics* refer to figures.

About the Author

Javier Lorenzo is an associate professor and chair of the Hispanic studies program at East Carolina University in Greenville, North Carolina. He is the author of *Nuevos casos, nuevas artes: intertextualidad, autorrepresentación e ideología en la obra de Juan Boscán*, and his articles on early modern Spanish literature have appeared in journals such as *Hispanic Review*, *Calíope*, *Bulletin of the Comediantes*, *Anuario Lope de Vega*, and *Cervantes*.

